Transforming Work

ReFormations

MEDIEVAL AND EARLY MODERN

Series Editors:
David Aers, Sarah Beckwith, and James Simpson

Transforming Work

EARLY MODERN
PASTORAL AND LATE
MEDIEVAL POETRY

KATHERINE C. LITTLE

University of Notre Dame Press
Notre Dame, Indiana

Copyright © 2013 by University of Notre Dame
Notre Dame, Indiana 46556
www.undpress.nd.edu
All Rights Reserved

Manufactured in the United States of America

Library of Congress Cataloging-in-Publication Data

Little, Katherine C., 1969–
　Transforming work : early modern pastoral and late medieval poetry / Katherine C. Little.
　　pages　cm. — (ReFormations: Medieval and Early Modern)
　Includes bibliographical references and index.
　ISBN 978-0-268-03387-3 (pbk. : alk. paper) —
　ISBN 0-268-03387-0 (pbk. : alk. paper)
　1. Pastoral poetry, English—History and criticism.
2. English poetry—Early modern, 1500–1700—History and criticism.
3. Literature, Medieval—Influence.　I. Title.
　PR509.P3L58　2013
　821'.309—dc23
　　　　　　　　　　　　　　　　　　　　　　　　　2013000467

∞ *The paper in this book meets the guidelines for permanence
and durability of the Committee on Production Guidelines
for Book Longevity of the Council on Library Resources.*

CONTENTS

	Acknowledgments	vii
	Introduction	1
ONE	Medieval Traditions of Writing Rural Labor	15
TWO	The Invention of the English Eclogue	49
THREE	The Pastoral Mode and Agrarian Capitalism	83
FOUR	Transforming Work: The Reformation and the *Piers Plowman* Tradition	111
FIVE	Spenser's *Shepheardes Calender* and a Poetry of Rural Labor	143
SIX	Reading Pastoral in Book 6 of Spenser's *Faerie Queene*	171
	Afterword: The Secret History of Pastoral	195
	Notes	201
	Works Cited	237
	Index	249

ACKNOWLEDGMENTS

This book has been a pleasure to write not least because of all the opportunities it has given me to learn from colleagues, students, and friends. In charting the continuities and disruptions between the Middle Ages and the Renaissance, I am indebted to the groundbreaking work of David Aers, Sarah Beckwith, and James Simpson. I thank them for inviting this book into their series, for their comments on my work, and for their advice and encouragement throughout the long process by which this book came into being. Particular thanks are due to David Aers for his remarkable generosity and candor and for providing a salutary example of how to break free of dominant critical narratives.

 I have written this book with specific conversations in mind: with early modernists, with theorists of pastoral, with Langlandians. I have benefited a great deal, therefore, from the responses of various audiences. I would like to thank Nigel Smith and Lynn Staley, who read a version of chapter 4 in manuscript. Thank you also to audiences at the Group for Early Modern Cultural Studies in Chicago (GEMCS) (2007); the Harvard Doctoral Conference (2007); the International Langland Conference in Philadelphia (2007); and Spenser at Kalamazoo (2008) for their thought-provoking responses. I am particularly grateful to James Simpson and his colleagues for inviting me to speak at Harvard and to Chi-ming Yang, Kim Hall, and Maureen Quilligan, my fellow panel participants, for stimulating discussion leading up to and at GEMCS.

I owe a great debt of gratitude to my former colleagues and students at Fordham University, where most of this project was completed. The idea for this study emerged out of several undergraduate and graduate courses on medieval romance that I taught there, and I thank my students for their curiosity. Comments from Jocelyn Wogan-Browne and Mary Bly in the early stages helped shape my thinking, and I thank them for their advice. On a more practical note, I am grateful to Nicola Pitchford and Eva Badowska, fabulous former chairs of Fordham's English Department, who helped me negotiate maternity leaves and research leaves, and to Heather Blatt for research assistance. I would also like to thank Mary Erler, Maryanne Kowaleski, and Nina Rowe, all of whom encouraged me in various ways as I pursued my work and helped make Fordham a very happy place to be. Thank you to my new colleagues at the University of Colorado, Boulder, especially William Kuskin, for their warm welcome.

One of my last, though not least, intellectual debts is to Annabel Patterson and her seminar on Sidney and Spenser that I took a very long time ago. I thank her for teaching me some of the rigor and delight with which she approached Spenser's poetry.

I would like to thank the two readers for University of Notre Dame Press, anonymous and Kellie Robertson, for the time and care they took in providing detailed and helpful comments. Thank you to Barbara Hanrahan, the former editor, and to Stephen Little, the present editor, for guiding me through the stages of publication, and, finally, to Rebecca DeBoer and Christina Lovely. I would also like to thank Wendy McMillen for her work on the cover and James Simpson for suggesting the image.

Generous financial support was provided by a Fordham Faculty Fellowship and a grant from the National Endowment for the Humanities, and I am deeply grateful for the time these grants afforded me for research and writing.

I could not have written this book without the loving support of my friends and family. Anna Katsnelson and Eric Rosenbaum were delightful companions whether in Texas or New York. Jennifer Bosson and Katrine Bangsgaard provided much-needed laughs and breaks from the solitary work of writing. Thank you to Paul Neimann and Diane Neimann for their generosity and good humor and for offering respite at their idyllic lakeside cabin. Thank you to my father, Silas Little, for his love and support, and to my mother, Mary Ann Beverly, who has encouraged me in every one of my pursuits. Finally, it would be difficult to describe the gratitude I feel toward my family. To Paul for being the staunchest of allies, for listening to every word, and for holding on to what is fun and funny amidst all of the hard work, and to Charlotte and Daisy, for being never-ending sources of delight: all of you remind me every day of how lucky I am.

An earlier version of chapter 4 appeared as "Transforming Work: Protestantism and the *Piers Plowman* Tradition," in the *Journal of Medieval and Early Modern Studies* 40 (2010): 497–526, and some material from chapters 1 and 5 previously appeared as "The 'Other' Past of Pastoral: Langland's *Piers Plowman* and Spenser's *Shepheardes Calender*," in *Exemplaria* 21 (2009): 161–79. I thank the editors at Duke University Press and Maney Publishing for permission to reproduce the work here.

Introduction

The divide between the medieval and the early modern (or Renaissance) periods is perhaps nowhere more apparent than in studies of the pastoral mode, in which the literature of the Middle Ages is often entirely absent. Either these studies begin with the sixteenth-century pastoral of Edmund Spenser's *Shepheardes Calender* or William Shakespeare's plays, or they begin with the eclogues of Theocritus (or Virgil) and then skip the Middle Ages entirely to focus, once again, on sixteenth-century texts.[1] More importantly, the underlying assumption of much of this work is that it is precisely the "newness" of the pastoral mode in the sixteenth century that makes it so rich and complex a literary mode, a position eloquently argued by Paul Alpers.[2] This focus on novelty appears even in studies that present themselves as historical, most famously the series of essays by Louis Montrose on Elizabethan pastoral.[3] For Montrose, the only history that matters is that of immediate context—that is, the social and political world of the Elizabethan court. Despite the wide range of approaches to pastoral, then, all of the studies implicitly reinforce a very traditional periodization: a clean break between the Middle Ages and the early modern period.

At first glance, the neglect of medieval literature in the study of pastoral makes perfect sense. It is relatively easy to argue that there was no pastoral—at least as far as this term refers to a classically influenced pastoral—before the rediscovery of Virgil's *Eclogues*, which were first printed in England by Wynkyn de Worde in 1512. Or before the popularization and dissemination of the *Adulescentia* (1498), the eclogues by Baptista (Spagnuoli) Mantuanus, who was known as Mantuan in England. Mantuan's eclogues quickly became a school text and were, therefore, read widely in sixteenth-century England.[4] Medieval authors were not, in contrast to their early modern successors, particularly interested in Virgil's *Eclogues*: although the *Eclogues* survive from the medieval period in almost as many manuscript copies as the *Aeneid*, very few authors allude to them or take them as a model.[5] Even if one defines the pastoral somewhat more broadly than imitations of Virgil's *Eclogues*—that is, to refer to any text with a similar interest in shepherds or shepherding—one is still hard-pressed to come up with anything resembling the pastoral of the sixteenth century and beyond. There are, of course, the nativity plays in the mystery cycles, which are commonly invoked to provide evidence of the continuity of pastoral, as in W. W. Greg's comprehensive but dated *Pastoral Poetry and Pastoral Drama* or Helen Cooper's *Pastoral: Mediaeval into Renaissance*. But it is worth noting the paucity of this evidence; the mystery plays are the only examples of medieval literature in the English vernacular that demonstrate any sustained interest in the shepherd as a character; even Greg notes that the "stream of pastoral . . . is reduced to the merest trickle" in the Middle Ages.[6] Moreover, the mystery plays are somewhat difficult to assimilate to a classically influenced pastoral. Cooper uses a different term altogether, "*bergerie*," to refer to them: *bergerie* "embraces both the realistic and artistic aspects of the shepherd world."[7] But her coining of a new term, one unfamiliar to an English tradition, also underlines, however unwittingly, the difference between these texts and the imitations of Virgilian pastoral that come later. Finally, perhaps the most recent study to compare the nativity plays to Renaissance pastoral finds them "alien" to it.[8] Indeed, the difficulty of arguing for a medieval pastoral that is in any significant way continuous with the pastoral of the early modern period is evident in the one study that attempts to link the two periods: Cooper's *Pastoral: Mediaeval into Renaissance*, which ends up reinforcing the very divide that it means to call into question, namely, that between medieval traditions and the Italian, Arcadian pastoral that "displaced" them.[9]

The absence of a medieval pastoral that is continuous with the early modern period does not mean, however, the absence of any medieval influences on early modern pastoral; perhaps the question has been posed the wrong way thus far. Instead of assuming that the first writers of pastoral understood it exclusively by means of Virgil and Mantuan because that is how we, as later readers, understand it, we could try to recover the specificity of these first encounters with the pastoral mode, encounters that were surely influenced by a knowledge of medieval literature as well. After all, on closer look, the first eclogues to appear in sixteenth-century England look backward to a pre-pastoral medieval period as well as forward to a mode that is recognizably pastoral: these are the eclogues of Alexander Barclay (composed ca. 1513–14; printed in 1548 and 1570), Barnabe Googe (1563), and Edmund Spenser (1579), whose eclogues are otherwise known as the *Shepheardes Calender*. While all of these texts certainly invoke the "new" pastoral, either of Virgil directly or of Virgil by way of Mantuan, they contain traces of what one can only call medieval literary traditions. Indeed, the editors of the two earliest eclogue collections, by Barclay and Googe, call these texts "medieval," and even Spenser's editor, who insists on the novelty of the *Calender*, acknowledges Spenser's debts to medieval traditions.[10] First and foremost, all make use of a particular form of allegorical pastoral, typically called "ecclesiastical" or "biblical" pastoral, in which the reader is meant to understand the shepherds as priests and the "shepherding" they discuss as referring to clerical duties and/or religious beliefs and practices. Ecclesiastical pastoral was, as the name suggests, a discourse for writing about the clergy, especially attacks on the clergy. Although the term *ecclesiastical* might suggest a kind of institutional association, this discourse was both ubiquitous and extremely flexible, appearing across a wide range of literary genres and audiences, both clerical and lay. Perhaps the most well-known example of this kind of pastoral is Chaucer's characterization of the Parson, in his *General Prologue* to the *Canterbury Tales*, as a "shepherde and noght a mercenarie."[11] One might say that *ecclesiastical pastoral*, the term I will use for ease of reference throughout

4 *Transforming Work*

this volume, is the primary medieval contribution to Renaissance pastoral: as Greg writes, "during the centuries that had elapsed since the days of Vergil the term 'pastoral' had gained a new meaning and new associations. . . . it was left to medieval Christianity to create a god who was in fact a shepherd of men."[12]

Nevertheless, the "medievalness" of this discourse has hardly been appreciated by theorists of pastoral. Instead, its presence in the early English eclogues is typically assigned to the influence of Mantuan, who famously fused it with the classical pastoral.[13] Patrick Cullen's discussion of Spenser is not only exemplary of this approach but has also shaped critical discussions:

> Spenser used not only pastoral, but also a division within pastoral. . . . While the pastoral tradition Spenser inherited undeniably possessed continuity, it was from one perspective divided. . . . By the time of the Renaissance one can discern two different, though related, strands within pastoral, the "Arcadian" and the "Mantuanesque." Arcadian pastoral for the most part takes as the pastoral ideal the *pastor felix* and the soft life of *otium*. . . . Mantuanesque pastoral, however minor it may be in the whole history of pastoral, was a major strand in the Renaissance. Emerging in part from the pastoral polemics of Petrarch and Boccaccio on the corruption of church and court, it found its culminating and definitive expression in the ten eclogues of Battista Spagnuoli. . . . [It] takes as its ideal the Judaeo-Christian *pastor bonus*, the shepherd unwaveringly committed to the flock and to the requirements for eternal salvation, and consequently one largely opposed to the shepherd of worldly felicity.[14]

Cullen's statement demonstrates the way in which a medieval form, the ecclesiastical pastoral, has been redefined in most studies of pastoral so that it is no longer medieval. First, Cullen assumes that there is a natural and obvious connection between ecclesiastical pastoral and classical pastoral, that both of these are ultimately the same form.[15] They are both "strands within" the larger category of pastoral "continuity" despite the fact that their literary histories suggest less a shared origin than an unceremonious linking of relatively disparate ideas.

Ecclesiastical pastoral grows out of a Christian, biblical tradition; it is less a mode or genre than a trope that appears in a wide range of genres; it is characteristically medieval, whereas Virgil's *Eclogues* are not; and it is far more "democratic" or popular than the *Eclogues* because it can be found in a wide range of lay and clerical texts, such as sermons, devotional treatises, and estates satires. Cullen's "by the time of the Renaissance" is here disingenuous, since only in the Renaissance (at least in England) was this form linked to classical pastoral. In positing a shared literary history, he can set aside how and why authors linked these forms in the first place and why they did not continue to do so; ecclesiastical pastoral is, as Cullen notes, only a "minor strand" in the whole history of pastoral. It is worth noting that another theorist of pastoral, Renato Poggioli, suggests, in contrast (although only quite briefly), that these forms might not have the natural connection Cullen assumes: "allegorical pastoral makes fully its own the Christian symbolic identification of the shepherd with the priest. This identification is, so to speak, so technical as to suggest that the allegorical pastoral is no pastoral at all."[16] Second, in assigning ecclesiastical pastoral exclusively to Mantuan and his influence, Cullen can exclude from consideration the large number of texts, both medieval and from the sixteenth century, that might resonate with the early eclogues, texts that use ecclesiastical pastoral but are not typically described as pastoral, most notably the *Piers Plowman* tradition. From Cullen's perspective, Mantuan discovered and popularized ecclesiastical pastoral just as he rediscovered and popularized Virgil's *Eclogues*. But this is not the case. The ecclesiastical pastoral was a familiar trope with a familiar set of meanings, meanings that would certainly be altered by its use in a new context to describe "real" shepherds who pipe and sing.

The medieval traces in early modern pastoral cannot, interestingly, all be assigned to Mantuan's influence, even if we wanted to assume that his *Eclogues* are the source of the ecclesiastical pastoral. The early eclogues also bear traces of what one might call a "plowman tradition," a tradition that includes William Langland's late-fourteenth-century poem *Piers Plowman* and the literary imitations it generated, such as the pseudo-Chaucerian *Plowman's Tale*. Simply put, there are traces of plowmen as well as shepherds in these texts. One might merely gesture toward the allusions to the *Plowman's Tale* and the presence of a shepherd named Piers in two eclogues of Spenser's *Shepheardes Calender* and to the extensive discussion of plowmen in Alexander Barclay's fifth and final eclogue, although the traces are far more complex and interesting (and will be discussed at length later in the volume) than can be argued here. These traces have led scholars to argue for a Langlandian influence on both Barclay and Spenser, although not, interestingly, on Barnabe Googe.[17] These Langlandian influences cannot be easily assimilated to the classical pastoral. Even more than the ecclesiastical pastoral, they suggest a literary tradition whose relationship with the new eclogue tradition has not yet been worked out or understood, either by the sixteenth-century writers themselves or by later critics. After all, *Piers Plowman* is in no way indebted to Virgil, and its particular mode of figuration (the plowman) is not the same as that of the ecclesiastical pastoral and its shepherds. Langland includes very little ecclesiastical pastoral in his text, although later texts, such as the pseudo-Chaucerian *Plowman's Tale*, tend to combine the plowman and shepherd-priests.[18] More importantly, the plowman tradition precedes and intersects with sixteenth-century pastoral: plowmen characters, unlike shepherds, did enjoy a kind of literary popularity in the late medieval period, one that extended into the sixteenth century. *Piers Plowman* alone survives in fifty-one manuscripts from the fourteenth and fifteenth centuries and was printed a number of times in the mid-sixteenth century: three times by Robert Crowley (1550) and once by Owen Rogers (1561).[19] For purposes of comparison, one might note that the Towneley *Second Shepherds' Play*, long used as evidence of medieval pastoral, only survives in one manuscript.[20] It would be difficult, then, to argue for its direct influence on the early writers of the eclogues. Finally, because of this vital tradition, in the sixteenth century plowmen were recognizable literary figures who carried with them a very specific set of associations. That is, they appear most commonly in texts that are concerned with a reform understood in both social and religious terms: a reform of the three estates and of the established church, as in Langland's dream vision; a reform of the friars in *Piers the Plowman's Crede* (ca. 1400); and then more pointedly the reform we know as the Reformation, as in the tract "I playne Piers which cannot flatter" (?1547).[21]

The fusion of these medieval modes—the ecclesiastical pastoral and the plowman tradition—with the eclogue form and its shepherds should be unsurprising. What unites them is obvious but worth stating: all are concerned with rural laborers or with using rural laborers to represent something else, whether priests or lovers. And yet, few scholars have read the shepherds within pastoral in relation to other rural laborers.[22] After all, what has been central to many studies of pastoral is the distinction between the shepherds of the pastoral tradition and all other representations of shepherds or other rural laborers. What informs this distinction is the process of "mystification," the retreat into innocence and happiness, or the idealization of shepherd life.[23] Greg, for example, long ago claimed that

> pastoral literature must not be confounded with that which has for its subject the lives, the ideas, and the emotions of simple and unsophisticated mankind, far from the centres of our complex civilization. The two may be in their origin related, and they occasionally, as it were, stretch out feelers towards one another, but the pastoral of tradition lies in its essence as far from the document of humble life as from a scientific treatise on agriculture or a volume of pastoral theology.[24]

Greg's distinction between the pastoral kind of shepherd and all other kinds of shepherds (and forms of "humble life") persists in studies of pastoral. Two influential studies of pastoral, by Paul Alpers and Louis Montrose, have asserted, quite persuasively and from very different perspectives, that what defines pastoral is the shepherds themselves.[25] Yet neither critic is interested in investigating the full range of what a shepherd could mean, either in literary traditions outside the pastoral or in terms of a "real" historical existence. For these critics, what is important about shepherds is their capacity to represent someone else.

Greg's clear distinction between the pastoral shepherd and other kinds of shepherds and rural laborers cannot, however, be found in the texts themselves, particularly in Virgil's *Eclogues*, which provide an important origin of the pastoral mode for sixteenth-century writers. Virgil's *Eclogues* reveal the shepherd as a rural laborer. As Annabel Patterson reminds us, "Meliboeus was as much farmer as shepherd, and the question of culture's relationship to agriculture was therefore inscribed in the same master-text that appeared, if read from a certain perspective, to privilege leisure."[26] Moreover, Samuel Johnson, who was a stickler when it came to classical texts (and influences), states "it is therefore improper to give the title of a pastoral to verses, in which the speakers, after the slight mention of their flocks, fall to complaints of errors in the church, and corruptions in the government, or to lamentations of the death of some illustrious person," thus implying that speakers must devote more than "slight mention" to sheep. He also defines pastoral, following Virgil, as "a poem in which any action or passion is represented by its effects upon a country life."[27] Johnson suggests thereby that true pastoral, at least the Virgilian pastoral, is, in fact, concerned with a "country life"—or, to use Greg's term, a "humble life"—even if he, like Greg, thinks this mode should not include pastoral theology.

Scholars' refusal to read shepherds in relation to "country life" should be seen for what it is: a rejection of the most obvious frame of reference for these texts as they entered the English literary tradition in favor of finding some universal and transhistorical "essence" (the term is Greg's). Shepherds are not an invention of either Virgil or Mantuan, and they had both a literary and a material existence in England long before texts about them became so popular. For all the novelty of the eclogue form, the subject matter could not possibly have been seen as new. Readers of Virgil in the sixteenth century would have been reminded of other shepherds—whether figurative, such as priests, or literal—and of other laborers who might do shepherdly activities, such as plowmen; in other words, they would have encountered this new mode in terms of familiar literary traditions and familiar figures from their social world.[28] As Alastair Fowler reminds us, "English pastoral has to be related to the consequential fact that from an early date England was Europe's major wool producer.... The English were then not yet a nation of shopkeepers, but of shepherds, wool-carders, dyers, weavers, fullers, and other of the sixteen occupations assignable to the wool trade."[29] The writers themselves certainly saw pastoral literature, and the eclogue form, as entirely compatible with "document[s] of humble life," treatises on agriculture, and pastoral theology (to use Greg's terms), as we shall see.

Mantuan's eclogues offer a case in point. As mentioned above, Mantuan stands at the beginning of the pastoral mode, at least in terms of the rediscovery of Virgil, whose influence can be found throughout his eclogues. But Mantuan clearly sees Virgil's shepherds in terms of contemporary rural labors, and readers have long pointed to his "rustic realism," a realism that involves labor.[30] Despite their "leasure" to tell tales, his shepherds repeatedly refer to their work; in the first few lines of the first eclogue, for example, we learn that the shepherds must "watch" for the "sauage beast" that lurks in the corn; how the speaker had "care" for his "cattell," how he took no delight in labor as a youth (here I follow George Turberville's translation of 1567).[31] These are precisely the kind of things that shepherds do. Indeed, Alpers notes briefly that Mantuan's world is one in which "human beings are subject to the curse of labor," such as the repair work done after the flooding of the River Po detailed at the opening of the second eclogue.[32]

Alpers describes Mantuan's interest in work as "georgic," and one might ask at this point whether the early eclogues' interest in rural labor might not usefully be described as georgic, instead of in relation to medieval literary traditions, as I'm suggesting here. Such a term would preserve the separation between sixteenth-century pastoral and other kinds of influences ("documents of humble life" or works of pastoral theology) because it would assign any interest in labor to a Virgilian literary tradition and not to the other influences. *Georgic* is, of course, the term typically used to refer to sixteenth-century representations of rural labor (and less often to medieval ones), as evident throughout Anthony Low's study, *The Georgic Revolution*.[33] This is true even when these representations of labor occur within texts otherwise deemed pastoral, and it seems that most scholars would agree with Fowler, who claims that "English pastoral is specially characterized by mixture with georgic."[34] But the term *georgic* would be misleading for this particular time period. First, Virgil's *Georgics* were not directly imitated until the eighteenth century in England.[35] To use the term *georgic* for any earlier period would suggest a chain of influence, a literary history, that does not, in fact, exist as it does for the pastoral, since Virgil's *Eclogues* were widely imitated. Second, and similarly, the term conflates all literary traditions for representing labor, whether classical or Christian, thus eliding precisely the kind of generic and ideological fissures that this study is interested in investigating. Low's Hegelian phrase "georgic spirit" is perhaps exemplary of the kind of ahistoricism that informs the common use of the term: it assumes that what a writer has to say about work preexists the discourses available for expressing it.[36] For Low (and others), an allusion to Langland's poem and the work described therein would therefore have exactly the same significance as an allusion to Virgil's *Georgics*. For these reasons, this study will set the georgic mode aside.

The intersection of the pastoral, both ecclesiastical and classical, and the plowman tradition in the early English eclogues suggests that like Mantuan, English writers understood Virgil's shepherds not only in terms of their novelty but also in relation to the rural laborers represented in what have long been called "native traditions": the mystery cycles, estates satire, sermons, and Langland's *Piers Plowman*.[37] This intersection of the new and the "native" was neither a particularly easy nor a happy one, as it has typically been understood, precisely because the meaning(s) of rural labor and rural laborers was so fraught during the sixteenth century.[38] As I shall argue here, in granting the shepherd a new identity, one borrowed from Virgil (or Virgil via Mantuan), these texts minimize or elide the traditional and potentially reformist significance of the rural laborer—the associations inherited from the medieval and Reformation period that surround both the shepherd/priest in the ecclesiastical pastoral and the plowman. Further, the process of rewriting the rural laborer that characterizes early modern pastoral texts consistently draws our attention to a historical shift in the range of meanings of labor, particularly labor's flexible capacity to be both literal and figurative: physical and social activity, on the one hand, or spiritual activity, on the other. In short, the emergence of pastoral reveals a change in what I'm going to call the symbolic imagination around work. In using the term *symbolic imagination*, I refer to the quite obvious capacity of words to function as symbols and, therefore, what seems to be a particularly medieval predilection for thinking symbolically. I also refer to the way in which those symbols participate in and reveal the structure of the social world. In this way, the term invokes both the Lacanian *symbolic order*—the abstract social structures into which people are born—and the related sociological term, *symbolic universe*, which refers to "the matrix of *all* socially objectivated and subjectively real meanings" and which "orders and thereby legitimates everyday roles, priorities, and operating procedures by placing them *sub specie universi*, that is, in the context of the most general frame of reference conceivable [and which imbues even the most trivial transactions of everyday life] with profound significance."[39] As much as both the symbolic order and the symbolic universe suggest a totality, they are not immune to the forces of historical change. To quote Marshall Sahlins, "'structure'—the symbolic relations of cultural order—is an historical object."[40] The "meaningful order" of culture is "always at risk" because, as Sahlins notes, "the old names that are still on everyone's lips [can] acquire connotations that are far removed from their original meaning." Sahlins calls this historical process "the functional revaluation of the categories."[41]

This study identifies and examines three major historical events (or processes) in the sixteenth century that caused a "functional revaluation of the categories" by introducing new languages of labor and laborers and thus both challenging and disrupting the late medieval symbolic imagination. First and perhaps most familiar is the "rediscovery" of the eclogue form and its "new" shepherds. Second is the "agrarian problem of the sixteenth century" (to use the title of R. H. Tawney's famous study): enclosure and the anxiety surrounding the introduction of agrarian capitalism into the countryside.[42] Third is the Reformation and its redefinition of good works, which led to a disruption of a long-standing cultural metaphor in which rural labor stood for good works.

I begin, in chapter one, before these historical disruptions, with an account of the native tradition into which we need to see pastoral inserting itself: what and how rural labor means in the Middle Ages. If we approach the pastoral mode, as sixteenth-century writers did, from the perspective of what comes before (not, as scholars have tended to do, from the texts that follow), then medieval literature is less a hodgepodge of random bits of pastoral, the various modes of *bergerie* and ecclesiastical pastoral identified by Helen Cooper, than a relatively coherent tradition of "writing rural labor." These texts are defined by their interest in using the symbolic meanings of rural labor inherited from a Christian exegetical tradition and a feudal approach to the social world: labor figures penance, the good deeds necessary for salvation, the proper functioning of society in its three estates, the reform of the social world. Each of these figurations is reformist: an individual or community is transformed for the better, and that change is imagined as physical labor. This reformism typically adheres to what we might consider a medieval understanding of reform—a return to an idealized version of the status quo—but it does have a radical potential, as demonstrated in William Langland's *Piers Plowman*. Chapters 2–4 then turn to the three sixteenth-century historical processes or disruptions identified above. Chapter 2 explores the first eclogues in English, by Alexander Barclay (1513–14) and Barnabe Googe (1563). These eclogues have typically been understood as too "medieval" to be proper pastoral, but what has been viewed as an aesthetic failure is important precisely because it reveals the ideological fault lines of what happens when the classical shepherd replaces the English laborer. On the one hand, their texts demonstrate a commitment to the new shepherd and his *otium*, his freedom to sing and woo; but, on the other, the shepherd continues to remind them of a medieval rural laborer, one who is defined by his "real" labor and who might also suggest the potential for the reform of the social world. The literary shift described in chapter 2, the emerging distinction between shepherds and plowmen, is all the more interesting for its "real world" equivalent, as demonstrated in chapter 3. The controversy over the enclosure of common lands for pasturing sheep also created a new language of shepherding in mid-sixteenth-century anti-enclosure treatises, such as *Pyers plowmans exhortation, vnto the lordes, knightes and burgoysses of the Parlyamenthouse* (1550), as the shepherd became a figure for agrarian capitalism, that is, the greed and individualism of noble landowners. This new social relation was thought to undermine the traditional three-estate structure and its mutuality, which were represented by the plowman. Chapter 4 takes up the last of the historical shifts: the Reformation redefinition of good works and its effect on the language of labor. Although early reformers insisted that they wanted to preserve traditional social structures even as they radically altered religious beliefs and practices, the early attempts at redefining the relationship between work and works by English theologians such as William Tyndale reveal a devaluing of rural labor. Such an unexpected and surprising side effect of the Reformation may go some way to explaining the popularity of William Langland's late medieval poem, *Piers Plowman*. This poem was printed four times in the mid-sixteenth century and also inspired a number of imitations, such as "I playne Piers which cannot flatter" (?1547). As I argue in this chapter, this popularity had less to do with Langland's proto-Protestantism than with his poem's glorification of the rural laborer. This glorification responds to and even resists the redefinition of good works, preserving a kind of spiritual meaning for rural labor.

My final two chapters take up the sixteenth-century author long associated with the "birth" of the pastoral mode in England, Edmund Spenser. While Spenser's debts to medieval literature have long been noted, these references have been seen as entirely harmonious with the "new" pastoral tradition. As the previous chapters will demonstrate, however, the native traditions of "writing rural labor" offer a potentially antagonistic (or at least potentially anxious) relationship with the new eclogue form. The plowman in particular had come to represent a desire to maintain an interdependent social order (against the shepherd and agrarian capitalism), the potential for class conflict, and a resistance to the breaking apart of the social and religious meanings of work during the Reformation. In short, the "native tradition" of writing rural labor as Spenser inherits it is far less unified and far less assimilable to the Virgilian pastoral than has been appreciated. In chapter 5 I argue that in Spenser's *Shepheardes Calender*, which is typically considered the first pastoral in English, he approaches labor consistently from a "medieval" perspective: through the *Piers Plowman* tradition and the ecclesiastical pastoral. In invoking an earlier symbolic imagination around labor, the rural laborers in the *Calender*, namely Piers and Davy, become a sign of what needs to be repressed and rewritten for the newly rediscovered pastoral to function. Finally, chapter 6 examines the pastoral episode in book 6 of Spenser's *Faerie Queene*, whose Arcadianism seems to reject entirely the medieval literary traditions that informed the *Calender*. Despite redirecting his pastoral toward the *otium* of the Arcadian tradition, Spenser prevents the reader from fully embracing this new "enamelled world," to borrow Raymond Williams's term for the pastoral.[43] Even as Spenser gestures toward the "enamelled world" of Arcadian pastoral, he reveals the dark side of a labor-free countryside: the violence of brigandage and slavery. In this way, Spenser suggests that reading pastoral can be dangerous both for courtly readers, who are trained to ignore the violence and exploitation in the countryside, and for the laborers themselves, whose reality has been appropriated and disguised.

From the perspective of the Middle Ages, the pastoral mode's self-conscious claims to novelty protest too much. To take these claims at their word, as most scholars have done, is to set aside the texts that "haunt" pastoral and that remind us that this mode is as much a meditation on disruption as on the felicitous possibilities of a new form.

ONE | *Medieval Traditions of Writing Rural Labor*

Medieval literature has played a minor role in the literary history of the pastoral mode for an obvious reason: medieval English writers neither imitated Virgil's *Eclogues* nor seemed particularly interested in writing about or in the guise of shepherds. This lack of enthusiasm for shepherds does not mean, however, that they are entirely absent. On the contrary, there are both the "real" shepherds in the shepherd plays of the mystery cycles and the figurative shepherds of ecclesiastical or biblical pastoral, that is, priests who are described in terms of shepherds. The question is whether or how these shepherds might fit in with the pastoral mode as it emerged and then flourished in the sixteenth century. For most scholars of pastoral, the answer has been that medieval shepherds do not fit, and they leave out the Middle Ages entirely in their literary histories. But if we take two of the most prominent theorists of pastoral, Paul Alpers and Louis Montrose, at their word—that it is the shepherds themselves, not the idyllic landscapes or any other elements, that constitute pastoral—then perhaps medieval literature should belong to the history of pastoral after all.[1] No study of pastoral thus far has adequately accounted for the strange status of medieval literature. There are shepherds, to be sure, but nothing that looks like either classical or sixteenth-century pastoral: either what Patrick Cullen (and others) have described as Arcadian pastoral or, to use Alpers's definition, an account of herdsmen and their lives that foregrounds *otium* or singing and wooing.[2] Helen Cooper's *Pastoral: Mediaeval into Renaissance* is the one study that attempts to place medieval shepherds in relation to later pastoral writing, but it does not do anything more than loosely group these texts together in a survey; it does not prove a continuity of influence or even of interest. In sum, all theorists of pastoral could be said to impose a literary history from without, by beginning with the pastoral mode as a given and then noting the few correspondences between medieval texts, on the one hand, and classical or early modern texts, on the other.

If we begin with the medieval texts themselves, however, we find a different story, a different literary tradition. The disparate medieval genres and forms in which literal and figurative shepherds appear—the estates satires, sermons, and plays—suggest that these writers did not understand the shepherd as associated with a particular literary mode or genre, unlike the writers of eclogues in the latter half of the sixteenth century. After all, ecclesiastical or biblical pastoral is an allegorical trope that can be (and is) deployed across a wide range of texts: the appearance of a priest described as a shepherd or shepherds who stand for priests tells us very little about either the form or the content of a piece of writing. Similarly, the shepherd plays are indebted to biblical narratives and do not, therefore, mark out a distinctive genre of their own. Medieval shepherds thus neither follow classical nor prefigure early modern pastoral. Instead, they belong to a tradition of "writing rural labor," whose literary history certainly intersects with but is not the same as pastoral. As such, medieval pastoral shares with other texts in the tradition (most famously William Langland's late-fourteenth-century poem *Piers Plowman*) an interest in the *labor* of rural laborers. In exploring this tradition, this chapter will make two related arguments: First, labor alone, not leisure, recreation, singing, wooing, nor idyllic landscapes (in short, any of the characteristics used to categorize classical and early modern pastoral), is the defining characteristic of rural life in the Middle Ages. Second, to write rural labor was to appropriate an extremely flexible and complex set of meanings: medieval representations of labor carry with them a reformist, even potentially radical, significance. It is this medieval past, of labor and its meanings, that haunts the emergence of early modern pastoral.

Writing Rural Labor

It is worth beginning with the obvious: medieval texts that represent rural life are interested primarily in labor, whether that labor is imagined as literal or figurative. For scholars of medieval literature, such an observation may be unnecessary; there are many medieval texts about rural laborers and very few about rural life without labor. More importantly, the characteristics considered definitive of pastoral—the idyllic landscape, the *otium*, and the piping, singing, and wooing—are almost entirely absent in medieval texts.[3] Such an observation is hardly surprising for the many texts that spring to mind with the phrase *writing rural labor*, such as the early fourteenth-century poem, *Song of the Husbandman*. This text is often considered a kind of ancestor of Langland's poem and other plowman writings, and it puts labor at the center of the "song."[4] Broadly speaking, the medieval view of rural life could be described as follows: labor is the lot of the peasant, and leisure that of the nobleman. When the peasant does not labor he is not leisurely; he is lazy, greedy, or sinful.[5] What is less noted, however, is that those texts that have long been assimilated into the pastoral mode, particularly the shepherd plays of the mystery cycles, are about laborers and their labor.[6] These are less shepherds than rural laborers, indistinguishable from plowmen. Even the recreation they represent becomes a sign of their labor and is, therefore, entirely distinct from the *otium* or the freedom to sing and woo that is typically associated with the classical tradition as it was taken up in the sixteenth century.[7] As Louis Montrose writes, "literary celebrations of pastoral otium conventionalize the relative *ease* of the shepherd's labors. Compared to other agrarian tasks, sheep farming requires very little investment of human resources."[8] The whole point of Virgilian pastoral for Montrose and other theorists is that shepherds do not resemble husbandmen or

18 *Transforming Work*

plowmen. This is not the case for the literal and allegorical shepherds of medieval texts.

My discussion will focus on the shepherd play in the Chester cycle and the first shepherd play from the Towneley manuscript. Dating the cycle plays, especially the Towneley plays, which exist only in one manuscript, is notoriously difficult, but both belong to what Martin Stevens considers the "second generation" of mystery cycles, written most likely in the fifteenth century.[9] For my argument, precise dates are unnecessary; what matters is that the plays were composed in the late medieval period and that they are, to a certain degree, exemplary of late medieval thinking about shepherds, both biblical and "real." The similarities between the shepherd plays in the surviving cycles—York, Chester, Towneley, and N-Town—suggest that writers did indeed draw on a shared tradition if not a shared text; Towneley, for example, seems to copy some plays from the York cycle.[10] Chester and Towneley are particularly suitable for discussing medieval pastoral because both include a kind of "first act" that explores the shepherds as shepherds before they move on to the central material of all the shepherd plays: the Annunciation and Adoration.

Both Chester and Towneley are clearly interested in the shepherds as characters: each play begins with a long speech by one of the shepherds. These opening speeches locate the shepherds in the audience's contemporary world through a discussion of labor, particularly the struggle with sheep rot.[11] Chester, for example, describes the hard work of the shepherd:

> On wouldes have I walked wylde
> under buskes my bowre to bylde,
> from styffe stormes my sheepe to shilde,
> my seemely wedders to save.
> From comlye Conway unto Clyde
> under tyldes them to hyde,
> a better shepperd on no syde
> noe yearthlye man may have.
> For with walkynge werye I have mee rought;
> besydes the suche my sheepe I sought.

> My taytfull tuppes are in my thought,
> them to save and heale
> from the shrewde scabbe yt sought,
> or the rotte, yf yt were wrought.
> (*Shepherds' Play*, 1–14)[12]

This shepherd is both physically and mentally exhausted—from walking around and from his anxiety about his sheep. In Towneley the interest in the "realism" of shepherd life is perhaps more pronounced: shepherding is an occupation, part of the economy of the countryside. When the first shepherd enters, he laments his "vnceyll [misery]" because all of his sheep are dead of the rot, and he has no money to pay his manorial rent:

> All my shepe ar gone,
> I am not left oone,
> The rott has theym slone;
> Now beg I and borow.
> My handys may I wryng
> And mowrnyng make,
> Bot if good will spryng,
> The countré forsake;
> Fermes thyk ar coming,
> My purs is bot wake,
> I haue nerehand nothyng
> To pay nor to take.
> (*First Shepherds' Play*, 5, 35–46)[13]

This passage is less interested in the labor itself than in establishing the shepherd as part of the laboring classes in terms recognizable to the audience: the shepherd must pay "fermes" (his manorial rent). Both plays suggest what a shepherd life meant to the medieval audience: a difficult life characterized by hard labor and poverty.

The feasting and wrestling, what we might consider recreation, are further indications that this is a hard job. The shepherdly activities appear as a necessary break from labor. Only after the shepherds introduce themselves as working men do they sit down together to eat and drink. As the first shepherd in the Towneley play states, "Sytt we downe all thre, / And drynk shall we then" (*First Shepherds' Play*, 276–77). Although the shepherds certainly enjoy themselves, the feasts—where they come together and share their food—function primarily as moments of community, a community that prefigures the kind of Christian community that will be established once Jesus is born. This Christian meaning is made explicit in the Towneley play, in which the shepherds decide to give the remnants of their feast to the poor. The first shepherd states,

> Then wold I we fest,
> This mete who shall
> Into panyere kest.
> (*First Shepherds' Play*, 405–7)

And the third shepherd replies, "For oure saules lett vs do / Poore men gyf it to" (409–10). In other words, even the break from work, the feasting, results in a kind of "work": feeding the hungry is one of the seven works of mercy.

The particular dependence of recreation on labor can be seen in the term used to describe it in the Chester play. The second shepherd turns to one of his fellows and asks, "Tudd, will we shape us to some solace?" (*Shepherds' Play*, 100). "Solace" in Middle English can mean joy and entertainment—a meaning that potentially underlines its similarity to the piping and singing of the pastoral tradition—but it can also mean comfort or consolation. This second meaning reveals the centrality of labor to any representation of leisure or enjoyment: labor is what comes first, and the hardships of labor must be alleviated in life through the comfort of eating and drinking with companions.

The strong, even inextricable, link between rural life and labor in medieval texts is perhaps made most apparent by the absence of depictions of a labor-free or leisurely rural life. Indeed, it seems that medieval writers have difficulty imagining rural life without labor, even when the context is the mythological Golden Age and not contemporary society, as it is in the shepherd plays.[14] Chaucer's "Former Age" offers one of the few medieval accounts of the Golden Age and, therefore, one of the few medieval instances where one might argue for a kind of Virgilian pastoral. Indeed, in his brief account of the poem in the *Oxford Guide to the Shorter Poems*, V. J. Scattergood describes the poem as offering a "pastoral simplicity."[15] Chaucer is not following Virgil's Fourth Eclogue directly; he is following primarily Boethius's *Consolation of Philosophy* and, to a lesser degree, the *Roman de la Rose*.[16] Nevertheless, Chaucer expands the Boethian text concerning how people will be fed without the cultivation of land, how the natural world will serve them, in a manner that brings his version closer to Virgil's poem than his source. Boethius dismisses cultivation quite quickly: "Blisful was the firste age of men. They heelden hem apayed with the metes that the trewe feeldes broughten forth."[17] Chaucer follows Boethius in the first stanza, but the second stanza introduces a focus on plowing (or the lack thereof): "Yit nas the ground nat wounded with the plough, / But corn up-sprong, unsowe of mannes hond."[18] Similarly, Virgil writes in his Fourth Eclogue: "But first, as little gifts for you, child, Earth untilled / Will pour the straying ivy rife, and baccaris" and "soft spikes of grain will gradually gild the fields."[19] Perhaps more interestingly, Chaucer describes the people in "The Former Age" as "lambish" (50), thus introducing a kind of pastoralism into his source. This odd term, which A. V. C. Schmidt thought was coined by Chaucer, certainly refers to the people's innocence, but in doing so it also invokes the world of the allegorical pastoral, in which the people are typically described as sheep.[20]

The potential conflation of Virgilian and allegorical pastoral in Chaucer's poem may be indebted to the *Roman de la Rose*, although not to the passage describing the Golden Age that is most commonly seen as the source of Chaucer's poem. It is indebted to Genius's mention of the Good Shepherd in Shepherd's Park, which occurs near the end of the poem. Genius's shepherd is informed by biblical pastoral (Jesus as the "pastor bonus" of John 10:11–18), but Genius also refers to Virgil's influence: "And as he who wrote the *Bucolics* says in the *Georgics*—for he found in Greek books how Jupiter acted—before Jupiter came there was no one who held a plow; no one had ever plowed, spaded, or cultivated a field. The simple people, peaceable and good, had never laid down boundaries."[21] Although Chaucer did not translate this particular passage of the *Roman*, he was quite familiar with it. It is possible that his account of the Golden Age is indirectly indebted to Virgil and is, therefore, the Middle English text that comes the closest to a Virgilian pastoral.

Despite its potentially "pastoral" elements, Chaucer's "Former Age" ultimately demonstrates how far he is from imagining the leisure or the idyllicism considered so fundamental to the pastoral mode. To be sure, the poem represents a life without labor, but it does not show that such a life is desirable in and of itself. Instead, Chaucer's poem demonstrates that such a life would be brutish and impoverished, not "golden" at all.

First, and most obviously, the subject of the poem is not the lack of labor itself. Instead, labor and its absence are signs of something else: greed and innocence, respectively. That absence is described through a series of negations: the corn is "unsowe of mannes hond" (10) and "no man yit in the morter spyces grond" (15). When labor emerges, it does so as a result of greed: the "swety bysinesse" of grubbing up metal (28). As a consequence of these links—between labor and greed, the lack of labor and innocence/virtue—the labor-free state is one of poverty. In other words, "blisful" (1) as this labor-free life might be, it is certainly not idealized as prosperous or even enjoyable. With one exception (that the corn grows itself) the poem's account of what people eat under such conditions seems entirely "realistic." They forage for food: "They eten mast, hawes, and swich pounage, / And dronken water of the colde welle" (7–8). Chaucer's list of foraged food is far more constricted and far less appetizing than the list appearing in one of his likely sources, the *Roman de la Rose*, in which the people find honey and all varieties of fruit (8355–80). For Chaucer, the limited description underlines the limited quantity of food. Although the people are satisfied with what they find—"They helde hem payed" (3)—they don't eat "half ynough" of the food that they "gnodded [shelled]" (11), a word that sounds like "gnauen" (gnaw) and therefore suggests the primitive, even animal-like existence during this time.[22] Virgil's Golden Age, in contrast, is fertile, filled with flowers, spices, goats with swollen udders, and trees sweating honey. No one has to forage in the Fourth Eclogue because the goats arrive home untended.

Finally, Chaucer's poem is pervaded by a sense that this mode of living has nothing to do with how people live in the countryside in his own time. In adding the lines on cultivation, Chaucer ties the poem more closely to Virgil's Fourth Eclogue and at the same time underlines the distance between the two poems. In Virgil's poem the people no longer need to plow, but they still live a pastoral life: "She-goats unshepherded will bring home udders plumped / With milk, and cattle will not fear the lion's might."[23] The desirability of this state only makes sense because it recognizes what shepherds already do: herd goats and protect livestock from predators. In other words, it is a wish fulfillment linked to a pastoral life. Because Chaucer does not include any pastoral activities in his poem, once he has negated plowing, nothing connects the former age to life in the countryside as it is lived in Chaucer's own time. The people sleep in woods and caves and they forage for their food, neither of which activities characterizes the peasants of Chaucer's "age."

The moment in the poem that is most idyllic is the account of the people asleep:

> In caves and wodes softe and swete
> Slepten this blissed folk withoute walles
> On gras or leves in parfit quiete
> (42–44)

Interestingly, Chaucer has transferred this moment from where it occurs in Boethius's text: immediately after the description of foraging, near the beginning of his account. Boethius thus sets up a clear contrast between then (foraging, sleeping) and the current moment (wars, difficulty), whereas Chaucer jumps back and forth between the Golden Age and his current moment, between positive descriptions of what the Golden Age was and negative descriptions of what it wasn't, thereby underlining what it is like now.[24] The description of sleeping happens in the middle of Chaucer's poem, marking out a tranquil place in the midst of the greed and destruction that surrounds it, just as the countryside, the woods and caves, is a tranquil place undisturbed by the intrigue and violence that characterize the city, the "paleis-chaumbres" and "halles" (41). Despite the pastoral feel to this passage, there is one very important difference: for Chaucer the contrast is between activity (including labor) and sleep, not between activity and leisure, as it is for Virgilian pastoral. The poem's most compelling account of the peaceful life in the former age is, therefore, not leisure at all but rest; this rest borders on a spiritual comfort or "solace," whose desirability for readers in his own time is made all the more potent because of their own labor.

Reform and Rural Labor

Chaucer's poem has a kind of reformist sensibility, although this reformism remains inert, limited to lamenting the state of things. As Andrew Galloway writes, the poem occupies a kind of middle ground, neither endorsing a Wycliffite "view of the Edenic past" nor taking the side of "those who would deny reformers like the Lollards the trenchancy of their disenchanted vision of history."[25] One might suggest that it is precisely the absence of rural labor in the poem that prevents it from articulating a positive sense of what must be done. Rural labor was powerfully associated with reform in the Middle Ages. This reformism stems from what I shall call the "symbolic imagination" around labor that appears repeatedly in medieval texts. That is, rural labor had both a real, historical referent (the activities of plowing and keeping livestock) and a symbolic significance that could be exploited by writers: a shepherd is a priest, a sower is a preacher, etc.[26] In referring to a symbolic imagination, I am purposefully invoking the tradition of exegetical criticism, which argued for a kind of cultural symbolic in the Middle Ages: literal actions and objects should always be read as figuring spiritual actions and objects. Stephen Barney, for example, has noted the "symbolization of agricultural imagery" in late medieval literature: the cultivation described in the Bible is read as penance.[27] That there are symbolic associations around rural labor in this period cannot be doubted: one cannot easily separate medieval discussions of labor into literal (such as the physical activity of plowing) and figurative (such as penance), as G. R. Owst long ago noted in his study of medieval sermons.[28] This is because there are very few discussions of rural labor that advertise themselves as being concerned only with the physical world, whether prescriptive, as in the husbandry manuals that appear with more frequency in the sixteenth century, or descriptive, as in attempts to capture the "reality" of the rural laborer.[29]

In referring to a symbolic imagination, this study does not claim, as did the exegetical critics, a single Christian vision for all of the Middle Ages, nor that we should always read figuratively.[30] As Marshall Leicester wittily states, "what really lies behind the objection [to exegetical criticism] is the feeling that if the exegetical critics are right our ancestors were, in their well-documented distrust of poetry, an impossibly reductive lot who were unable to distinguish clearly between a daisy of the field and the Virgin Mary and who preferred (perhaps rightly) to see the latter whenever they encountered the former."[31] If recent scholarship has shown us one thing, it is the great variety and richness of late medieval religious belief and, indeed, of all late medieval engagements with "authority," whether religious doctrine or practices.[32] Nevertheless, it is worth returning to the exegetical critics' interest in the symbolic precisely because, according to Fredric Jameson's helpful formulation, the symbolic level is where ideology is located and contested, "if we take the term *ideology* here in Althusser's sense as a representational structure which allows the individual subject to conceive or imagine his or her lived relationship to transpersonal realities such as the social structure or the collective logic of History."[33] As Jameson writes, "it is precisely by way of the *moral* and *anagogical* interpretations that the textual apparatus is transformed into a 'libidinal apparatus,' a machinery for ideological investment."[34]

Jameson reminds us that there can be no such thing as a disinterested representation of rural labor, whether literal or figurative. The texts in which one finds popular conceptions about "real" labor—such as sermons, estates satire, and the complaint tradition—are also deeply invested in ideas about how the social world should function and the beliefs and practices of the Christian church. As Stephen Knight writes, "actual representations of those who labour" are "hegemonic in impact, even though apparently positive towards labour."[35] The popularity of "writing rural labor" in the late Middle Ages can certainly be tied to "real" concerns about labor in this period, particularly vagrancy and the upsets of the Peasants' Revolt of 1381, even if these representations themselves ultimately have little to do with reality.[36]

To understand the way in which discussions of rural labor illustrated and encouraged social/economic ideology, one might turn to late medieval sermons on the parable of the laborers in the vineyard (Matthew 20:1–16). This parable is ubiquitous, and it is consistently expounded to explain the ideal social-economic relationship of the Middle Ages: the three-estate model. John Mirk writes in his *Festial* (ca. 1400):

> So mot [must] vch [each] seruand of God enforson [compel] hym to laberon yn þys gre [degree] þat God hath set hym yn: men of Holy Chyrche schuld laberen bysyly in prayng and studying forto techen Goddes pepul; lordus schuld laberen, and oþur rentud [endowed] men schul bysy ham to kepe Holy Chy[r]che in pesse [peace] and in reste, and al oþur comyn [common] pepul; þe comyn pepul schuld labore bysyly to geton lyflode [livelihood] to hemself and for al oþur. For no mon ne wommon schuld excusen ham [himself] of oþur labor, God in þe gospel of þys day ȝeueþ [gives] ensampul, seyng þys [and here Mirk provides the parable].[37]

As this exposition makes clear, rural labor refers both to physical, agricultural labor and, symbolically, to the duties of the clergy and nobility. More importantly, the interpretation of the parable uses rural labor to imagine the proper functioning of society—the mutuality associated with the three-estate structure in which everyone upholds his obligations.

Similarly, expositions of this parable link rural labor to religious beliefs and practices, specifically the spiritual works (penance, prayers, good deeds) necessary for reintegration into the church and, ultimately, for salvation. For example, the priest John Mirk demonstrates this conflation of work, good works, and penance in his account of Adam and Eve, which follows his exposition of the laborers in the vineyard, "Þus ȝe schul know wel þat Adam and Eve were ful holy er [before] þei dyed, and thouthon [thought] on deth inwardely, and labordon bothe besely, and schastysid [chastised] here body re[so]nabully, and so moton [must] alle þat comon of hem þat wil com to þe ioy of paradice and to þe lyue that eure schal laste."[38] For Mirk, as for many other sermon writers, work is a continuous spectrum of physical, mental, and spiritual activities: the "busy" labor of cultivation, the penitential contemplation of mortality, and the punishment of the body through fasting.

Allegories of work in sermons thus have an overt ideological purpose—to ensure that the individual's participation in the social world and the church, what Jameson calls "transpersonal realities," is understood as basic and as central to survival, even as natural, as farming for one's sustenance. Or, one could reverse the direction of the allegory; listeners are trained to understand that working for one's living is always already working to support the status quo—the three-estate structure and the authority of the church/clergy. This ideology is, importantly, always in the process of being created (as well as demonstrated) because the figuration of work carries with it an inherent reformism. This is a typically medieval reformism, understood as a return to an earlier, ideal social and religious state: the three-estate model, in which mutuality is emphasized, greed is condemned, and repentance (and satisfaction) for sins is community-wide. In other words, the reformism does not threaten "transpersonal realities"; it only asks that everyone reform within them. The best example of this is the famous sermon preached by Thomas Wimbledon in 1388, in the wake of the Peasants' Revolt, at St. Paul's Cross. In this sermon, entitled *Redde rationem vilicationis tue*, Wimbledon uses agricultural metaphors taken from biblical parables, such as the dishonest steward (Luke 16:1–10) and the laborers in the vineyard, to urge his listeners to repent both as individuals and as laborers within the three estates, each of whose duties he details. For Wimbledon, the social world (the three estates) has been corrupted by covetousness, and this sin can only be corrected by a reordering of society in which everyone does his job properly in tending the vineyard: "Herfore [therefore] 'euery man see to what astaat God haþ clepid hym [called him to] and dwelle he þer inne' by trauayle acordyng to his degre."[39] That this labor is explicitly penitential is made clear in his directions to yield a reckoning of one's "bailey" [domain]—*redde rationem vilicationis tue*—which is the language of the parable of the dishonest steward. And Wimbledon ends his sermon with a call for penitence in those terms: "Loke þerfore now what þyng is writen in þe bok of þy conscience whyle þou art here. And ʒif þou fyndest out [anything] contrarie to Cristis lif oþer to his techynge, wiþ þe knyf of penaunce and repentaunce scrape it awey, and write it beterer, euermore hertily þynkynge þat þou schalt ʒelde rekenynge of þy baylie."[40] Here Wimbledon links the "thinking" and "reckoning" that go with the sacrament of penance with the "baylie," the site of one's office and where one labors. This sermon demonstrates perfectly how the figurative meanings traditionally assigned to rural labor—penance and working within one's estate—help generate specifically reformist associations around it.

Piers Plowman

The most striking meditation on the meanings of rural labor and the rural laborer in the late medieval period is, of course, William Langland's late-fourteenth-century poem, *Piers Plowman*. At the center of this meditation is the figure Piers, who is clearly indebted to what Stephen Barney calls the "symbolization of agricultural imagery," in that he has both a literal and a spiritual level: he is a plowman (a "real" worker) and a "folwere," a servant of Truth.[41] He is also a figure of some complexity and ambiguity, and scholars have long debated his meaning. For exegetical critics, for example, the fact of rural labor is easily dismissed: Piers is a priest, or priesthood more generally.[42] More persuasive are the discussions that argue for the novelty of Piers's figurative meaning and, therefore, its continued link with a literal level, that is, "real" rural labor and laborers. From this perspective, Piers is not an unproblematic representative of the feudal economy and its values or the practices of the Christian church; rather, he gives us some insight into both the "traditional ideologies" of labor and the contradictions generated by those ideologies.[43] In creating this figure, Langland appropriates the reformism inherent in the language of rural labor: the figurative meanings of penance and the proper functioning of the social world, as discussed above. I shall argue here that by assigning these figurative meanings back to a "real" rural laborer (that is, re-literalizing them as the laborer's duties), Langland suggests that social and religious reform *should* come from the laborer and not only from the estate (or persons) more typically invoked as reformers—namely, the clergy or the king. As Paul Freedman notes, conventional representations of labor can, in certain contexts, have an "anti-hierarchical edge."[44] That the poem establishes a connection between reform and the rural laborer seems glaringly obvious: after all, Piers is an ideal figure who reforms the social world twice, once in the Plowing of the Half-Acre and once in Passus 19 of the B-text, near the end of the poem. And yet, critics have long insisted on the social and religious conservatism of the poem and its upholding of traditional ideologies. It is worth remembering that the poem certainly was not perceived as conservative either by the participants in the Peasants' Revolt of 1381, who invoked it in their letters, or by sixteenth-century readers, as Larry Scanlon has recently observed.[45] What I'd like to suggest here is that Langland's poem, however unconsciously, recognizes, and is made possible by, an odd ideological contradiction in the language of labor: that the same clerical and exegetical tradition that insists upon the status quo (the three-estate structure and the dominance of the clergy over the laity) has assigned a value to "figurative" rural labor that can be appropriated to change that status quo. In other words, the reformist associations surrounding rural labor, which reflect, of course, the conventional ideology, threaten a radical rethinking of the social world when set into motion in Langland's poem. When a Middle English sermon writer states, "And lower men shuld hold hem contente with þe questions and þe sotelte of þer own labour," he clearly means to deny laborers any intellectual or spiritual labor; these are pursuits typically characterized by both questions and "subtlety," whereas ditch-digging most certainly is not.[46] What Langland shows is that the language of "labor" does, in fact, possess a "subtlety" that would allow "lower men" to engage in precisely the intellectual and spiritual labor that is prohibited by the sermon writer. One does not need to reject the language of labor in order to modify its ideological function.

Piers himself functions as a kind of "re-literalization" of spiritual labor, in that he embodies the values that are assigned to the rural laborers in the biblical parables: he is the figure who reforms the social world in the Plowing of the Half-Acre (Passus 6 in the B-text) and the institutional church near the end of the poem (Passus 19 of the B-text). The first of these episodes recalls to a certain degree expositions of the parable of the laborers in the vineyard:

> Now is Perkyn and [þe] pilgrimes to þe plow faren.
> To erie þis half-acre holpen hym manye;
> Dikeres and Delueres digged vp þe balkes;
> Therwiþ was Perkyn apayed and preised hem [yerne].
> Oþere werkmen þer were that wroȝten ful [faste],
> Ech man in his manere made hymself to doone,
> And somme to plese Perkyn piked vp þe wedes,
> At heiȝ prime Piers leet þe plowȝ stonde
> To ouersen hem hymself; whoso best wroȝte
> Sholde be hired þerafter whan heruest tyme come.
> (B6.105–14)

Each person works "in his manere," which could be understood as his "kind," or estate. Despite the divisions of labor, the project requires mutuality: that is, an entire society embarks on the same project. But we should not jump too quickly to allegory, because this account of a properly functioning society is not a parable; the labor is meant to be "real" agricultural labor and the laborers "real" laborers, not priests cutting branches of sin, for example.[47] And the "real" laborer, not the figurative laborers (priests and nobility), is the reformer. That Piers is in charge is made apparent in the exchange between Piers and the knight: the knight offers to plow and Piers declines, instead telling him,

> I shal swynke and swete and sowe for vs boþe,
> And [ek] labour[e] for þi loue al my lif tyme,
> In couenaunt þat þow kepe holy kirke and myselue
> Fro wastours and wikked men þat [wolde me destruye].
> (B6.25–28)[48]

As James Simpson has noted, this is a "bottom-up" view of reform, which simultaneously preserves the content of the tradition (the three-estate structure) and removes it from the hands of those in power (the clergy who preached the sermons, the knights who enforced the peasants' labor).[49]

Such a positive view of the laborer seems, at first glance, to be undercut by the appearance of Wastour, the laborer who refuses to work and who threatens both the knight who attempts to control him and Piers and his men: "'I was noȝt wont to werche,' quod Wastour, 'now wol I noȝt bigynne!'/ And leet liȝt of þe lawe and lasse of þe knyȝte" (B6.167–68). This is a figure drawn from the perspective of the governing classes (not the laborers themselves), the same governing classes who attempted to enforce how much a laborer could be paid and where he could work in the Statutes of Laborers.[50] Piers's harsh treatment of Wastour, calling on Hunger so that he might starve Wastour into working, suggests that Langland is more interested in a kind of reformism shared with Wimbledon, for example, than in any radical rethinking of the role of the laborer. But the appearance of Wastour does not, in fact, result in the expanded power of clergy and knighthood (who are entirely absent or useless, respectively), as we might imagine. Rather, Wastour's threat to the community on the Half-Acre serves to underline the importance of the "libbynge laborers þat lyuen [by] hir hondes, / That treweliche taken and treweliche wynnen" (B7.62–63). As much as Langland recognizes (or fears) the "bad" laborer for whom the collapse of the social world is blamed, he also insists on the "true" laborer as the foundation of that social world.

The reform on the Half-Acre is, of course, a failed experiment: Piers famously abandons his plowing for penance after tearing the Pardon sent from Truth and then disappears from the poem until near the end. When he returns, his literal meaning (as laborer) is far more attenuated; the plowing he supervises seems exclusively an allegory for the founding of the church.[51] We could say, then, that Langland has shown that work doesn't work, that it doesn't return the social world to its proper functioning. As David Aers has argued, this is "an abandonment of attempts to equate the work ethos [of employers] . . . with Christian moral theory and faith."[52] While it is certainly true that the poem rejects a defining aspect of the reformism associated with work—that each person must only fulfill the "labor" and duties associated with his degree—it does not abandon work entirely. Indeed, it is precisely the figurative meanings of rural labor, particularly penance, that allow Langland to transform Piers's meaning when he reaches the limit of the Half-Acre, when "real" labor fails to return society to its proper functioning.

To a certain degree, Piers is always associated with penance. He appears when the pilgrims are seeking Truth, and the episode on the Half-Acre can be read as a form of satisfaction that replaces the pilgrimage.[53] But this link between Piers and penance is made explicit when Piers tears the Pardon sent from Truth, an event that occurs only in the B-version:[54]

> And Piers for pure tene pulled it [asonder]
> And seide, "*Si ambulauero in medio vmbre mortis*
> *Non timebo mala quoniam tu mecum es.*
> I shall cessen of my sowyng," quod Piers, "and swynke noȝt so harde,
> Ne aboute my bely ioye so bisy be na moore;
> Of preieres and of penaunce my plouȝ shal ben herafter,
> And wepen whan I sholde [werche], thouȝ whete breed me faille."
> (B7.119–25)[55]

This dramatic moment has been read as a rejection of the tradition that informs Piers's metaphor: the equation of work with good deeds. Langland does not like the consequences of this metaphor in the social world, its co-option by those in power and the equation of the work ethic with Christian moral theory and faith, to paraphrase Aers. Therefore, he dramatically replaces it with another tradition: an appeal to poverty and *ne solicitii sitis*, Jesus's instruction in Matthew 6:25 to give no thought to the means by which one would be clothed and fed.[56] But the strangeness of this moment in Langland's poem should be appreciated. For Piers to abandon the link between literal and spiritual labor is to abandon the very "ground" of his metaphor. This odd conundrum is made explicit in Piers's speech. First, Piers claims that in the future he will not be concerned with his "bely ioye"; in other words, he will not work for food (as in the directive *ne solicitii sitis*). Then, he gives plowing what seems to be a purely metaphorical (and therefore spiritual) meaning: prayers and penance. But this separation of labor into a literal part (for his belly) and a spiritual part (prayers) should bring us up short, for Piers's work has never been purely literal or concerned only with the body. Rather, we have understood Piers as a penitential figure from the moment that he arrived on the scene. His "sowing" and "swynking" in that instance definitely were not for the purpose of filling his belly but rather in his service to Truth. When Piers then says, in essence, that he's going to abandon the plowing for penance, this reader certainly wonders, What was the plowing if not penance? To be sure, this episode suggests a problem with pardons and with penance; the kind of penance that the church seems to require in this world, that everyone work hard within the three-estate structure, is deeply problematic. All of its rules are called into question by the historical conditions under which work takes place, such as Wastours and market forces. But this episode also presents another kind of challenge to the language of labor. Langland's desire to make Piers more spiritual (purely penitential) is also a desire to make him more literal. After all, only a real plowman can give up plowing to do penance.

Indeed, Piers must remain a plowman throughout the rest of the poem—during the Dreamer's search for Dowel—precisely because Langland is interested in the reformist possibilities of linking the rural laborer, and not the priest, with penance and good deeds. In emphasizing the spiritual capacity of the laborer, Langland departs from traditional sermons and devotional texts for the laity, which consistently draw limits around what the "lewd" (the unlearned) are permitted to know. For example, the author of a late medieval sermon writes, in an extremely illogical fashion, "Sir, ryght as Criste is well payed [satisfied] with euery man þat can [knows] is [his] lawe, and þe more þat he can [knows] þer-of, þe bettur he is apeid [satisfied], ryght so euery lewde [unlearned] man and laborere is exscused generally to beleue as all holychurche dothe with-owte more lernynge þer-of."[57] Such an approach to lay learning, in which the basic information is understood as the upper limit, should be familiar to readers of Wycliffite texts of the late fourteenth and early fifteenth centuries, which consistently accuse the established church of "fencing off" scripture from those who would like to read it, as private gardens inside the commons.[58] Indeed, the motivation for *Piers the Plowman's Crede*, a poem written in imitation of Langland's between 1393 and 1401, is that the speaker does not know his Creed, one of the basic elements of faith:[59]

> *A* and all myn *A-B-C* after have I lerned,
> And patred in my *Pater Noster* iche poynt after other,
> And after all myn *Ave Marie* almost to the ende.
> But al my kare is to comen, for I can nohght my Crede.[60]

But Langland does not "excuse" the laborer from knowledge, nor does he show him to be the victim of incompetent clergy and friars (as do the Wycliffites and the author of the *Crede*); instead, he appropriates him to present complex religious ideas. Piers's alternative to clergy is not one that rejects knowledge entirely ("lewed" instead of "lerned"), and it must, therefore, be differentiated from "holy simplicity," the idea that simple people are holy precisely because they are simple, a view that Elizabeth Kirk has seen to be influential, in some part, in how Piers was understood.[61] First, we should note that the one appeal to holy simplicity in the poem does not hold much authority. This appeal is made by Will, a highly questionable speaker, who confronts the allegorical figure Scripture with a gloss on "*Ecce ipsi ydiot[e] rapiunt celum vbi nos sapientes in inferno mergimur* [Lo, the unlearned themselves take heaven by force while we wise ones are drowned in hell]":[62]

> And is to mene to [Englissh] men, moore ne lesse,
> Arn none raþer yrauysshed fro þe riȝte bileue
> Than are þise [kete] clerkes þat konne manye bokes,
> Ne none sonner saued, ne sadder of bileue,
> Than Plowmen and pastours and [pouere] commune laborers,
> Souteres and shepherdes; [swiche] lewed Iuttes
> Percen wiþ a Paternoster þe paleys of heuene
> And passen Purgatorie penauncelees at hir hennes partyng
> Into þe [parfit] blisse of Paradis for hir pure bileue,
> That inparfitly here knewe and ek lyuede.
> (B10.461–71)

Will raises a compelling question about the importance of learning, one that Langland clearly found significant because he ended the A version of his poem with this passage.[63] But this position should not be assigned to Langland, since Will is scorned for it by the allegorical figure Scripture at the opening of the next Passus. Second, we should recall

Medieval Traditions of Writing Rural Labor 35

that it was precisely Piers's (the plowman's) anxiety about salvation, his tearing of the Pardon, that has led to this point in the poem. We can hardly think that plowmen are "sonner saved" after that experience.

If Piers is neither clergy nor "simple" laborer, then he offers a third way that recognizes the capacity of the humble and simple to understand complicated religious ideas about salvation. This "third way" of Piers's learning stands in a sometime hostile but always dependent relation to clerkly learning; it is not the simple rejection of learning that Will has outlined in his account of holy simplicity. This connection can be found in Piers's first appearance, when he sets his knowledge equal to the clergy: he knows Truth "as kyndely as a clerc doþ hise bokes" (B5.538). And it can be found when the figure Clergie describes Piers's significance:

> "For oon Piers þe Plowman haþ impugned vs alle,
> And set alle sciences at a sop saue loue one;
> And no text ne takeþ to mayntene his cause
> But *Dilige deum* and *Domine quis habitabit*;
> And [demeþ] þat dowel and dobet arn two Infinites,
> Whiche Infinites wiþ a feith fynden out dobest,
> Which shal saue mannes soule; þus seiþ Piers þe Plowman."
> (B13.124–30)[64]

It is no accident that Clergie understands Piers and can explain his significance because Clergie here is learning, not just the institution or occupation "clergy."[65] Although both of these passages hint at a kind of anti-intellectualism, an opposition to clergy, this opposition must be distinguished from the knee-jerk reaction of the dreamer, who is ready to dismiss learning entirely and must realize that knowledge can be useful, as the man who knows how to swim has an advantage over the man who does not.

The potential radicalism of Piers as a "re-literalization" of the spiritual meanings of labor, first suggested by his alternative to "clergie," is made most apparent at the end of the poem in Passus 19 of the B-text, when Langland returns to the social world and the concerns of the Half-Acre. At the end of his narration about Jesus' life and death, Conscience says:

36 *Transforming Work*

> And whan þis dede was doon do best he [þouȝte],
> And yaf Piers [pardon, and power] he grauntede hym,
> Myght [men] to assoille of alle manere synne[s],
> To alle maner men, mercy and forȝifnesse
> In couenaunt þat þei come and knewelich[e] to paie
> To Piers pardon þe Plowman *redde quod debes*.
> Thus haþ Piers power, b[e] his pardon paied,
> To bynde and vnbynde boþe here and elli[s],
> And assoille men of alle synnes saue of dette one.
> (B19.183–90)⁶⁶

Here Jesus has given Peter's role as confessor—the power to pardon, to bind and unbind—to a plowman. This is, of course, a quite radical message, in that it denies the clergy their distinct role, their special knowledge and authority, and, in suggesting that Piers is now pope, the poem fills the highest office in the church with a laborer. Indeed, Langland here quite pointedly reminds us of his laboring status by repeating his occupation—"Piers pardon the *Plowman*." It is important to note the way in which this description of Piers's new role reverses the familiar mode. In the parable of the workers in the vineyard, "real" priests are figurative rural laborers, in that they "cut" the branches of sin, for example. In Langland, "real" rural laborers are figurative priests, in that they have the power over confession. That it is the penitential system that is explicitly being reformed by a laborer should come as no surprise. What Piers, as the laborer, brings to his new office is, precisely, his association with the figurative meaning of work: penance. Piers will ensure that everyone pays what he owes, that is, performs the work of penance.⁶⁷

Radical Plowmen

The potential radicalism in Langland's poem lies in the fact that it locates the spiritual labor of reform in the "real" rural laborer, instead of in the clergy and the nobility (who are only figurative laborers). For Langland, this radicalism remains only a potential; this is, after all, a dream vision, not a sermon or a treatise. But Langland's contemporaries clearly perceived this potential as well, aided as they were by the pressures of the fraught historical moment in which Langland's poem emerged: the Peasants' Revolt of 1381. The revolt certainly also raised questions about the radicalism of "real" plowmen given the Piers who appears in a sermon attributed to the rebel priest John Ball, quoted in Thomas Walsingham's account of the revolt in his chronicle.[68]

Like Langland's poem, Ball's sermon demonstrates in brief a change in the expected relationship between literal and figurative labors: the rebels (who are, one would imagine, literally peasants) are told to become figurative husbandmen as well. Walsingham claims to quote Ball's sermon:

> Quapropter monuit ut essent uiri cordati, et amore boni patrisfamilias excolentis agrum suum, et extirpantis ac resecantis noxia gramina que fruges solent opprimere, et ipsi in presenti facere festinarent. Primo, maiores regni dominos occidendo, deinde, iuridicos, iusticiarios, et iuratores patrie, perimendo postremo, quoscunque scirent in posterum communitati nociuos [He therefore urged them to be men of courage, and out of love for their virtuous fathers who had tilled their land, and pulled up and cut down the noxious weeds which usually choke the crops, to make haste themselves at that present time to do the same. They must do this first, by killing the most powerful of the lords of the realm, then by slaying the lawyers, justiciars, and jurors of the land, and finally, by weeding out from their land any that they knew would in the future be harmful to the commonwealth].[69]

Ball here follows precisely the expositions of parables of rural labor: real labor, of plowing and uprooting weeds, has the figurative meaning of reform (rooting out). The difference is, of course, that Ball has assigned (and limited) these figurative meanings; they are re-literalized so that uprooting weeds (a physical activity), which is typically read as reform (a spiritual activity, such as "cutting sin"), is read as another physical activity: killing. Those who literally uproot weeds, the "real" rural laborers, should also uproot people. As Steven Justice writes, "In Ball as in Langland, 'delving' is a figure for action, and the weeds are its frustration. . . . the *structure* of meaning is identical: both use the concrete vocabulary of labor as a vocabulary of reform."[70] In exploiting this ambiguity of literal and figurative labors, Ball has changed the ideological impact of the parable to authorize rebellion instead of obedience and an overturning of the status quo instead of its support. The radical restructuring imagined here is quite startling and seems to be unique to the peasants of the Peasants' Revolt. As Rodney Hilton writes, the rebels' "rejection of the concept of a society composed of a balance of hierarchically arranged estates is not easy to explain," and he considers their "determination to end the system of lordship" to be a "remarkable breakaway from traditional thought."[71] One could certainly imagine a revolt that would insist on the traditional obligations of lords to peasants or one that would resist taxation. In both of these, the rebels would invoke the same language as their perceived oppressors: reminding them, perhaps with the parable of the laborers in the vineyard, that each estate has obligations to the other. But the rebels of the Peasants' Revolt abandon those obligations, using the same language within which they've found new possibilities, apparently inspired by Langland's poem.

In their representations of laborers, Langland and Ball both demonstrate that the inherent slipperiness of figurative language can be put to ideological uses. As much as exegetes might inform their listeners and readers to read in one direction, from the literal to the figurative, the levels always threaten to collapse, to break down the exegetes' carefully constructed categories.

Medieval Pastoral

That the medieval plowman is, at least in part, an expression of and meditation on the reformist potential inherent in the language of rural labor should hardly come as a surprise to readers of Langland's poem. But my focus on the plowman—who is, of course, the most popular rural laborer in Middle English literature—has perhaps obscured my larger argument that *all* medieval representations of rural laborers, including, most importantly for this study, shepherds, belong to a tradition of writing rural labor that recognizes a reformist potential even if it does not embrace it. As mentioned above, the medieval pastoral includes essentially two kinds of medieval shepherds: the shepherds of ecclesiastical pastoral and those appearing in the medieval mystery plays. These two types of shepherds are, as I shall argue here, related in terms somewhat similar to biblical agricultural laborers (the sower or the workers in the vineyard) and literary plowmen. That is, shepherds in medieval mystery plays are attempts to think through a "real" rural laborer specifically in light of the range of symbolic meanings that accompany him; in this case those meanings are generated by the ecclesiastical pastoral, in which the shepherd is a priest. This allegorical mode is similarly loose, capable of working in both directions—from the literal to the symbolic, as it should do according to the exegetes, and vice versa, in that it threatens to endow the "real" shepherd with learning and authority far beyond his status as a simple, humble layperson.

The ecclesiastical pastoral appears in a wide range of texts—medieval sermons, estates satire, and devotional writings—and its roots are in the parable of the good shepherd (John 10:11–18), in which Jesus calls himself a shepherd: "*Ego sum pastor bonus*." One might say that the shepherd-priest was (and indeed remains) the governing metaphor for imagining and describing the relationship between clergy and laity within the Christian church. A brief survey of some examples will demonstrate that this metaphor, like the "symbolization of agricultural imagery" discussed above, is focused on labor and, ultimately, reformist in its interests. Shepherding provides a language for priestly duties (caring for the flock) and for the dereliction of duty (hired shepherds do not protect the sheep from wolves). The equation between priestly duties and shepherding is demonstrated in a sermon by Bishop Thomas Brinton, preached to other clergymen in ca. 1376–77, in which he details priests' three main duties: keep the sheep together, govern and guard them, and even suffer death for them.[72] And Brinton is quite explicit about what the "governing" and "guarding" consist of: "predicacionis verbo, conuersacionis exemplo, et temporali subsidio [by preaching the word, providing an example, and temporal assistance]."[73] It is worth emphasizing that the details (the "reality") of labor are absolutely central to this form of pastoral. This mode could not possibly make sense if one does not understand the particular tasks necessary in keeping sheep, such as putting salve on (anointing) those that are scabbed. As a late-fourteenth-century sermon states, "Hit [It] falluþ to a good herde [shepherd] to ledon hise schep in hoole pasturis, and whanne hise schep ben hurte or scabbude to heelon hem and to greson hem."[74]

In more popular expressions of ecclesiastical pastoral—those accounts of the clergy that appear in estates satire, for example—the emphasis tends to fall on what priests should do but do not.[75] It is this anticlericalism that gives ecclesiastical pastoral its reformist tone. In the brief estates satire with which John Gower begins his late-fourteenth-century collection of tales, *Confessio Amantis*, he describes the failings of the clergy using the pastoral:

> Lo thus tobroke is Cristes folde,
> Wherof the flock withoute guide
> Devoured is on every side,
> In lacke of hem that ben unware
> Schepherdes, which her wit beware
> Upon the world in other halve.[76]

This account of the clergy as failed shepherds is entirely conventional and is matched almost exactly in a late-fourteenth-century sermon by a follower of John Wyclif, who claims that "Crist telluþ in þis gospel þe maneris of a good herde [shepherde], so þat herby we may wyten how owre herdis faylen now."[77] We could say that the only potentially radical aspect of these examples is that they appear in English and thus give the laity a language with which to criticize their priests.

In its conventionality the reformism of ecclesiastical pastoral matches that of the agricultural parables, such as the laborers in the vineyard: the comparison of priests to shepherds, or the three estates to laborers, reflects a desire to return to an idealized status quo rather than a desire to challenge the authority of the clergy or change the church (or any aspect of the social world) as such. But the reformism of ecclesiastical pastoral is both broader and more limited in scope than that of the agricultural parables. On the one hand, the critique of the church and clergy generated by the ecclesiastical pastoral, what one might even call its anticlericalism, appears in a wide range of writings: Gower, Brinton, and the Wycliffites all make use of this trope. On the other hand, its very popularity implies its limitations: it can only go over familiar ground, not articulate a new role for the clergy or for the laity. William Langland's brief use of ecclesiastical pastoral in the C-text of *Piers Plowman* is illustrative of both the appeal of this discourse and its limits. In the Pardon sent from Truth, the "wretched villainy" in the church is blamed on the bishops, whose dereliction of duty is described in detail in terms of shepherds who do not protect their flocks (C9.255–81). But Langland does not stay with the pastoral; he interjects a command to "Redde racionem vilicacionis" (C9.274) into his address to the "herde," thus raising the stakes by underlining that his shepherd is a laborer who must account for his "huyre" (C9.275). Similarly, the pseudo-Chaucerian *Plowman's Tale*, a late-medieval, anticlerical poem revised and circulated in the sixteenth century, puts the ecclesiastical pastoral within a "plowman" frame. It is as if the later author, inspired by Langland, thinks that the plowman can make the reformist argument more effectively than the ecclesiastical pastoral.[78] One could speculate that shepherds did not inspire as much experimentation and innovation as the plowman precisely because the shepherd figure was already so firmly and clearly defined as a priest by biblical precedent. There is not the same figurative (and potentially ideological) ambiguity as there is in the plowman, in which the spiritual and the literal overlap and shift around: the "real" rural laborer performing spiritual works.

Nevertheless, the potential for figurative (and, therefore, ideological) ambiguity around shepherds does appear at the end of the medieval period in the shepherd plays of the mystery cycles, perhaps because of the influence of Langland's poem and its expanded role for rural laborers. Both Elizabeth Salter and, more recently, Ruth Nisse argue for a relationship between Langland's poem and the shepherd plays. Salter writes, "both Langland and the authors of the religious plays, to some degree and in some areas, are uneasy about the preservation of the status quo; both raise awkward questions"; and Nisse claims that the Wakefield Master, the author of the Towneley shepherd plays, borrows directly "from the literary culture of *Piers Plowman*."[79] The shepherds who appear in the medieval mystery plays are certainly attempts to think through shepherds as shepherds. Readers have long noticed what they typically refer to as "realism."[80] In this sense, the plays re-ground the pastoral metaphor in its literal level.[81] But the plays are also informed by ecclesiastical pastoral, the equation of shepherds and priests. In this sense, we could say that the plays cannot help but see "real" shepherds in terms of priests: they re-literalize the spiritual aspects of shepherds (their priestliness) by assigning these back to shepherds. In doing so, they allow an expanded role for the laity, evidence of a desire to imagine religious knowledge for "real" herdsmen, a topic quite suitable for religious plays performed in English for the townspeople.[82] The plays' use of pastoral thus demonstrates how the changing devotional situation of the laity in the late medieval period (that desire for knowledge associated with the clergy) can and cannot be contained within a traditional language. In other words, the language of labor once again provides a kind of ideological ambiguity that can be exploited to challenge (or at least question) the status quo, in which humble, simple people should not have access to the knowledge that belongs to priests.

As discussed above, the opening of both plays makes clear that we are to see these shepherds primarily in terms of their literal meaning— as rural laborers—because they contain details recognizable from the audience's social world: discussions of sheep keeping, eating and drinking, wrestling. At the same time, the shepherds also have a symbolic significance outside time, as the shepherds of the Bible. As such, they have access to sacred knowledge (the angel's revelation of Christ's birth) and biblical texts, particularly those of the prophets. In this way, the plays suggest that the shepherds are, in some sense, "clergie" (in the sense of educated). Medieval audience members probably would have seen this link between shepherds and clergy as natural or at least normal because they would have already been trained by the ecclesiastical pastoral to read shepherds as priests. In other words, the plays cannot help but confer a kind of priestliness on these shepherds precisely because of their shepherdliness. The plays do not necessarily negotiate the shepherds' expanded role smoothly, and the representation of the shepherds' learning suggests a discomfort about what it means for lay people, especially laborers, to be "clergie." As I shall demonstrate here, the Towneley play is far more radical in re-literalizing the shepherd, whereas the Chester play seeks to contain the shepherd within his figurative (and ideologically secure) significance.

Although both plays detail shepherding activities, the Towneley play understands these within all the specificity of the contemporary social world. In other words, shepherding is not some timeless duty mapped onto England but part of the economy of the countryside—the loss of sheep to the rot is translated into the loss of money—and may reflect concerns about the enclosures of the fifteenth century.[83] In his opening speech the first shepherd discusses his poverty and his inability to pay his rents ("fermes") because his sheep have died. In its attention to the economic conditions of the shepherd, particularly his vulnerability, the *First Shepherds' Play* in the Towneley cycle (and its more famous successor, the *Second Shepherds' Play*) bears some resemblance to texts typically placed in the "plowman tradition," such as the early fourteenth-century *Song of the Husbandman*, which details the laborer's vulnerability to those in power. For this reason, some readers have seen a connection between "shepherd literature" and social injustice or the literature of dissent.[84]

At the same time that the play insists on a kind of heightened literalism around its shepherds (in that these are not the biblical shepherds but shepherds in late medieval England), it also assigns them knowledge of their biblical role. These shepherds are familiar with the prophets—"That same childe is he / That prophetys of told" (*First Shepherds' Play*, 478–79)—as if they themselves can read. This expansion of lay knowledge works both within the play and outside it, if we read the play as a kind of "vernacular theology," in that the play translates the Bible for the laity, informing them of what happens in scripture. The angel appears and speaks to the shepherds in English, not Latin: "Herkyn, hyrdes! Awake! (*First Shepherds' Play*, 426). From this perspective, the play undercuts precisely that simplicity of the vulnerable poor that is thematized in the Bible. These shepherds may be shepherds, but they are not merely following the angel blindly.

Moreover, the shepherds' knowledge of Christ's birth and Mary's virginity is never co-opted by the clergy (or anyone else); it remains the property of the rural laborers. We could say, then, that the shepherds have become both literal and spiritual shepherds, thus making the priests unnecessary. The potential for opposition to the clergy is made clear in a moment of anticlericalism and antifraternalism near the end of the play, when one of the shepherds "reads" his experience in light of Virgil:

> Virgill in his poetré
> Sayde in his verse,
> Even thus by grameré,
> As I shall reherse:
> "*Iam noua progenies celo demittitur alto;
> Iam rediet Virgo, redeunt Saturnia regna.*"
> (*First Shepherds' Play*, 556–59)

This quotation of Virgil's Fourth Eclogue aligns these shepherds with learning and therefore lays claim to a knowledge that must certainly be described as "clergé," as it is in the citation below. But the appropriation of "clergie" is not unambiguous; it earns a vociferous anticlerical response:

> Weme! tord! what speke ye
> Here in myne eeres?
> Tell vs no clergé!
> I hold you of the frères;
> Ye preche.
> (*First Shepherds' Play*, 560–64)[85]

What has generated the antipathy is the Latin, and perhaps the classical reference, not "clerical knowledge" itself. Indeed, the content of the Latin is discussed in English without a problem, as is the content of all the other Latin (what the prophets have said). It would seem that "clergie" (in terms of biblical knowledge) has been successfully separated from the clergy and assigned to the laity as long as it appears in

English. This allusion to Virgil is, somewhat surprisingly, a meditation on ecclesiastical pastoral, not classical pastoral. Virgil's Fourth Eclogue lends authority to the shepherds' prophetic role, but the author is entirely uninterested in the similarity of the pastoral world itself. In other words, the author uses Virgil only to claim an expanded role for the shepherds and their religious knowledge, not as a model for what shepherds do and say regarding their sheep.[86] It should be noted that this invocation of Virgil is not typical in the shepherd plays; in fact, this is the only identifiably Virgilian moment in all of the vernacular literature that is typically described in terms of medieval pastoral.

The Chester play, in contrast, attempts to control the meaning of the shepherds by linking them firmly to their figurative meaning as a kind of clergy, or at least a "spiritual pastorate," to use the editors' terms.[87] To be sure, these shepherds are, like the shepherds in the Towneley play, supposed to be "real" in their working and feasting and wrestling. But the specific references to their shepherding, their labor, can also be read allegorically. For example, the opening speech, quoted above, establishes the first shepherd as a "good shepherd": every detail of this speech—the saving and healing, the earthly shepherd—can be read in terms of the parable. Only the brief reference to geography distinguishes it from ecclesiastical pastoral. In addition, the author denies his shepherds access to "clergie," the knowledge gained by the shepherds in the Towneley plays. The Chester shepherds exhibit a kind of "holy simplicity." They do not know what the light means—"What is all this light here" (*Shepherds' Play*, 300)—but they want to follow it anyway, "That starre if it stand / to seek will I fond" (*Shepherds' Play*, 318–19). More importantly, their encounter with the angel underscores both their lack of knowledge and their unsuitability for learning. After the angel sings in Latin, they begin to imitate the sounds without understanding them:

> What songe was this, saye yee,
> that he sang to us all three?
> Expounded shall yt bee,
> erre wee hethen passe;
> for I am eldest of degree,

and alsoe best, as it seemes mee,
hit was "grorus glorus" with a "glee."
Hit was neyther more nor lasse.
          (*Shepherds' Play*, 376–83)

The term "expounded" invokes the clergy, only to distance these shepherds from them, since the shepherd imitates the sounds without translating the words. In a sense this author offers them a kind of half-knowledge, in which one shepherd interlards his account of the song with untranslated Latin words. It's not clear whether the shepherd understands them or not:

Yett and yett he sange more to;
from my mynde yt shall not starte.
Hee sange alsoe of a "Deo";
me thought that heled my harte.
And that word "terra" hee tamed—
therto I toke good intent.
And "pax" alsoe may not be blamed;
for that to this songe I assent.
          (*Shepherds' Play*, 428–35)

The audience understands this speech in a general sense—the angel's song proclaims a glorious event—even if they do not understand Latin. All of the words generate a positive response on the part of the shepherd; what matters, therefore, is the effect of the words on the shepherd, not their specific meaning. In fact, the author is not interested in translating them, in making "clergie" accessible to everyone.

The final, and definitive, attempt to control the shepherds and their access to "clergie" occurs at the end of the play, when all of the shepherds become associated with a religious life. The second shepherd states that he will "preach all that I can and knowe" (*Shepherds' Play*, 654), and the third shepherd will go over the sea "to preach this thinge in every place" (659). At first glance, these vows seem relatively independent of both clerical status and the institutional church, but each shepherd also identifies a new vocation to replace his status as worker. Garcius becomes an "anker" (667) and the first shepherd a "hermitte" (669). All of them give up "sheppardes craft" (666). In other words, the shepherds cannot be both shepherds and preachers; their new vocations revise their extra-clerical status in a form recognizable to the audience as "religious." In this way, the play asserts that these shepherds cannot remain rural laborers and also "knowe" about Jesus's birth.

As the only surviving examples of what can definitively be called "shepherd literature" in medieval England, the mystery plays are strikingly uninterested in establishing or upholding the conventions associated with the pastoral mode, whether classical or ecclesiastical. They belong instead to what we might call the literature of rural labor, related to both the plowman tradition and the "symbolization of agricultural imagery." The wide variety of texts that belong to this literary tradition—expositions of parables, the literature of complaint, mystery plays, the plowman tradition, estates satire—reinforces that rural labor in the medieval period is never merely about the literal (a physical activity that earns a wage) but inextricably connected with ideas about the way in which society and the church should function. This connection is created symbolically, in the tradition of attributing an "extra" meaning to sowing or plowing or shepherding. But we hardly need reminding that figuration of all kinds is never stable, that no matter what the tradition, metaphors are slippery and can be reversed. If it is conventional to call a "real" priest a shepherd, it is far more radical to call a "real" shepherd a priest. The medieval poetry of rural labor, in its very conventionality, always carries with it a reformist, even radical, potential.

TWO | *The Invention of the English Eclogue*

*I*nterest in the eclogue form and its shepherds seems to appear (or reappear) almost entirely out of nowhere in early sixteenth-century England. Although Virgil's works were certainly known to medieval authors, the *Eclogues* had very little influence on the development of vernacular literature in fourteenth- and fifteenth-century England.[1] The origins of the sudden interest in the *Eclogues* in the sixteenth century can be traced to two important literary events: first, the publication of Mantuan's *Eclogues* in 1498, which took Virgil as their model, and then the first printing of Virgil's *Eclogues* in 1512.[2] Both of these became popular school texts and were used throughout the sixteenth century; Michael Drayton, an Elizabethan pastoralist, underlines their role in his own education, when he writes that his tutor

> first read to me honest Mantuan,
> Then Virgil's Eclogues being enter'd thus,
> Methought I straight had mounted Pegasus.[3]

Eclogues written in English in imitation of Virgil and Mantuan followed shortly after the appearance of the Latin texts: Alexander Barclay composed five eclogues in 1513–14 (printed in part in 1548 and in full in 1570); Barnabe Googe's eclogues were printed in 1563; and finally and most influentially, Edmund Spenser's *Shepheardes Calender* appeared in 1579. The novelty of the eclogue form is, perhaps, most self-consciously expressed at the opening of Spenser's *Shepheardes Calender*, in which E. K., who introduces and comments on Spenser's poetry, defines the eclogue, or "AEglogue," commenting that this is a word that is "unknowen to most."[4] Spenser has, of course, received credit for introducing the eclogue and its version of pastoral to England, but it is worth remembering that his attempts were preceded by both Barclay and Googe.[5] Their eclogues have, in contrast to Spenser's, received very little attention from scholars and are discussed almost solely in terms of their inferiority to the *Calender*.[6] Perhaps more importantly, their works have not figured at all in influential theories of pastoral, including Paul Alpers's *What Is Pastoral?* and Louis Montrose's essays.[7] This omission may have to do with uncertainty about the lines of influence: there is no definite evidence that Spenser or any of the later pastoral poets knew the work of Barclay and Googe, whereas they certainly knew Virgil. But it also smacks of a kind of literary hermeticism: the history of pastoral consists only of those writers who come closest to the classical tradition.[8] But, if we agree with Alpers and Montrose that pastoral is about "herdsmen and their lives," then these early eclogues surely belong to the pastoral tradition.[9] As the first English attempts at a new literary form, they lend particular insight into the conditions of its emergence. Barclay and Googe, and even Spenser, whose eclogues will be discussed in a later chapter, encountered the pastoral of Virgil and Mantuan not as we do—within a defined literary form, however porous the boundaries—but as at least partly intelligible within the medieval literary traditions of writing rural labor, as I shall demonstrate here. It is precisely because of their contradictions and inconsistencies, what Fredric Jameson calls "discontinuous and heterogeneous formal processes," that the eclogues reveal the ideological struggle that marks the emergence of the pastoral mode.[10]

The most important aspect of this novelty, one borrowed from both Mantuan and Virgil, is a re-literalization of the shepherd, what one might otherwise describe as that interest in "herdsmen and their lives." In other words, the shepherds in the eclogue are supposed to be first and foremost shepherds; they are not merely substitutes for priests, as in the most common form of pastoral in the Middle Ages (the ecclesiastical), nor are they ultimately revealed to be the biblical shepherds at Christ's birth, as in medieval nativity plays. Their distance from medieval texts is most immediately evident in their names, which recall the shepherds of Virgil and Mantuan: Cornix, Coridon, Amintas, and Menalcas. More importantly, both Googe and Barclay include details about the labor of the shepherds: the state of the weather, the condition of their sheep, what they plan to eat (these details are far more attenuated in Googe, for reasons discussed below). None of these details should be read allegorically, as are the wolves that prey on sheep or the tar used to heal them in the purely ecclesiastical pastoral found in medieval estates satires and sermons. This is not to say that the sixteenth-century authors avoid allegory completely: their eclogues also take up wolves and shepherd-priests. But the framework for understanding shepherds has shifted away from a primarily Christian or biblical tradition. Although the re-literalization of shepherds is fundamental to the new form, it also presents a challenge to its authors and readers: How literally should these new shepherds be taken? The authors (and the readers) are thus confronted with precisely those historical and social questions that the metaphoricity of the ecclesiastical pastoral had set aside: to what extent do these figures represent rural laborers in the English countryside, laborers who belong to the same social world inhabited by the readers and authors?[11]

Such questions were, at the time Barclay and Googe were writing, particularly fraught. As discussed in the previous chapter, "writing rural labor" had a reformist significance, both religious and social, from the late medieval period well into the mid-sixteenth century. This reformism is most obvious in the *Piers Plowman* tradition: plowmen are often spokesmen for anticlericalism, associated first with Wycliffism, as in *Piers the Plowman's Crede* (ca. 1400), and then with Protestantism, as in the *Plowman's Tale* (a late medieval poem with a Henrician prologue) and "I playne Piers" (?1547).[12] In addition, plowmen were typically used to represent the commons in the late Middle Ages, as the *General Prologue* to the *Canterbury Tales* makes clear. They have the potential to be, therefore, figures demanding the redress of grievances against the commons, as in the letters of the Peasants' Revolt, which made use of *Piers Plowman*, and the anti-enclosure tract *Pyers plowmans exhortation, vnto the lords, knightes and burgoysses of the Parlyamenthouse* (1550). Even shepherds, who are far less common in medieval texts, appearing only in nativity plays, reveal a potential reformism that is linked with their status as laborers, as discussed in the previous chapter.

Barclay and Googe are at first glance clearly uninterested in invoking either the plowman tradition or the shepherds of the nativity plays. Indeed, the appeal of the eclogue seems to be precisely that it is a mode for writing rural laborers untainted by a tradition of social reformism (but not necessarily untainted by the kind of religious reformism found in ecclesiastical pastoral). And yet, these new inventions cannot help revealing the traces of what the authors are writing against. This chapter shall explore the way in which the radical potential of rural laborers, in the tradition of *Piers Plowman*, haunts the emergence of pastoral and how these authors attempt to limit this capacity, and ultimately to limit the literalization in which they are otherwise so invested.[13] In using the term *haunt* to describe the early eclogues' relation to their medieval past, I am invoking the work of Pierre Macherey in *A Theory of Literary Production*. Macherey offers a particularly compelling account of the relationship between a text and the historical conditions out of which it emerges:

> it is not a question of introducing a historical explanation which is stuck on to the work from the outside. On the contrary, we must show a sort of splitting within the work: this division is its unconscious, in so far as it possesses one—the unconscious which is history, the play of history beyond its edges, encroaching on those edges: this is why it is possible to trace the path which leads from the haunted work to that which haunts it. Once again, it is not a question of redoubling the work with an unconscious, but a question of revealing in the very gestures of expression that which it is not. Then, the reverse side of what is written will be history itself.[14]

The unconscious of the early eclogues is, as I shall demonstrate here, rural labor, which must be repressed because this is the aspect of the medieval tradition that carries with it a reformist significance. After all, no one is threatened by the "real" pursuits of the rural laborer that do not involve labor—his wrestling, feasting, or wooing—and these literal aspects remain; indeed, they begin to dominate a characterization that once had been largely focused on labor.

Barclay and the Medieval Pastoral

Barclay's eclogues are a kind of pastiche of medieval literary modes, such as satire, allegory, didactic treatise, and lament, within the new eclogue form. Despite Barclay's evident interest in novelty, his work is more often associated with the medieval period than the early modern. As his editor writes, "the cast of Barclay's mind was entirely mediaeval. He has much more in common with Lydgate than with Spenser."[15] Nevertheless, Barclay seems to share a certain degree of self-consciousness about his eclogues as a transitory text with Spenser (or, rather, E. K., Spenser's commentator), about "the olde name" and the "new worke."[16] Barclay does not advertise this transition explicitly, as Spenser does, but he marks it in the structure of the eclogues themselves, which can be divided into two parts. The first three eclogues offer old into new: Barclay's translation of Aeneas Sylvius's *Miseriae Curialium*, a mid-fifteenth-century treatise, which has been reshaped and adapted into a dialogue between two shepherds about the miseries of the court.[17] In other words, Barclay takes a work that is not at all pastoral (along either ecclesiastical or classical models) and fashions it into eclogues. The final two eclogues adapt Mantuan's fifth and sixth eclogues, on the poet-patron relationship and the contrast between the country and the town, respectively. Barclay's eclogues are thus characterized by what one might call a "moral" interest, to follow the terminology typically used to describe Mantuan, in that they use the shepherd speaker to attack corruption (as opposed to the "Arcadian" or idealized mode, which is primarily interested in love).[18] They also are strikingly detailed in their depiction of shepherdly life: Barclay's pastoral is unique in his attention to the labor as well as the poverty of his shepherds. This particular intersection between a moral message and attention to social conditions should suggest that at its emergence the pastoral had an interest in the social world that aligned it with the plowman tradition: the virtuous hard worker whose poverty offers a critique of corrupted institutions. One might think of the late medieval poem *Piers the Plowman's Crede*, which opposes the poverty of the plowman, "a sely man . . . [who] opon the plow hongen," with the wealth of the friars.[19] After all, there is nothing in the pastoral as Barclay inherits it from Virgil or from Mantuan that requires it to be singularly unconcerned with social realities. As Raymond Williams observes, "we find a continuity of pastoral [in Hesiod, Theocritus, and Virgil] which in and through its literary elaboration maintains its contact with the working year and with the real social conditions of country life."[20] But, as I shall argue in this section, even as Barclay's eclogues hold out the possibility of what one might call a social, even a materialist, reading, they explicitly attempt to forestall it. As the first eclogues in English, then, Barclay shows that the emergence of pastoral is thus characterized by a contradiction about the literalism of the rural laborer—he is meant to be "real" but not "real" enough to evoke contemporary concerns about rural labor.

Barclay's uncertainty about the mode through which he wants his reader to approach his shepherds is apparent from the opening of the text. The eclogues begin with an explanatory prologue that gives an account of some of the conventions governing classical pastoral. Barclay notes that "the famous Theocrite" wrote,

> Certayne Egloges or speeches pastorall,
> Inducing Shepherdes, men homely and rurall.
> Which in playne language, according to their name,
> Had sundry talking, sometime of mirth and game,
> Sometime of thinges more like to grauitie,
> And not exceeding their small capacitie.
> Moste noble Uirgill after him longe while
> Wrote also Egloges after like maner stile.
> His wittes prouing in matters pastorall.
> (Prol.19, 21–29)

Such an account describes what I've been calling the *literalization* that is associated with classical pastoral, which is another way of describing what scholars have called *realism*: the shepherds are simple ("homely and rurall") and use "playn language." Barclay would most likely have understood this literalization in terms of decorum, what is suitable for a shepherd. George Turberville, who translated Mantuan's eclogues in 1567, also underlines the centrality of decorum in his preface:

> I haue not chaunged the Authors meaning or sense in any thing: but played the part of a true interpretor, obseruing that which we terme *Decorum* in eche respect, as far as the Poete and our mother tong wold giue me leaue. For as the conference betwixt Shephierds is familiar stuffe and homely: so haue I shapt my stile and tempred it with such common and ordinarie phrase of speach as Countreymen do vse in their affaires.[21]

What looks like realism in this literalization is interestingly limited: according to decorum, shepherds speak either of recreation or of serious issues to the extent that can fit in a "small capacitie," not, interestingly, of matters particular to shepherds. In this way, the discussions of decorum emphasize that what is distinctly shepherdly is a mode of speech, not actions or a livelihood or some other "real" aspect that we might choose. The point of using shepherds as characters is not to explore shepherds as such, then, but to prove one's wits (one's mastery of language), as made clear in the reference to Virgil. Barclay's account thus matches William Empson's definition of pastoral—"the complex into the simple"—almost exactly because it is a calculated effort to describe what is homely both to prove his own sophistication and the sophistication of his themes.[22]

Yet when Barclay turns to his eclogues proper, his literalization conforms less to this classical model—in which the shepherd is a voice, a vehicle for exploring recreation and the "complex into simple"—than what appears to be a medieval model, in which what is important about the shepherd is his *labor*. For example, at the opening of the first eclogue, Coridon states,

> Forsooth frende Cornix nought can my heart make light
> When I remember the stormes of yester night,
> The thunder and lightning, the tempest and the hayle
> Hath playnely wasted our profite and auayle,

> The fearefull thunder with greeuous clap and sounde
> Our Corne hath beaten downe flat vnto the grounde,
> With tempest after and violence of rayne
> That it as I doubt shall neuer rise agayne.
> The hayle hath beaten our shepe within the folde,
> That all be febled aswell the yong as olde,
> Our milke is turned and waxen pale and soure,
> The storme and tempest vpon our couches poure.
> (1.174–86)

Barclay is here loosely following the opening of Mantuan's third eclogue and its focus on bad weather. What is offered in Mantuan as a secondhand account (in Turberville's translation, D2r–D2v) becomes a dire first-person lament about shepherds', indeed all peasants', vulnerability to bad weather. Moreover, Barclay understands this vulnerability specifically in terms of the social/economic world—the "profite" that has been destroyed. Whereas Mantuan's shepherds abruptly set aside the reality of shepherdly life (the weather) after the opening speech to discuss love (D4v), Barclay uses the miseries of the shepherd as a transition into the material for the eclogue: the critique of the court. In this way, Barclay insists that the shepherd is a rural laborer, like a plowman, who is concerned neither with mirth and game nor with discussing grave matters (generally) but with the very material basis of his existence.

Barclay's interest in the material realities of shepherdly life seems, at times, to threaten pastoral conventions. Perhaps the most obvious of these is *otium*, that particular state of leisure that is considered to be typical of shepherds and, therefore, of pastoral from its origins.[23] Even Mantuan, whose shepherds describe labor in some detail, demonstrates the fundamental association between leisure and shepherdly conversation: "synce we are at leasure both, / and pleasaunt is to tell" (B1v). But Barclay clearly disavows *otium* in Cornix's long account of shepherdly life that follows the opening complaint about the weather:

> *Some nought doth labour and liueth pleasauntly*,
> Though all his reason to vices he apply:
> But see with what sweat, what busines and payne

> Our simple liuing we labour to obtayne:
> Beholde what illes the shepheardes must endure
> For flocke and housholde bare liuing to procure,
> In feruent heate we must intende our folde,
> And in the winter almost we frese for colde:
> Upon the harde ground or on the flintes browne
> We slepe, when other lye on a bed of downe.
> A thousande illes of daunger and sicknesse,
> With diuers sores our beastes doth oppresse:
> A thousande perils and mo if they were tolde
> Dayly and nightly inuadeth our poore folde.
> Sometime the wolfe our beastes doth deuour,
> And sometime the thefe awayteth for his hour:
> Or els the souldiour much worse then wolfe or thefe
> Agaynst all our flocke inrageth with mischefe.
> See howe my handes are with many a gall,
> And stiffe as a borde by worke continuall.
> (1.217–36, emphasis added)

Although, again, some of this description is borrowed from Mantuan's third eclogue, the opening line of the quotation is not. In this line Cornix provides a clear description of *otium*, of pleasant living, and assigns it somewhat surprisingly not to the shepherds but to others. The shepherdly life, in contrast, is characterized by unending labor, a labor whose deleterious effects are detailed at great length for more lines than are quoted here. Given this description, and the others throughout the eclogues, one would hardly think that Barclay's shepherds had enough time to sing.

This rejection of *otium*, both the leisure and the pleasant living described by Mantuan, is certainly interesting in and of itself, particularly because Barclay ultimately reverses himself (on which more below). But it is also the sign of a larger problem with the pastoral convention that Barclay is most interested in using—the contrast between the countryside and the court that should drive the critique of that court. Typically, the life of shepherds is construed positively, whether in terms of leisure, or "mirth and game," or a vaguer sense of "pleasant living," all of which can then be contrasted with the miseries and vices

58   *Transforming Work*

of town life. While it is true that the majority of Barclay's poetry is, in fact, devoted to the miseries of the court, the shepherdly frame does not work as one might expect, as the place of "non-misery," whether that non-misery is understood in terms of *otium* or something else. Indeed, the shepherds' attention to the difficulty (not the simplicity or virtue) of their own conditions makes it almost impossible to discern where, in fact, the moral contrast with the court lies. The problem arises at the beginning of this series with an odd kind of reversal. When the shepherd, Cornix, complains about their labor (as cited above), he is reprimanded by Coridon for questioning the fairness of the situation: "Ho there frende Cornix, thou wadest nowe to farre, / Thy selfe forgetting thou leapest ouer the barre" (1.255–56). Up to this point Barclay is following Mantuan loosely, but where Mantuan abruptly changes the subject to love, Barclay keeps the focus on the social and economic context of shepherding. Coridon underscores the difficulty of the shepherding life when he goes on to argue for removing to the court:

> If thou findest here no easement, wealth ne rest,
> What then, seke farther, for playnely so shall I,
> In some place fortune beholdeth merily.
> I bide no longer by saint Thomas of Kent
> In suche bare places where euery day is Lent,
> The Frers haue store euery day of the weke,
> But euery day our meat is for to seke.
>   (1.288–94)

As the reference to Lent demonstrates, being a shepherd is a kind of penance, a state of fasting. It is then, oddly enough, Cornix who begins a long attack on the court, which continues through three eclogues. This is the same Cornix who has begun the eclogue by lamenting the unending hardship of shepherdly life, and his framing of the debate does nothing to change our understanding of the countryside as a place of hardship:

> Onely bare nede is all our payne and wo,
> But these Towne dwellers haue many paynes mo,

> Our payne is pleasour nere in comparison
> Of their great illes and sore vexation.
> Of all suche thinges haue I experience,
> Then mayst thou surely geue to me credence:
> Whither wilt thou go to liue more quietly?
> Man all the worlde is full of misery.
>
> (1.307–14)

The question at line 313 suggests a pastoral impulse. The pastoral is supposedly the place of retreat. But for these shepherds every place is full of misery; the shepherd life is only less bad than that of the court.

The shepherd life is largely set aside, although its status in relation to the court is never clearly resolved, once the attack on the court begins. The reader is presented only with the vices of the court, through the mouths of the shepherds, not with the virtues of the countryside. There is nothing, in fact, particularly shepherdly or pastoral about these parts of the poem. At the end of the third eclogue (the end of this initial project—adapting the treatise *Miseriae Curialium* to the eclogue form), however, Barclay finally returns to the shepherds themselves. It is here that he sets aside the attention to the social realities that concerned him at the opening and invokes pastoral conventions for the first time: the simplicity of the shepherdly life and *otium*. Coming as it does after such a long interlude, this section is not, at first glance, disruptive, but read against the beginning, it seems to conclude an entirely different poem. That the poem is ending is indicated when Coridon is finally convinced to stay in the countryside. He states,

> Beleue me Cornix thou turned hast my minde,
> Farewell all courting, adewe pleasour vnkinde,
> Thou playne hast proued that all they fooles be
> Which folowe the court seking captiuitie,
> And might els where an honest life purchase,
> Hauing suffisaunce and moderate solace.
>
> (3.757–62)

With the terms "suffisaunce and moderate solace," Coridon describes a kind of life that one might describe as typically pastoral, if we consider Virgil's or Mantuan's eclogues as a model: shepherds have enough to eat, although they are not rich, and they have the solace, or the "mirth and game," that Barclay identifies in his prologue. But neither of these terms has appeared earlier, and, in fact, they both directly contradict the account of "nede," "povertie," and "paynes" with which the first eclogue began.

More importantly, this final description of shepherds elides their status as laborers, which was so central to the opening characterization. Cornix rewrites the opposition between shepherds and the court as one between the merry life of ease and the vulnerability of courtly life:

> Then let all shepheardes from hence to Salisbury,
> With easie riches liue well, laugh and be mery.
> Pipe vnder shadowes, small riches hath most rest,
> In greatest seas moste sorest is tempest.
> The court is nought els but a tempesteous sea,
> Auoyde the rockes, be ruled after me,
> There is more daunger then is vppon the lande.
> (3.763–69)

This passage offers the first account of shepherdly *otium* in the text. To be sure, this is not a description of how things are but a wish for the future: "let all shepherds . . . ." Nevertheless, it brings "easie riches" as well as "mirth and game" into the realm of possibility. In this way the speech returns to the aims of the prologue—to write pastoral in the manner of Virgil—and it does so by rewriting the storms described at the beginning. The initial reference to storms had to do with the economic difficulty of being shepherds. Now these storms are metaphorical, affecting the court instead of the livelihood of the shepherds. Both the literal labor and the literal (material) vulnerability of shepherds have now been replaced with their ease and security in relation to the court.

Barclay's pastoral conclusion does not, however, succeed entirely in erasing shepherdly labor. Coridon asks one last time what he should do and, in doing so, returns to the "miseries" of shepherd life with which the poems began:

> But tell me Cornix one thing or we departe,
> On what maner life is best to set my harte?
> In court is combraunce, care, payne, and misery,
> And here is enuy, ill will and penury.
> (3.811–14)

At this point the reader might well throw up her hands in despair since the entire poem has been dedicated to answering the question. This time Cornix's answer does not appeal to the pastoral convention (shepherds have an easy life) nor the exhaustive detail of the court's vices, which have occupied most of the poem, but a new moral register:

> Sufferaunce ouercommeth all malice at the last,
> Weake is that tree which can not bide a blast,
> But heare nowe my counsell I bid thee finally,
> Liue still a shepheard for playnly so will I.
> (3.815–18)

In invoking "sufferaunce," Barclay once again sets aside *otium* and preserves the hardship of shepherdly life; however, he does it not for the purposes of realism (as, presumably, he has done before) but in order to assign that hardship a particularly Christian meaning: endurance. This is the "vertuous suffraunce" that one finds in Geoffrey Chaucer's *Clerk's Tale*; indeed, the first two lines of the quotation could easily serve as the moral of that tale.[24] Such a moral reading of the shepherds' poverty and their labor has not previously guided our reading of the eclogues, and its appearance here is somewhat disconcerting. After all, the first three eclogues have studiously avoided assigning the shepherds any religious significance, whether that of ecclesiastical pastoral or merely the holy simplicity found in the medieval cycle plays. In turning to a Christian interpretive framework for the final word in the eclogue, Barclay draws attention to a kind of moral failure at the heart of the pastoral mode, an insistence on the "reality" of the shepherd without an account of how to read either his poverty or his labor.

Pastoral's Radical Potential

Barclay's first three eclogues offer a version of pastoral in which the shepherd remains a rural laborer. The eclogues thus bring together detailed attention to labor with the pastoral convention of opposing the countryside and the court, as well as a certain degree of sympathy for laborers with a sense of their moral superiority. For this reason, this version of pastoral should be read as opening up a potentially radical literary role for laborers—both the capacity of a "real" laborer (even if "small") to speak of serious things and the moral superiority lent by his poverty and labor. This radical potential resembles that offered by a literary tradition contemporary with Barclay, that is, by Langland's poem and its imitations, which also expand the laborer's role. Such a potential for pastoral may seem surprising given the studies of pastoral that have dominated the field, studies that emphasize the *otium* and the recreation of the shepherds above all, but it is worth remembering that for Barclay the pastoral was an entirely new form whose ideological ramifications were still being shaped, at least in part by Barclay himself. Nevertheless, if the first three eclogues raise the possibility of a literary social radicalism for pastoral, then this is a possibility that Barclay wishes to close off. He does so in the fifth and final eclogue, which simultaneously distinguishes shepherds from other rural laborers and reinforces the traditional social hierarchy in which laborers are characterized by their limitations.

The fifth eclogue, which follows Mantuan's sixth, returns to the pastoral convention that governed the first three eclogues: the contrast between the country and the city. Here that convention is framed explicitly in terms of whether peasants ("husbandes") are morally superior:

> Namely they [the shepherds] pleaded of the diuersitie
> Of rurall husbandes and men of the citie.
> Faustus accused and blamed citizens,
> To them imputing great faultes, crime and sins:
> Amintas blamed the rurall men agayne.
> (5.53–57)

The debate turns not on the vices of the citizens, as do the first three eclogues, even though they are listed in this passage, but on the nature of "rurall men." For this reason the eclogue can be read as a kind of meditation on the questions, Why write pastoral? Why valorize shepherds (or peasants)? Although the classical tradition has provided one answer—that through shepherds, the poet proves his wits (which Barclay gives in the prologue)—he does not refer to that tradition in this eclogue. Instead, he demonstrates that these questions must be answered in terms of the "reality" of shepherd existence.

The two shepherd speakers can be understood as different modes for confronting that reality, what I'll call the "pre-pastoral" (medieval) and "pastoral" (classically influenced), and ultimately as a correction of the approach in the first three eclogues, which attempted to link these together. Amintas offers the pre-pastoral understanding, in which shepherds belong to the general category of rural laborers. Indeed, Amintas describes the contrast between country and city not in terms of countrymen and citizens, as it is in Turberville's translation of Mantuan (D5v), but *plowmen* and citizens:

> God first disposed and made diuersitie
> Betwene rude plowmen and men of the citie,
> And in what maner Cornix thine owne mate
> As we went talking recounted to me late.
> (5.183–86)

This pre-pastoralism evokes a powerful class consciousness, even class hatred, in a story that asserts the inferior status of all rural laborers. This is a very long story based on a similar speech in Mantuan's sixth eclogue, in which God visits Eve one day, and, because she is embarrassed at the number of her children, she hides some of them. God assigns the children he meets an occupation in order of their birth—emperor, princes, earls, and so on. Eve then discloses the hidden children so that they might also receive "honor" from God. The story reaches its climax (or low point?) when God assigns these children the status of peasants:

> No more will I make, howbeit that I can,
> Of a vile villayne a noble gentleman,

Ye shall be plowmen and tillers of the grounde,
To payne and labour shall ye alway be bounde,
Some shall kepe oxen, and some shall hogges kepe,
Some shall be threshers, some other shall kepe shepe,
To digge and to delue, to hedge and to dike,
Take this for your lot and other labour like,
To drudge and to driuell in workes vile and rude,
This wise shall ye liue in endlesse seruitude.
(5.363–72)

In this pre-pastoral mode, rural laborers, whether plowmen or shepherds, are known by their labor. Their labor is not, as it is in the first three eclogues, either assimilable to the pastoral tradition or viewed favorably. Instead, the passage offers a conventional denigration of the peasant, who is characterized by rudeness and servitude. On the one hand, this denigration of the laborer is not surprising. Late medieval literature is filled with condemnations of peasants. One must only look at the description of peasants in John Gower's late-fourteenth-century estates satire, the *Vox Clamantis*: "Hec est gens racione carens vt bestia, namque / Non amat hec hominem, nec putat esse deum [This is a race (the waged laborers) without power of reason, like beasts, for it does not esteem mankind nor does it think God exists]."[25] For all of its shock value (contemporary as it is with Langland's poem), Gower's analogy between peasants and beasts is utterly conventional. Medieval literature is filled with similarly contemptuous descriptions of peasants, as Paul Freedman makes clear.[26] On the other hand, such an attack on the laborer, which in Barclay's poem specifically includes shepherds, does not seem entirely compatible with the pastoral mode. Shepherds are simple, yes, but not rude or bestial. It is perhaps telling that in Mantuan's sixth eclogue, from which this speech is taken, the other shepherd dismisses it as the product of an entirely self-interested townsman and spends the rest of the eclogue attacking the townsmen and their vices.

Barclay's desire to rewrite a pre-pastoral perspective in terms of hostility to rural laborers makes sense only if we understand it as at least in part a response to the dangers of pre-pastoralism and its emphasis on the reality of rural labor. Perhaps the most obvious example of the radical potential of pre-pastoralism is William Langland's *Piers Plowman* and the *Piers Plowman* tradition, but it's not entirely clear whether Barclay's plowmen are in any way indebted to these texts. More telling, perhaps, is the odd story about Adam and Eve and their offspring. Adam and Eve were typically described as providing a common origin for all mankind. Even Gower, who is far from subtle in his class consciousness and his antipathy for peasants, observes that "Al was aliche gentil tho," that is, during the time of Adam and Eve, in his discussion of "gentilesce" in the *Confessio Amantis*.[27] Yet Amintas's story does not invoke that common origin; instead it imagines Eve in terms of a class division authorized by God himself out of what seems to be nothing more than pique. While medieval authors certainly justified servile status by claiming it to be a punishment for sin, this account does not even mention anything so weighty as sin: God is merely annoyed that Eve has hidden some of her children from him but still wants his blessing. The glibness of the story—its attempt to be an "amusing anecdote," in the words of Douglas Bush, the editor of Turberville's translation—makes it all the more chilling.[28]

But this glibness seems calculated to distract from the far weightier associations between Adam and Eve and class division that were circulating at this time. In late medieval England, Adam and Eve were famously invoked as an argument for egalitarianism, specifically for the rights of peasants over and against the lords. As Paul Freedman notes, they were "used to justify equality in both radical and commonplace observation."[29] This perspective is summed up in the rhyme that was famously assigned to John Ball in the Peasants' Revolt of 1381 and was well-known throughout the medieval period: "Whan Adam dalf, and Eve span / Wo was þanne a gentilman?"[30] For John Ball, this proverb meant that "ab inicio omnes pares creatos a natura, seruitutem per iniustam oppressionem nequam hominum introductam, contra Dei uoluntatem; quia, si Deo placuisset seruos creasse, utique in principio mundi constituisset quis seruus, quisue dominus, futurus fuisset [all men were by nature created equal from the beginning, and that servitude had been brought in wrongly by the unjust oppression of human beings, contrary to the will of God; that if God had intended that men should be made serfs, he would certainly have established it at the beginning of the world who was to be a serf, and who a master]."[31] In imagining precisely what Ball rejects—God's role in class division—the eclogue anticipates and then prevents the potential social radicalism (and egalitarianism) associated with the rural laborer. Perhaps even more pertinent, because contemporary with Barclay's eclogues, is Edmund Dudley's "Warning to the People against Rebellion" (1509–10). In this text Dudley responds precisely to the egalitarianism associated with Adam and Eve in the same manner as Barclay, by invoking "degree" as divinely ordained. First Dudley warns of Arrogance, who "will tell you that ye be the children and right inheritovrs to Adam, as well as they. Whie should they haue this great honour, royall castels and mannors with soe much landes and possessions, and you but poore Tenementes and cotages?" Then, he warns, "mynde you not this purpose or intent, that is the equallitie of the mouldes betwene the nobles and you, nor the cognisaunce of the petegree from Adam, nor the indifferency of their soules in theire creacions. . . . But let vs all consider that god hath set a due order by grace . . . betwene man and man."[32] Dudley's warning, like John Ball's sermon, should remind us that thinking about peasants and their labor was never very far removed from thinking about rebellion.

This association between peasants and rebellion (or social radicalism) is as much (if not more) a part of the history of pastoral, for Barclay, as decorum. Moreover, his eclogues demonstrate that the prepastoral attitude toward the rural laborer (from which social radicalism stems) certainly could have been harnessed to the pastoral and its capacity for critique. Any discussion of the superiority of rural laborers (vis à vis the citizens of the town), the position with which the eclogue begins, raises the specter of radical social change: if workers are more virtuous than townspeople (or anyone else), then class division makes no sense.

While Amintas's speech dispels any social radicalism associated with rural laborers, his position undermines the pastoral as a mode. Given Amintas's position, why would anyone write about shepherds? They are only vile, rude slaves. Barclay provides an answer in the rest of the eclogue, which is devoted to the "pastoral" perspective: in order to recuperate the shepherd and his superiority. Before he can be held superior to the townsmen, however, he must be distinguished from the plowmen and other laborers. Here the speaker, Faustus, also invokes biblical figures, in this case Cain and Abel, to prove his point:

> This is true history and no surmised fable.
> At the beginning of thinges first of all,
> God made shepheardes and other men rurall,
> But the first plowman and tiller of the grounde
> Was rude and sturdie, disdayning to be bounde,
> Rough and stubborne, and Cayn men did him call,
> He had of mercy and pitie none at all,
> But like as the grounde is dull, stony and tough,
> Stubborne and heauy, rebelling to the plough.
> So the first plowman was strong and obstinate,
> Frowarde, selfewilled, and mouer of debate;
> But the first shepheard was meke and nothing fell,
> Humble as a lambe, and called was Abell.
> (5.434–46)[33]

Faustus's account of shepherds is far more authoritative, as he notes, because it is a familiar biblical story, while Amintas's most definitely is not. Although the story begins with shepherds in relation to other rural men, it quickly separates them by character, as Cain and Abel. Moreover, the list of biblical shepherds that follows this story distinguishes them from rural laborers even more forcefully by underlining their high status—King David is a notable example. By the end of the list, the shepherd has become a primarily literary figure. The sense that there are no "real" shepherds in the defense of shepherds—as there were in Amintas's speech, which insists upon the reality of both labor and class division—is more pronounced because of the gestures toward the shepherd-priests of ecclesiastical pastoral. It would seem that Barclay wants to define his shepherds via ecclesiastical (or biblical) pastoral, with all of the positive associations therein, but then he insists that these are, in fact, the literal shepherds in the countryside. This movement to ecclesiastical pastoral is more apparent in the source,

Mantuan's seventh eclogue, which narrates Pollux's decision to enter a cloister. But in Barclay the biblical shepherds are invoked not to discuss religious matters but in order to argue for the superiority of the country:

> But I shall proue thee that rurall people be
> More wise and noble then they of the citie,
> And that the citie is full of fraude and strife,
> When we in village haue good and quiet life.
> (5.419–22)

In a sense we could say that Barclay is cheating by avoiding the topic of "real" shepherds entirely. Perhaps a more charitable interpretation is that on some level Virgil simply remains too foreign or too removed from his experience. Unlike Virgil, he does not make the argument that "rurall people" are nobler than city folk using the details of shepherdly life that he has spent a great deal of time cataloging elsewhere in the eclogue. Rather, he resorts to the biblical shepherds, so that the nobility of shepherds stems not from the pastoral tradition he imitates but from the biblical tradition, in which the shepherds bear little relation to the shepherds of his own time.

With all their contradictions and inconsistencies, Barclay's eclogues demonstrate that the invention of the pastoral mode, in which "rurall people" are characterized by "good and quiet life," did not come particularly easily. As much as his poetry attempts to see the English countryside through pastoral conventions, he cannot set aside the labor that is for him its dominant characteristic.

Googe's Laborers

Whereas Barclay fills his eclogues with details of shepherdly life, particularly shepherdly labor, Googe consciously sets these details aside; his eclogues often begin by assigning the sheep and the duties of sheep keeping to someone else. In the first eclogue, the shepherd Daphnes says to Amintas,

Begin therefore, and I give ear,
for talk doth me delight,
Go Boy: go drive the beasts to feed
while he his mind recite.[34]

In lieu of his identity as laborer, the shepherd is given an identity as lover. Indeed, six of the eight eclogues in the collection concern love, whether the dangers of overmuch passion or the tragedy of unrequited love. The remaining two might be characterized as "moral": the third on the vices of the town and the eighth and last on "the wicked man." From this perspective, Googe's version of pastoral bears little or no resemblance to the English poetry of rural labor that precedes it, whether the *Piers Plowman* tradition or the medieval cycle plays.[35] Even ecclesiastical pastoral, a common feature of the eclogue tradition due to Mantuan's influence, is found only briefly in the third eclogue, despite the "moral" focus. Indeed, Googe is far more successful than either Barclay or Spenser (who will be discussed in chapter 5) in rewriting the countryside as a place of leisure, where the primary activity of shepherds is speaking poetically. It is easy to see in Googe, then, the beginning of a new tradition that separates shepherds from their labor in order to appropriate this figure for the courtly pursuits of love. Although Montrose does not discuss Googe, his poetry exemplifies what Montrose describes as "the process by which literal pastoralism [animal husbandry and agrarian life] is variously appropriated by and excluded from the discourse of figurative pastoralism."[36]

But on closer look, Googe's eclogues do, in fact, maintain a connection to "literal pastoralism," to traditions of writing rural labor. His eclogues include a woodcut that precedes the "Preface to Blundeston" (A7v); this is the only illustration that appears in the text besides Googe's coat of arms, which is not, properly, an illustration (see figure 1).[37] This woodcut depicts the two shepherds of the first eclogue in conversation. We know that they are shepherds because their names, Daphnes and Amintas, appear above the frame. The woodcut connects the eclogues not to Virgilian pastoral or the pastoral of Jorge Montemayor's romance *Diana*, both of which Googe is imitating, but to another tradition entirely, one that purports to represent "real"

Figure 1. Woodcut of two shepherds from Barnabe Googe, *Eglogs, epytaphes, and sonettes* (London, 1563; STC 12048), A7v. Courtesy of Huntington Library, San Marino, California. Image produced by ProQuest as part of *Early English Books Online*. Published with permission of ProQuest. Further reproduction prohibited without permission.

rural laborers: namely, *The Shepherds Kalender*, which was printed by Thomas Pynson in 1506 and from which the block for the woodcut appears to have been taken.[38] The *Kalender* is not, of course, a collection of eclogues but rather an almanac containing advice about farming, one that understands shepherds in terms of their labor, not as lovers or poets. That Googe, or his printer, included the woodcut suggests that the framework for reading pastoral at this point was not only Virgil's poetry but *all* writing about shepherds. In other words, the shepherd is not yet a purely literary figure or a figure who has been entirely appropriated for the court. As much as Googe might desire to cleanse the taint of labor from the shepherds so that they might be appropriated by gentlemen—a transformation that, as Montrose has described, is essential to Elizabethan pastoral—the transformation itself is not uncomplicated given the controversial topic of rural laborers (or peasantry more generally) during the mid-sixteenth century.[39] The mid-sixteenth century witnessed a great deal of unrest among rural laborers, notably Kett's Rebellion in 1549, to which I'll return below. Inasmuch as a shepherd could (and probably did) still remind readers of rural laborers, whether real or imagined, or agrarian controversy, he had a socially radical potential that had to be negotiated when it could not be excised. For these reasons Googe's eclogues reveal, as I shall argue, a certain caution about shepherdly activities. When Googe's material confronts shepherding itself, whether literal or figurative (in the ecclesiastical pastoral), he anxiously seeks to distinguish shepherds from other laborers and, indeed, from labor more generally.

In most of Googe's eclogues shepherding itself receives very little attention and seems almost entirely irrelevant to the characterization of the speakers, who could just as easily have any or no occupation at all. The eclogues themselves register this disinterest: in eclogues 1, 2, and 4 one or both of the speakers sends the sheep away (in 4, amusingly, they run away) so that the shepherds may converse. Eclogues 5, 6, and 7 do not contain any descriptions of shepherdly activities; one only knows that these characters are shepherds because they call each other shepherd. In these eclogues Googe has excised those aspects of shepherds that might prevent readerly identification or courtly appropriation: their poverty, their labor, their participation in the rural economy—all of which, of course, appear in Barclay's eclogues. Were it not for two of the eclogues, the third and the eighth, the reader might consider Googe's rewriting of shepherds as lovers, not laborers, to be entirely successful. All that is needed to write the new shepherd is to repress certain aspects of shepherding (almost all aspects), to make shepherding only the thinnest of disguises. Even the absence of any account of the eclogue form, what it is that Googe is doing, suggests the success of this repression. Whereas both Barclay's and Spenser's texts include some introductory material to explain the role of shepherds in the eclogue, Googe's does not.[40] But the third and the eighth eclogues do take up shepherding itself, and it is in these eclogues that Googe's anxiety about the relationship between the pastoral mode and its capacity to represent (or contain) rural laborers emerges.

The third eclogue is the first to detail the activities of the shepherds, and for this reason it could be seen as a kind of meditation on pastoral. Menalcas's observation about the weather, which pertains to working conditions ("A pleasant weather, Coridon, / and fit to keep the field" [3.1–2]), is followed by a long account of a ram and ewes, the only discussion of sheep in the entire series. Moreover, this eclogue takes up one of the most conventional topics of pastoral in the Virgilian and Mantuanesque tradition: the virtuous simplicity of the countryside contrasted with the vices of the town. An affecting account of this simplicity appears at the end of the eclogue, when Coridon says,

> Menalcas, best we now depart;
>   my cottage us shall keep,
> For there is room for thee and me,
>   and eke for all our sheep.
> Some chestnuts have I there in store
>   with cheese and pleasant whey;
> God sends my victuals for my need,
>   and I sing care away.
>   (3.165–72)

These lines offer the most satisfying image of shepherd life in all of Googe's poetry: they contain references to the shepherd as singer, to his care of the sheep, and to the simplicity (but adequacy) of his meal and shelter. The shepherd is not so much free from care as having the enviable capacity (or skill) of dismissing it through his singing.

Although this eclogue is, for these reasons, perhaps the most conventional of the series, it contains notable disruptions in tone. The contrast between the countryside and the city quickly seems to give way to what one can only call class consciousness. Googe begins typically, with Menalcas referring to the leisure of pastoral life:

> Well, Coridon, let him go halt,
>   and let us both go lie
> In yonder bush of juniper;
>   the beasts shall feed hereby.
> A pleasant place here is to talk:
>   good Coridon, begin,
> And let us know the town's estate,
>   that thou remainest in.
>   (3.45–52)

Coridon responds: "The town's estate? Menalcas, O, / thou mak'st my heart to groan" (3.53–54). The pleasantness of shepherdly life, as voiced by Menalcas, is juxtaposed with the groans of Coridon at the thought of the town. At this point readers familiar with Mantuan (or with Barclay) might guess what comes next—a condemnation of the town for its materialism, lust, corruption, and so on and an articulation (however contradictory, for Barclay at least) of the virtues of the countryside, particularly its simplicity. Googe's Coridon does, in fact, begin with the expected condemnation of the town—"vice hath every place possessed / and virtue thence is flown" (55–56)—but he quickly shifts to a surprising diatribe against the townspeople not for being corrupt (and the opposite of peasants and their virtuous simplicity) but for being rustics themselves: "Nobility begins to fade, / and carters up do spring" (65–66).

It is as if in characterizing shepherds for the first time in detail, Googe is reminded that shepherds have a socioeconomic identity outside his text; shepherds are, in fact, more similar to carters than to courtly lovers, and that identity threatens to complicate the eclogue conventions he has set into motion. The rest of the eclogue both confirms the status of the shepherd as a kind of rural laborer and attempts to distinguish shepherds from "real" rural laborers, who, for Googe, carry a socially radical meaning. Coridon notes,

> Menalcas, I have known myself,
>   within this thirty year,
> Of lords and ancient gentlemen
>   a hundred dwellng there,

> Of whom we shepherds had relief:
>   such gentleness of mind
> Was placèd in their noble hearts,
>   as none is now to find.
> But haughtiness and proud disdain
>   hath now the chief estate,
> For Sir John Straw, and Sir John Cur
>   will not degenerate.
> And yet, they dare account themselves
>   To be of noble blood.
>   (3.69–82)

The mention of the lords' treatment of shepherds strikingly reminds the reader of an aspect of rural life (and labor) that goes almost entirely unmentioned in many of the early eclogues: the shepherd's position in the socioeconomic relations of the countryside. In other words, Googe is far more specific (and explicit) than William Empson's formulation, that pastoral should imply "the beautiful relation between rich and poor," would have it.[41] Coridon describes shepherds as part of an idealized feudal relationship, dependent on lords and gentlemen for "relief," thus implicitly confirming their status as peasants. At the same time, the passage reveals another, far more problematic, relationship between lords and peasants, one in which the peasants are no longer content to be peasants, in which rural laborers represent social radicalism. The new (and corrupted) social relationships, in which haughtiness and disdain have replaced true nobility, are blamed on Sir John Straw and Sir John Cur. The reader knows that these figures are peasants because of the resonant names: *cur* is a term of abuse for the lower classes (see the discussion of "An Epitaph of the Lord Sheffield's Death" below), and John Straw certainly refers to Jack Straw, one of the leaders of the Peasants' Revolt of 1381, whose "confession" famously appeared in Thomas Walsingham's *St. Albans Chronicle*.[42] What characterizes this confession, and indeed most of the writing on the Peasants' Revolt, is the desire to alter the existing social order radically and violently: the "determination to end the system of lordship," as Rodney Hilton notes.[43] The consequence of ending the system of lordship is, of course, egalitarianism, the very same threat that underlies the reference to Adam and Eve in

Barclay's eclogue discussed above. In this way, the passage maps the distinction between bad and good peasants onto the distinction between those who labor (carters and others) and those who do not (shepherds).

This attack on peasants suggests that Googe's pastoral cannot escape or repress "what the country was really like" so easily. As if to assert control over the meaning of his laborers (whether shepherds or others), Googe ends his eclogue with an allegory. The "moral" is difficult to ascertain, however, because the movement to allegory is so confused. Coridon begins with an attack on social mobility by recounting the story of a "neatherd" also named Coridon:

> The chiefest man in all our town
>   that bears the greatest sway
> Is Coridon (no kin to me),
>   a neatherd th' other day.
> This Coridon, come from the cart,
>   in honour chief doth sit
> And governs us. Because he hath
>   a crabbèd, clownish wit,
> Now see the churlish cruelty
>   that in his heart remains.
> The seely sheep that shepherds good
>   have fostered up with pains,
> And brought away from stinking dales
>   on pleasant hills to feed,—
> O cruel clownish Coridon!
>   O cursèd carlish seed!—
> The simple sheep constrainèd he
>   their pasture sweet to leave,
> And to their old corrupted grass
>   enforceth them to cleave.
> Such sheep as would not them obey,
>   but in their pasture bide,
> With cruel flames they did consume
>   and vex on every side.
> And with the sheep, the shepherds good
>   (O hateful hounds of hell)

> They did torment, and drive them out
>   in places for to dwell.
> There dièd Daphnes for his sheep.
>   (3.109–37)

At its opening the attack rehearses what has been said about Sir John Straw: Coridon is a "churl" and should not, therefore, be in charge, should not be the chiefest man in town. But by line 131, if not earlier, the reader becomes aware that this is an allegory, that Coridon is not a "real" neatherd but a religious leader who has persecuted others, both priests (good shepherds) and people (the flocks). Although it invokes familiar elements—the hills and dales, the innocent sheep, the corrupted grass—the allegory does not quite fit the mode of ecclesiastical pastoral. That is, the vitriol against the peasantry, the repeated references to "clownish" and "carlish," is distinctly jarring when read against more conventional examples of this mode. Although the bad shepherds in ecclesiastical pastoral may be venal, what makes them bad is not their class status but the fact that they do not labor (do not care for their sheep) as the good shepherds do. Good shepherds are, in fact, allied with peasants precisely because they labor, as any reader of Chaucer's *General Prologue* to the *Canterbury Tales* is well aware: the Parson's brother is the Plowman. The strangeness of this passage might best be assessed if it is paraphrased thus: Googe's bad shepherd is bad because he is literally a peasant. For Googe, the peasants, with their demands for social mobility, draw attention to the particular economic relations that characterize the countryside (and the town) and, for this reason, jeopardize the pastoral itself, whether the Virgilian or the ecclesiastical mode. The only way to write pastoral is, then, to ensure that the reader (and writer) is never reminded that shepherds have a socioeconomic identity. But in assigning this upstart the same name as one of the shepherds, a name that is drawn from Virgil's own eclogues, Googe maintains a link between the new literary shepherd and the "clowns" that occupy the countryside.

Googe's ambivalence about the moral value of shepherds, which confuses his ecclesiastical pastoral in eclogue 3, is also apparent in the eighth and final eclogue. This eclogue begins typically for Googe, with the shepherds "resting," but these songs explicitly focus on God, not the "wretched lovers" of the previous eclogues (8.23). Cornix praises God,

> Who gives us pasture for our beasts
>   and blesseth our increase;
> By whom, while other cark and toil,
>   we live at home with ease;
> Who keeps us down, from climbing high
>   where honour breeds debate,
> And here hath granted us to live
>   in simple shepherd's state:
> A life that sure doth far exceed
>   each other kind of life.
>   (8.25–34)

Such a "religious" turn is, of course, not at all uncommon in the eclogue tradition. Both Mantuan and Barclay are very much concerned with the shepherds' Christian meaning, certainly as much as they are with the elements borrowed from Virgilian pastoral. At first glance Googe's eclogue seems to match those of Mantuan and Barclay: the simplicity of the shepherd's life, his humility, is explicitly tied to God's favor and considered more virtuous than other kinds of life. We can see here a kind of dim echo of the mystery plays, in which God shows his favor to the shepherds by making them the first witnesses of Jesus's birth. Probably for this reason, the editor notes that in this eclogue "the carefree pastoral life is now presented in a fully religious light."[44] But it is worth noting that this particular reading of the moral (and Christian) superiority of shepherds puts a new spin on shepherdly simplicity, associating it with ease. For Googe ease is a sign of God's favor and contrasts with the "cark [care, pains, responsibility] and toil" of other "states." In other words, Googe has moralized the "ease" of the Virgilian tradition, making it superior to labor. The novelty of this "morality" in the pastoral form should be appreciated. In the eclogues that detail the superiority of the shepherdly life, Barclay's fifth (discussed above) and Mantuan's sixth, the shepherds' labor is contrasted with the laziness and corruption of the townsfolk.

In broad strokes the discussion that follows of the opposition of the good and the wicked man can be read in terms of the pastoral convention, the contrast between the shepherds and the men of the town. But after setting the pastoral scene, Googe abandons the world of shepherds for over two hundred lines, until the end of the poem. After a long discussion of the importance of pleasing God, which begins with an address to shepherds but then does not mention them or their particular sins/virtues again, the speaker proceeds to attack the "brainless fool" who has run away from "virtue's school" (8.146, 148). This discussion of the vice-ridden man does not invoke pastoral language, as with the bad shepherd Coridon in eclogue 3, but rather makes use of an allegory of the sinful man on "vice's barge" (8.152). Here the reader again encounters a concern familiar from the third eclogue, social mobility. The sinful man claims:

"I will be proud, and look aloft;
   I will my body deck
With costly clothes above my state:
   who then dare give me check?"
          (8.169–71)

This allegory has nothing to do with shepherds, nor is the potential parallel between the shepherd and the good man (perhaps of the Bible) ever elucidated, as in Barclay's fifth eclogue. It is as if the pastoral mode is somehow inadequate for moralizing. Such a perspective certainly does not fit with earlier writers of ecclesiastical pastoral, but, as mentioned above, Googe is almost entirely uninterested in invoking that mode. Instead, he attempts to keep his shepherds literal, albeit a kind of "literary" literal, removed from any indication of socioeconomic condition.

If one were in any doubt that Googe's eclogues reflect a hostility toward the peasantry and a fear of agrarian controversies associated with the shepherd, one might turn to the first poem that appears after Googe's eclogues: "An Epitaph of the Lord Sheffield's Death," which describes the death of Lord Sheffield in Kett's Rebellion in 1549. The reader thus moves from the eclogues—poetry idealizing rural laborers, however contradictorily—to a poem condemning them. This movement is purposeful; Googe arranged his own poetry, and his editor notes his "self-conscious divisions."[45] Such a juxtaposition can be read as a kind of return of the repressed, that is, the historical conditions that define rural labor in this period that must be disguised or occluded for the shepherd to be appropriated. After all, Googe did not know Lord Sheffield personally; there is no particular reason that he would have begun the section of epitaphs with this one. Kett's Rebellion deserves far more attention than I can give it here, but what's important to my discussion is perhaps its most obvious point: it was an uprising of rural laborers, peasants, and yeoman farmers and, as such, bears a resemblance to the Peasants' Revolt of 1381, which haunts Googe's eighth eclogue. Indeed, the most recent study characterizes it as "at the end of a long tradition of medieval popular revolts."[46] Moreover, this revolt was, in an odd sense, caused by shepherds and sheep: the revolt began as a response to enclosure.[47] I quote the poem in its entirety:

> When brutish broil and rage of war
>   in clownish hearts began,
> When tigers stout in tanner's bond
>   unmuzzled all they ran,
> The noble Sheffield, Lord by birth
>   and of a courage good,
> By clubbish hands of crabbèd clowns
>   there spent his noble blood.
> His noble birth availèd not,
>   his honour all was vain,
> Amid the press of masty curs
>   the valiant Lord was slain;
> And after such a sort (O ruth!)
>   that who can tears suppress?
> To think that dunghill dogs should daunt
>   the flower of worthiness.
> Whileas the ravening wolves he prayed
>   his guiltless life to save,
> A bloody butcher big and blunt,
>   a vile unwieldy knave,

> With beastly blow of boisterous bill
>   at him (O Lord) let drive,
> And cleft his head, and said therewith
>   "Shalt thou be left alive?"
> O Lord, that I had present been,
>   and Hector's force withal,
> Before that from his carlish hands
>   the cruel bill did fall.
> Then should that peasant vile have felt
>   the clap upon his crown
> That should have dazed his doggèd heart
>   from driving Lords adown;
> Then should my hands have saved thy life,
>   good Lord whom dear I loved;
> Then should my heart in doubtful case
>   full well to thee been proved.
> But all in vain thy death I wail,
>   thy corpse in earth doth lie.
> Thy king and country for to serve
>   thou didst not fear to die.
> Farewell, good Lord, thy death bewail
>   all such as well thee knew,
> And every man laments thy case,
>   and Googe thy death doth rue.[48]

We can see in this epitaph the same kind of antipeasant feeling that informs the third eclogue, but here the association between peasants and outright rebellion is made startlingly clear.[49] Indeed, the poem reads as a compressed version of John Gower's account of the Peasants' Revolt of 1381, particularly in its insistence that the peasants are beasts: tigers, curs, dogs, wolves. As Gower writes, "Cutte que Curre simul rapidi per deuia currunt [Cut and Cur ran swiftly together through the alleys]" and "Hii quibus in nocte solito fimus extitit hospes, / Mollibus in lectis sordida membra fouent [Dogs to which a heap of dung had ordinarily been host at night kept their filthy limbs warm in soft beds]."[50] But Googe does not limit himself to dehumanizing the rebels by associating them with animals; he also ensures that readers understand that these are peasants by repeating a series of terms used to describe them: "clowns," "carlish," "peasant," and "knave." Just as Gower's description of the rebels of 1381 is characterized by an odd "vernacular" poetic tic—including the English names in Latin, such as "Cutte and Curre"—so is Googe's description of the peasants in Kett's Rebellion characterized by a "vernacular tradition," that is, alliterating lines: "To think that dunghill dogs should daunt" and "With beastly blow of boisterous bill" (15, 21).[51] These alliterated lines are not regular, either in frequency or in the number of alliterated words, and they interrupt the regular verse form and meter of unrhymed lines of eight syllables that alternate with rhymed lines of six syllables. In this way, Googe links peasants and the details of their rebellion with a native verse form, alliteration, a form associated with reform through the poem *Piers Plowman* and its tradition.

If this epitaph signals its connection with the eclogues that precede it, it also distinguishes itself from those that follow. Only in this epitaph does Googe imagine himself taking part in the events described and ensuring a different outcome—namely, saving the life of Sheffield by striking down a peasant. In drawing attention to himself, Googe creates an odd analogy between writing the eclogues and defending Lord Sheffield: the peopling of the countryside with shepherds, who float free of any social relations, or who evoke only idealized feudal relations, parallels the violent repression of the "churls," at least on the level of imagination.

In choosing to read the eclogues of Googe and Barclay as the first pastorals (and not merely attempts at pastoral encumbered by medievalisms), this chapter has emphasized the way in which pastoral emerged in dialogue with "native traditions." Such a recategorization is not just a matter of literary historical importance but of ideological importance as well.[52] The transitional nature of these texts reminds us that to write about rural life and laborers in terms of the pastoral was hardly a "natural" choice. That is, to write pastoral was both an ideological choice reflecting the authors' interest in promoting or repressing what laborers might "mean" and a choice with ideological consequences, affecting how readers would be encouraged to "see" rural laborers. The specifically political aspect of that ideology will be the subject of the next chapter on enclosure.

THREE | *The Pastoral Mode and Agrarian Capitalism*

The emergence of the pastoral mode has long been understood as a decisive moment in the history of literature but not, interestingly, as a decisive moment in the history of shepherds.[1] Yet the rediscovery of Virgil's *Eclogues* and the subsequent flourishing of literary imitations, a process that began in the early sixteenth century and continued through its end, coincided with an agricultural crisis, or "problem" (to borrow from the title of R. H. Tawney's seminal study, *The Agrarian Problem in the Sixteenth Century*), that had much to do with shepherds and sheep keeping. The "problem" to which Tawney refers was the enclosure of common fields for pasturing sheep, a problem that was seen to affect landholding, farming practices, and the living and working conditions of rural laborers of all kinds. As Tawney notes, enclosure was the "most serious" economic question occupying the Crown from 1489 to 1656, and the government repeatedly introduced statutes to prevent land from being converted to pasture.[2] That enclosure and, therefore, the agrarian problem should be understood in terms of sheep farming and sheep is made clear in Karl Marx's famous account of "primitive accumulation":

The prelude to the revolution that laid the foundation of the capitalist mode of production was played out in the last third of the fifteenth century and the first few decades of the sixteenth. A mass of "free" and unattached proletarians was hurled onto the labour-market by the dissolution of the bands of feudal retainers. . . . [More importantly,] the great feudal lords . . . created an incomparably larger proletariat by forcibly driving the peasantry from the land, to which the latter had the same feudal title as the lords themselves, and by usurpation of the common lands. . . . The new nobility was the child of its time, for which money was the power of all powers. Transformation of arable land into sheep-walks was therefore its slogan.[3]

Marx's polemical account of enclosure is helpful for demonstrating the way in which sheep keeping became a symptom (for Marx, a slogan) of a greater social and economic transition. Joan Thirsk underlines this point in her chapter on enclosure in *The Agrarian History of England and Wales*: "the sins of the government were at once laid at the door of the pasture farmer, and particularly the sheepmaster."[4] In short, sheep keeping gained a distinctive notoriety in this period, and, as a result, the language surrounding sheep and shepherding became inflected with socioeconomic controversy.

Despite what seems to be a tantalizing coincidence between the two "new" approaches to (or languages of) shepherding in the sixteenth century—the literary and the economic, the pastoral and the anti-enclosure polemic—scholars otherwise interested in the history of pastoral have been reluctant to read these phenomena as related. Raymond Williams was, perhaps, the critic most ideally suited to this kind of analysis because of his interest in recovering "what the country was really like," or what had been repressed in accounts of the countryside.[5] In *The Country and the City* he famously argued that "the Renaissance adaptation of just these classical modes is that, step by step, these living tensions are excised, until there is nothing countervailing, and selected images stand as themselves: not in a living but in an enamelled world."[6] But Williams sets aside the pastoral literature of the sixteenth century entirely because he finds it primarily courtly in its interests: "the pastoral of the courts and of the aristocratic houses was not, as it came through, the really significant development."[7] The most influential historicist reading of sixteenth-century pastoral, that of Louis Montrose, also focuses on the court.[8] Although Montrose acknowledges that the flourishing of pastoral follows the "moral, economic, and ecological controversy" around sheep farming, he states that these two phenomena have nothing to do with each other. The pastoral appears after a "period of decontamination," when sheep farming no longer carries with it the taint of agrarian controversy.[9] For Montrose, what is significant about pastoral is not its agricultural interest (or setting) but its "cultural work" regarding class status: "Elizabethan pastoral forms may have worked to mediate differential relationships of power, prestige, and wealth in a variety of social situations, and to have variously marked and obfuscated the hierarchical distinctions—the symbolic boundaries—upon which the Elizabethan social order was predicated."[10] In dismissing Williams's materialist model in favor of "culture" more generally, Montrose also dismisses any "direct correlations between socioeconomic and literary change" as "the reductionism of reflection-theory."[11]

But a historical approach would seem to demand an investigation of the correlations between accounts of the "agrarian problems" of the sixteenth century and the pastoral mode precisely because they lay claim to the same language: both are about shepherds and keeping sheep. It is true that sheep keeping did become less controversial during the later Elizabethan period, certainly by the time the pastoral began to flourish. Joan Thirsk observes that after the mid-sixteenth century the attack on sheep masters died away, and concerns about enclosure began to fade.[12] It is nevertheless worth noting that "the last large scale inquiry" into enclosure occurred in 1607. Moreover, one can find the familiar rhetoric against enclosure in epigrams by the Rev. Thomas Bastard, which were printed in 1598, or in a sermon given by Robert Wilkinson in 1607 in Northampton.[13] Exactly how long the controversy persisted into the sixteenth century is, to a certain degree, irrelevant. It would be foolish, in any case, to argue that Elizabethan pastoral is directly "about" the agrarian problem of enclosure. But the choice is not, as Montrose implies, between a crude reflection theory and a historicism that sets aside the agrarian controversies entirely.[14] Even if sheep keeping underwent a "period of decontamination" during which it was cleansed of its controversial nuances, the symbolic imagination (what sheep keeping, sheep, and shepherds could and did mean) was nevertheless irrevocably altered by these controversies. More to the point, Montrose does not provide any evidence that shepherding became less controversial *before* the emergence of pastoral; the pastoral itself, therefore, could well be the mode of decontamination.

This chapter will explore the sixteenth-century enclosure controversy in order to recapture a sense of the cultural framework through which readers would have encountered shepherding and, therefore, the literary pastoral, which was, as we should remember, a new mode in the sixteenth century. I shall demonstrate that attacks on sheep farming, which appear with some frequency in sermons and treatises from the beginning to the middle of the sixteenth century, generate a new approach to, even rhetoric of, shepherding that is parallel to and contemporary with the new rhetoric of shepherding derived from Virgil's and Mantuan's eclogues. Like the eclogues, these treatises draw attention to the conditions of sheep keeping and thus ultimately to "real" (not allegorical) shepherds. Both also serve, for very different reasons, as a means to separate the shepherd from his past identity—both his past literary identity, as has been discussed in the previous chapter, and his past economic identity, as a rural laborer among other rural laborers, such as plowmen.[15] Thus severed from traditional ideas of social order, the shepherd becomes a representative of an emerging and threatening new economic order: agrarian capitalism. The chapter will then return to the first pastorals of Alexander Barclay and Barnabe Googe to argue that the pastoral mode serves a cultural function, not just to disguise social mobility, as Montrose has persuasively argued, but also to disarm the critique of capitalism with which discussions of sheep keeping were so closely associated. To use a more pointedly Marxist language, from its beginning the pastoral mode works, however indirectly, re-imagine the site of violent expropriation as an idyll, to make the countryside safe to write about again or, to some degree, for the first time.[16] This is not merely the general mystification of the "reality" of country life—the idealization that readers have long attributed to the pastoral—but a specific response to the polemic surrounding the enclosure controversy.

A New Economic Identity

The anti-enclosure tracts of the mid-sixteenth century respond to the first wave of enclosures, which occurred from 1450 to 1525 and during which "about one-tenth of the villages in the midlands were destroyed."[17] It is this first wave that Sir Thomas More famously describes in his *Utopia*:

> your shepe that were wont to be so meke and tame, and so smal eaters, now, as I heare saye, be become so great devowerers and so wylde, that they eate up, and swallow downe the very men them selfes. They consume, destroye, and devoure whole fieldes, howses, and cities. For looke in what partes of the realme doth growe the finest and therfore dearest woll, there noblemen and gentlemen, yea and certeyn abbottes, holy men no doubt, not contenting them selfes with the yearely revenues and profytes, that were wont to grow to theyr forefathers and predecessours of their landes, nor beynge content that they live in rest and pleasure nothinge profiting, yea much noyinge the weale publique, leave no grounde for tillage, thei inclose al into pastures; thei throw doune houses; they plucke downe townes, and leave nothing standynge.[18]

As More's vivid account makes clear, this first wave of enclosures generated a great deal of anxiety that traditional agricultural practices, those of the "forefathers and predecessours," were threatened and must be shored up.[19] I've used Robynson's translation of More because it dates from midcentury and, therefore, shares its vocabulary with the polemical treatises that will be discussed further below: for example, "tillage" for the Latin "arvus." Following More, whose account certainly informs that of Marx, we might note that this anxiety equated enclosure and sheep keeping with a changed economic role for the nobility: the separation of their financial interests from those of the yeoman and small landowner. The nobility are no longer content with the old system—which is understood implicitly as benefitting everyone—and desire to have more profit just to themselves. In this way, the anti-enclosure polemic associates sheep keeping, and, ultimately, the shepherd, with precisely what Marx describes in "Primitive Accumulation": the emergence of agrarian capitalism.[20]

Although the emergence of a full-blown agrarian capitalism has typically been assigned to the eighteenth century, especially in discussions of enclosure, some historians have followed Marx in emphasizing the role of the fifteenth and sixteenth centuries.[21] For Robert Allen, changes in agriculture that benefitted the nobility, which he calls the "landlords' revolution," began in the fifteenth century and continued somewhat sporadically until the eighteenth, when this revolution reached its height.[22] Similarly, in his study of Kett's Rebellion of 1549, Andy Wood agrees that "the late fifteenth and early sixteenth centuries represented the key decades in the emergence of capitalist relations of production in the countryside."[23] Finally, James Holstun invents the term "aristo-capitalism" to describe this early form of capitalism, which "integrated an imperial and capitalist aristocracy with its non-noble functionaries and the laborers they aimed to exploit more systematically, leaving little room for popular participation in politics."[24] Even Jane Whittle, who comes to a more cautious assessment of the sixteenth century, agrees with Marx that the two processes central in the development of agrarian capitalism had begun by the period in question: "the end of serfdom and the expropriation of the rural population from the land."[25] The writings on the agrarian crisis in the sixteenth century certainly demonstrate an awareness of the latter of these processes and, therefore, an incipient awareness of a "new" economic order, as will become apparent below. As Tawney noted long ago, "the fact that statistical evidence reveals no startling disturbance in the area enclosed or population displaced, is no bar to the belief that, both in immediate consequences and in ultimate effects, the heavy blows dealt in that age at the traditional organisation of agriculture were an episode of the first importance in economic and social development."[26] As the shepherd gains his new economic identity in the polemic around enclosure, an identity representative of "aristo-capitalism," the plowman, the traditional rural laborer to which the polemic opposes the shepherd, remains a figure for an interdependent social structure (the three estates) and communal farming, the traditional model that Holstun calls "monarcho-populism." This is a "postfeudal but precapitalist economy and culture based in small production" that reserved "a substantial place for popular participation in politics."[27] In this way, these rural laborers become signs of the contemporary economic and, ultimately, moral crisis: the struggle between a traditional and an emergent order.

Until the early to mid-sixteenth century, shepherds did not have what one might call an economic (or political) identity distinct from other rural laborers, although they could certainly have a distinct figurative identity. That is, when writers describe the occupation of "real" shepherds, they are often grouped with or understood in terms of other kinds of rural laborers, under the larger rubric of husbandmen and peasants, whereas descriptions of allegorical shepherds (priests) insist upon the special characteristics of shepherds. In William Langland's late-fourteenth-century poem, *Piers Plowman*, the dreamer Will famously groups several types of laborers together in opposition to the clergy:

> Arn none raþer yrauysshed fro þe riȝte bileue
> Than are þise [kete] clerkes þat konne manye bokes,
> Ne none sonner saued, ne sadder of bileue,
> Than Plowmen and pastours and [pouere] commune laborers,
> Souteres and shepherdes; [swich] lewed Iuttes
> Percen wiþ a Paternoster þe paleys of heuene
> And passen Purgatorie penauncelees at hir hennes partyng
> Into þe [parfit] blisse of Paradis for hir pure bileue,
> That inparfitly here knewe and ek lyuede.[28]

There can be no doubt that these shepherds (and "pastours") are meant to be understood as rural laborers; the speaker is contrasting "lewed" laborers with "konnynge clerkes" in making an argument for "holy simplicity"—that the workers are "sooner saved" precisely because they are not educated. This association between shepherds and other workers is apparent even in the texts that concern shepherds specifically, such as the medieval mystery plays about Christ's nativity, as discussed in chapter 1. In the York plays, the shepherds are "herde-men" who keep "catell," which means livestock generally (not just sheep).[29] Moreover, at the end of the play one of the shepherds addresses Jesus as a "swete swayne," underlining their shared status as servants/commoners.[30] Similarly, in the first shepherd play of the Towneley cycle, one of the shepherds bemoans his inability to pay the rents he owes:

> Bot if good will spryng
> The countré forsake;
> Fermes [rents] thyk ar comyng,
> My purs is bot wake,
> I haue nerehand nothyng
> To pay nor to take.[31]

This is not the shepherd found in Mantuan, Barclay, or Googe who exists free of social and economic bonds but rather a figure enmeshed in the medieval economic relation of lord and tenant.

Even texts concerned with the occupations of the social world, such as estates satire, do not understand shepherds in terms of a distinct category; rather, they tend to represent all rural laborers either as plowmen, as in Chaucer's *General Prologue* to the *Canterbury Tales*, or as "rustici," as in John Gower's *Vox Clamantis*. One must look at one of the very few husbandry manuals that survive from the Middle Ages, such as the *Seneschaucie*, to find the duties of shepherds distinguished from other laborers. The *Seneschaucie*, an Anglo-Norman text dated to the late thirteenth century, is devoted to describing the various offices on the manor, beginning with the seneschal. In this text the shepherd is "companion to the miller," and the description of his duties appears between the "office of cowherd" and the "office of dairymaid."[32] It is clear that the shepherd is part of the manorial economy, keeping sheep for the lord. In the midst of describing the shepherd's responsibilities, the author ensures that we know whose sheep these are and for whom the shepherd is working: "Let all the lord's sheep be marked with one mark."[33] The absence of a distinct occupational identity for shepherds in this period matches to a great degree "what the country was really like." Most farmers, both great and small, kept sheep.[34]

Based on the dearth of descriptions of them, we could say that shepherds in the medieval period do not carry much symbolic weight, except, of course, when they are meant to stand for priests or when they are biblical shepherds. Because of the figurative associations (with the priesthood), the shepherd cannot consistently represent the "common man." Nevertheless, when the shepherd does appear in his literal capacity as a peasant, he can be assimilated to the reformist and radical tradition with which the plowman is more typically associated, such as in the shepherd plays discussed in the first chapter. Ultimately, it is the shepherd's class status that is the most important point: medieval representations of peasants, whether shepherds, plowmen, or the people/commons more generally, invariably remind readers of the interdependent nature of the medieval social order. This is an interdependence imagined both horizontally and vertically, so to speak. That is, peasants are characterized by a kind of communalism, such as the groups of shepherds in the nativity plays who eat and drink and sing together. This is true even when only one peasant is taken as representative; Chaucer's Plowman in the *General Prologue* to the *Canterbury Tales* is defined by his charity toward his neighbor:

> God loved he best with al his hoole herte
> At alle tymes, thogh him gamed or smerte
> And thanne his neighebor right as hymselve.[35]

In addition, peasants are consistently represented as part of a larger social order: the emphasis falls on their obligations to lords or their responsibility to tithe to their priests. That "vertical" interdependence might be seen from a positive perspective, as in the loving mutuality between lords and commons described by John Gower in the prologue to his *Confessio Amantis*:

> He [Arion] broghte hem alle in good acord;
> So that the comun with the lord,
> And lord with the comun also,
> He sette in love bothe tuo.[36]

Or that interdependence might be understood as exploitative and oppressive, as in the shepherd's complaint about the "rents" he must pay in the first of the Towneley shepherd plays (quoted above) or the husbandman's complaint about taxation in *Song of the Husbandman* (ca. 1330):

> Ich herde men upo mold [earth] make muche mon,
> Hou he [they] beth itened [weary] of here tilyynge [plowing]:
> Gode yeres and corn bothe beth agon;
> Ne kepeth here no sawe ne no song synge.
> Nou we mote [must] worche, nis ther non other won [way],
> Mai ich no lengore lyve with mi lesinge [lying];
> Yet ther is a bitterore bid [command] to the bon:
> For ever the furthe peni mot [must] to the kynge.[37]

For this writer, the difficulty of the husbandman's job has not only to do with crop failure and hard work but with the penny that must be given to the king. That his work profits someone else is more bitter than the other hardships.

At a certain point in the first part of the sixteenth century, the symbolic imagination around shepherds and, consequently, plowmen changed dramatically. The activity of keeping sheep began to be distinguished from and opposed to other kinds of traditional rural labor—namely, plowing. It is important to note that this opposition between plowing and keeping sheep is a relatively new one in the early sixteenth century.[38] The transition is made clear in an oft-quoted sermon by the Protestant preacher Hugh Latimer, as he preached before King Edward VI in 1549. He describes his father as a "yeoman" who had a farm that he tilled and "a walk for a hundred sheep."[39] For his father, then, being a farmer (and tiller of the soil) is entirely compatible with sheep keeping. But times have changed, and in the same sermon Latimer goes on to attack those who keep sheep as "graziers, inclosers, and rent-rearers" who are "hinderers of the king's honour."[40] These "graziers" are not, of course, the yeomen or hired hands (that is, those who are actually keeping the sheep); they are in opposition to the farmers. The sermon thus demonstrates the emergence of a new category of "sheep masters" who ultimately distinguish shepherdly activities from other kinds of rural labor, and therefore other rural laborers, who fit a traditional model of yeoman or plowman, such as Latimer's own father. Indeed, the polemic against enclosure is consistent in opposing tillage and shepherding, with the former standing for tradition or the status quo and the latter for the new conditions.

This opposition was made forcefully by the participants in the Lincolnshire Rising of 1536. Although the rising was on the face of it motivated by anger at Henry VIII's religious policies, it also reflected a great amount of distress with agrarian conditions, particularly changes in lordship and landownership.[41] According to R. H. Tawney, "the men of Lincolnshire marched under a banner embroidered with a ploughshare and laggards were spurred forward with the cry, 'What will ye do? Shall we go home and keep sheep?'"[42] For these men keeping sheep had taken on a new meaning: acceptance of the new order, in which lords could enclose lands and the commons had to give up their traditional role as farmers (and part-owners) of that land, a role represented by plowmen. A more sustained discussion of this new opposition can be found in the anti-enclosure tract *Certayne Causes gathered together wherin is shewed the decaye of England, only by the great multitude of shepe, to the vtter decay of household keeping, mayntenaunce of men, dearth of corne, and other notable dyscommodityes approued by syxe olde prouerbes* (1552), in which the author writes:

> Manye of these worshipfull men, sette no store, nor pryse, vpon the mayntenaunce of tyllage of their landes, as before tyme hath bene vsed, neyther breadynge nor leadynge of catle, but many of them doeth kepe the most substaunce of theyr landes in their owne handes. And where tyllage was wont to be, now is it stored wyth greate vmbermente of shepe.[43]

The passage assigns "tillage" a kind of timelessness, with the phrase "before time," which the author repeats elsewhere: "tyllage is not vsed, occupyed, and mainteyned as it hath bene before tyme" (A5r). Sheep keeping, in contrast, belongs to the "now" (and is, therefore, a threat). The author of another anti-enclosure tract, *Pyers plowmans exhortation, vnto the lordes, knightes and burgoysses of the Parlyamenthouse* (1550), underlines the opposition between "tillage" and the new practices of enclosure and sheep keeping by pointedly borrowing a figure from medieval literary tradition: Piers Plowman.[44] In William Langland's late-fourteenth-century poem, Piers is both a part of and an advocate for the traditional three-estate structure: he retains this traditional social order when he organizes the Plowing of the Half-Acre in Passus 6.[45] As the appearance of Piers, a recognizable figure from the past, makes clear, tillage stands for what the author consider tradition, what we might call a pre-capitalist economy of small producers. The rhetoric around this economy is shaped by concerns about subsistence (the "dearth of corne" mentioned in the title to *Certayne Causes*), however much, in reality, farming was a money-making venture. As Jane Whittle reminds us, what distinguishes "peasant societies" (the term she uses instead of *feudalism*) from capitalist ones is "the fact that peasants possessed land, used mainly family labour [not waged labor], and had the dominant aim of subsistence rather than marketing produce."[46] Indeed, the repetition of the term *maintenance* in *Certayne Causes* offers a kind of window into this pre-capitalist worldview: the desire for continuity (*maintaining* understood as preserving the status quo) is closely linked to subsistence (*maintaining* understood as providing for oneself). For the authors of both texts novelty threatens both the social order and the very livelihood of the farmers. Neither author can imagine that there could be another way besides agriculture to provide for the population of England.

If tillage stands for traditional economic relations—or the "maintenance" of all classes in England—then sheep keeping stands for new economic relations characterized by individualism. In the passage from *Certayne Causes* cited above, the author laments that the "worshipfull men" "doeth kepe the most substaunce of theyr landes in their owne handes" instead of turning them over to tillage. Here is recognition that the land, when it was being farmed under the traditional model, might have belonged to the lords but was not actually in their hands. It was in the hands of—that is, worked by—the tenants. The phrase "in their own hands" appears throughout the anti-enclosure writings, its presence suggesting an anxiety about the change in the nobility's perspective on their lands. For example, it is used to describe the "new" individualism of farmers in Robert Crowley's tract *The Way to Wealth* (1550), which offers itself as a "present remedy for Sedition." Crowley notes that the "pore man of the contrey" would identify the first "cause of Sedition" as oppressive farmers ("the great fermares, the grasiers") and goes on to say that these are "Men that would haue all in their owne handes."[47] The repetition of this phrase in the sixteenth-century tracts underlines what historians have also observed: a sudden (and somewhat surprising) interest on the part of landowners in farming their own lands and a subsequent (or simultaneous) change in the understanding of landownership. Joan Thirsk writes, "[f]rom the Black Death until about 1500 gentlemen shed the toil and trouble of farming their home farms and leased them to others"; she then asks, "What persuaded them, after a long period of a century and more, to take on the onerous business of farming their demesnes once again?"[48] According to Tawney,

> if one were to seek the watershed where the mediaeval theory of land tenure, as something contingent on the fulfilment of obligations, parts company from modern conceptions of ownership, as conferring an unlimited right to unconditional disposal by the owner, one would find it in the century and a half between 1500 and the final abolition of feudal tenures in 1660.[49]

This new individualism is, of course, linked to the desire for profit, which fuels the interest in sheep farming. In Thomas Tusser's *Five Hundred Pointes of Good Husbandrie* (1580), a supporter of enclosure states the reasoning behind it:

More profit is quieter found
(where pastures in seuerall bee)
Of one seelie aker of ground,
than champion [common ground] maketh of three.
Againe what a ioie is it knowne,
when men may be bold of their owne![50]

Tusser's links between profit, joy, and the boldness of claiming possession of land read as a kind of reassurance, particularly in light of the attacks on enclosure that occurred throughout the middle of the sixteenth century. But the desire for profit (and, of course, the individualism) long associated with enclosure was, for many, not in the least admirable, and in most of the writings of this period sheep keeping is repeatedly associated with the "covetousness" of the lords.[51] The author of *Pyers plowmans exhortation* writes,

> And for as much as it is wel nygh impossyble for them to ouersee so manye seruauntes as might kepe so great quantite of grounde in tyllage and desiringe to haue the whole profight of their grounde themselues they are driuen (by their insaciable couetousnes) to conuert al their groundes vnto the pasturing of shepe and such kynde of beastes as they maye receyue the whole proffyght with very litell charge of seruauntes so that one man hauing in his occupying so much ground as fiue hundredth parsons haue heretofore with their labour gayned their lyuinge vppon shall kepe perchaunce ten or twelue shepehardes and fower or fyue neatherdes. (A6v–7r)

For this writer, the "shepehardes" are occupying the same "ground" that would have previously been given over to five hundred persons. In other words, shepherds are now clearly identified with lords and not with "persons," that is, the commons. The passage on enclosure in Thomas More's *Utopia*, translated by Robynson, uses an almost identical formulation:

> Therefore that on covetous and unsatiable cormaraunte and very plage of his natyve contrey maye compasse aboute and inclose many thousand akers of grounde together within one pale or hedge, the husbandmen be thrust owte of their owne.... For one shephearde or heardman is ynoughe to eate up that grounde with cattel, to the occupiyng wherof aboute husbandrye manye handes were requisite.[52]

Here, too, the shepherd replaces the husbandmen because of the "insatiable greed" of the lords. Similarly, the author of *Certayne Causes* associates sheep keeping with exploitative practices and profit-oriented thinking: "we do partlye knowe, that there be some dwellynge withyn these thre shyres, rather then they wyll sell their woll at a lowe pryse, they wyll kepe it a yeare or twayne, and all to make it deare, and to kepe it a deare pryse" (A4v). The use of the term *pryse* should recall the passage quoted above, in which the author claims that rich men "sette no pryse" upon tillage, as if to suggest that it does not have a monetary value, only a time-honored value.

The new view of shepherding introduces a kind of rupture or set of contradictions in the language of rural labor. Previously, labor belonged literally to the peasantry; it was what characterized them. In Chaucer's *General Prologue* to the *Canterbury Tales*, the Plowman is a "trewe swynkere."[53] The growing association between shepherding and the nobility would seem to reflect and encourage the sense that shepherds do not labor. At first glance the anti-enclosure treatises do suggest that shepherding is not labor; just as shepherds have replaced plowmen, so their lack of labor replaces honest rural labor. For example, the quotation from *Pyers plowmans exhortation* demonstrates that "ten or twelue shepehardes"—who, significantly, are not said to labor—now occupy the same ground from which five hundred persons gained their living with "labor." The very fact that the author uses Piers Plowman, who is a figure for rural labor, to attack sheep keeping underlines that this new rural activity does not fit into the traditional model for understanding labor in the countryside. In the same way, *Certayne Causes* distinguishes sheep keepers from all other laborers in its appeal to the king:

> take al craftesmen dwelling in cyties and tounes, daye laborers that laboreth by water or by land, cottygers and other housholders, refusing none, but onely them that hath al this aboundaunce, that is to saye, shepe or woll masters and inclosers, the lamentacyons of the Kynges maiesties subiectes wil make anye true herted body to seke and call for remedy. (B2v)

This hoped for alliance between the king and the workers to the exclusion of the nobility, who are the "woll masters and inclosers," conforms exactly to what Holstun calls "monarcho-populism"—that is, the king should support a tradition that favors the small farmer.

98 *Transforming Work*

But this shift is slightly more complicated. It is not that shepherds and their masters (the enclosers) do not labor but that their labor has a different meaning, and fits into a different economic system. It is oriented toward profit, not toward subsistence or the maintenance of the three-estate structure. Thus, we find in William Harrison's *Description of England* (1577; 1587) an assertion that the nobility have become the shepherds, thereby ensuring that their farmers will not earn any money at all: "[I am] most sorowfull of all to vnderstand that men of great port and countenance are so farre from suffering their farmers to haue anie gaine at all, that they themselues become grasiers, butchers, tanners, sheepmasters, woodmen, and *denique quid non*, thereby to inrich themselues, and bring all the wealth of the countrie into their owne hands, leauing the communaltie weake."[54] For Harrison, what distinguishes the "men of great port" from the "farmers" is not labor but the desire to profit and to possess their own lands at the expense of the greater community.

Harrison's fears about the weakness of the "communaltie" were shared by many. The changes in the countryside were thought to be destroying the mutuality that was considered a fundamental aspect (however imaginary) of lord/peasant relations. For the writers of the anti-enclosure pamphlets, one class (the rich) profits by destroying the other, the commons. Instead of mutuality, there is class war. These tracts repeatedly invoke the term *decay* (as in the title to the tract *Certayne Causes*) to describe the process by which the nobility have ruined the commons, and even England itself: towns have been pulled down, laborers sent begging, rents raised, fields enclosed. The author of *Pyers plowmans exhortation* uses Piers, the voice of the traditional order, to warn of its destruction, particularly the destruction of the third estate, the laborers: "a fewe riche men haue ingrossed vp so many fermes and shepe pastures and haue decayed so many whole townes that thousandes of the poore comens can not get so muche as one ferme nor scant any litell house to put their head in" (A2r).[55] This is, interestingly, not only a material destruction (of the means by which the commons support themselves) but a symbolic one as well, in that it destroys their very place in the social structure, the identity of the commons, as made clear in a ballad dating from ca. 1520:

> We Englisshemen beholde
> Our aunciet customs bolde,
> more preciouser then golde,
> be clene cast away,
> And other new be fownd
> the which (ye may vnderstand)
> that causethe all your land
> So gretly to decay.[56]

The anti-enclosure pamphlets were, of course, entirely unsuccessful in their attempt to reverse history and return to their desired goal: the socioeconomic world of Henry VII. That the changes were perceived not just in terms of their novelty but in terms of loss is made clear by the author of *Certayne Causes*, who details the "nine losses" in the second half of the treatise; for example, the loss of plows translates into the loss of livelihood for "twelfscore persons" in Oxfordshire (A6v). The attempts to imagine the consequences of this loss in these pamphlets, for all of their stridency about towns decaying and families sent begging, seem to fall short. As Joan Thirsk observes,[57] the most powerful argument for common lands, the "co-operative spirit" it generated, was never made, although it is suggested in some of the tracts:

> but excepte in shortt tyme
> we drawe by one lyne,
> and agre with one accorde,—
> bothe the plowgh-man and the lorde,—
> we shall sore Rewe
> that ever this statte we knewe.[58]

Thirsk offers an account of this "accorde" at some length by way of conclusion:

> common fields and pastures kept alive a vigorous co-operative spirit in the community; enclosures starved it. In champion country people had to work together amicably, to agree upon crop rotations, stints of common pasture, the upkeep and improvement of their grazings and

meadows, the clearing of ditches, the fencing of fields. They toiled side by side in the fields, and they walked together from field to village, from farm to heath, morning, afternoon, and evening. They all depended on common resources for their fuel, for bedding, and fodder for their stock, and by pooling so many of the necessities of livelihood they were disciplined from early youth to submit to the rules and customs of their community. After enclosure, when every man could fence his own piece of territory and warn his neighbours off, the discipline of sharing things fairly with one's neighbours was relaxed, and every household became an island unto itself. This was the great revolution in men's lives, greater than all the economic changes following enclosure.[59]

The Pastoral Mode

Anti-enclosure tracts of the sixteenth century already reveal concerns with what Raymond Williams considered the "new order," in which the nobility were associated with agrarian capitalism and, therefore, the destruction of the traditional socioeconomic relations in the countryside. For these writers the sign of that transformation is sheep keeping. Given the economic significance of sheep keeping in this period, it is worth asking how early pastorals, whose "courtliness" has long been assumed, might still be "about" agriculture, particularly the transition to agrarian capitalism. This is not to look for the representation of working conditions in the pastoral because we will not find them, except, perhaps, in Alexander Barclay's *Eclogues*. Nevertheless, the pastoral mode can, indeed, be read as a kind of account of "what the country was really like" if we are willing to read the text's unconscious and to see the pastoral as a veiled representation of the dissolution of traditional labor relations—that is, of the obligations between lord and tenant and the increase in waged labor in the countryside.[60] In referring to the unconscious of the pastoral, I am, of course, invoking both Pierre Macherey's *A Theory of Literary Production* and Fredric Jameson's *The Political Unconscious*. The text's unconscious is where "history" is located, what Macherey describes as "latent knowledge" of the conditions of its emergence.[61] For Jameson the "unconscious" is "the repressed and buried reality of this fundamental history"—that is, the history of class struggle.[62] From this perspective the pastoral is a document of disruption, and its much-heralded novelty is precisely the point. The pastoral rewrites the transition to agrarian capitalism, which was described as a loss in the anti-enclosure pamphlets, in almost entirely positive terms: the happy and self-sufficient shepherds in the English countryside.

To make this argument one must pay close attention to what one might call the "economy of pastoral," that is, the world of labor relations and commodity production represented in these texts. At first glance, such a discussion would seem to miss the mark entirely. Isn't the point of pastoral, after all, its refusal to face the material basis of life? In Alpers's eloquent formulation shepherds must be "simply free to sing and woo," even if such a "pretense" seems to be "callow and in bad faith."[63] As Alpers's use of the word *free* suggests, pastoral is (or is understood to be) about a space apart from materialism. But in sixteenth-century pastoral, as well as in Virgil's *Eclogues*, economic considerations are not set aside completely.[64] After all, the shepherds are not shepherding merely for the fun of it but rather to produce both commodities (milk and wool) and livestock (more sheep), for reasons that are made intermittently clear. The details of this economy are entirely compatible with the agrarian capitalism described by writers in the enclosure controversies, as I shall demonstrate here. Perhaps the most obvious economic aspect of pastoral is its individualism, or interest in the independent producer. The shepherds labor for themselves, not for another nor together. As Alexander Barclay writes in his fourth eclogue,

> Nedes must a Shepheard bestowe his whole labour
> In tending his flockes, scant may he spare one houre:
> In going, comming, and often them to tende,
> Full lightly the day is brought vnto an ende.
> Sometime the wolues with dogges must he chace,
> Sometime his foldes must he newe compace:
> And oft time them chaunge, and if he stormes doubt,
> Of his shepecote dawbe the walles round about:

When they be broken, oft times them renue,
And hurtfull pastures note well, and them eschue.
Bye strawe and litter, and hay for winter colde,
Oft grease the scabbes aswell of yonge as olde.
For dreade of thieues oft watche vp all the night,
Beside this labour with all his minde and might,
For his poore housholde for to prouide vitayle,
If by aduenture his wooll or lambes fayle.
                    (4.163–78)

In its emphasis on the details of labor, Barclay's account of shepherdly life points backward to the traditional model, in which labor is what defines the laborer, including the shepherd. But this labor is not linked to anything outside the individual, whether the city or the marketplace (as in Virgil's *Eclogues*) or lord/tenant relations (as in the nativity plays); rather, it sustains the individual "housholde." There is no mention of any other beneficiary of the shepherds' labor or his risk ("aduenture"), nor any obligations other than to his sheep.

This emphasis on individualism has consequences for the social order represented in these texts. Early pastorals tend to imagine their shepherds in a kind of hermetic community, in which shepherds are subordinate to none. As Barclay's poetry reminds us, these shepherds are not keeping sheep for a lord. In addition, there are few references to the social world outside of the shepherding community. This independence certainly suggests the compatibility of the pastoral mode with agrarian capitalism (as discussed above), but it also serves to erase the interdependence that characterized the countryside at the time, an interdependence imagined both horizontally (the groups of shepherds in the nativity plays) and vertically (the subordination of plowmen to the nobility and clergy). Indeed, it is worth noting how radical the pastoral approach to rural laborers looks when compared to medieval and even mid-sixteenth-century texts, in which to represent a laborer independently of the social order, such as the three estates, would have been almost unthinkable. Chaucer's Plowman, we might remember, is brother to the Parson; the plowman of "I playne Piers which cannot flatter" complains about both the clergy and the lords (see further discussion in the following chapter).

Central to this focus on the individual shepherd is, of course, his ownership. All early eclogues follow Virgil in describing the shepherd speakers as owners of the sheep; the shepherds repeatedly refer to the sheep as "mine." For example, in Barnabe Googe's second eclogue, Dametas says, "My beasts, go feed upon the plain, / and let your herdman lie" (2.1–2) This aspect is not in itself significant, but the eclogues also imagine this ownership in terms of a kind of self-sufficiency; the shepherd is a producer of all that is needed and, therefore, independent of any other kind of economic relationship. In Googe's third eclogue, which explicitly takes up the relations between the country and the town, Coridon retreats to his home:

> I would not leave the pleasant field
>   for all the townish lands.
> . . . .
> Menalcas, best we now depart;
>   my cottage us shall keep,
> For there is room for thee and me,
>   and eke for all our sheep.
> Some chestnuts have I there in store
>   with cheese and pleasant whey;
> God sends me victuals for my need,
>   and I sing care away.
>   (3.151–72)

These foods are produced by the shepherd himself (the cheese and whey) or found in nature (the chestnuts). From this perspective, the fantasy is that of the shepherd as a producer who does not need "tillage," in the words of the anti-enclosure treatises, nor does he need the town. Similarly, Barclay describes the shepherd life as "sufficient" in terms of material goods at the end of his third eclogue:

> Thou playne hast proued that all they fooles be
> Which folowe the court seking captiuitie,
> And might els where an honest life purchase,
> Hauing suffisaunce and moderate solace.
>   (3.759–62)

This "suffisaunce" is produced, of course, by the shepherd himself. In short, individual ownership and independent production in the countryside replace the communalism associated with the "traditional order."

Of course, the pastoral includes not only the shepherd speakers but also "boys," who are mentioned in the eclogues of Mantuan, Googe, and Spenser (although not, interestingly enough, in Barclay). For example, in Googe's first eclogue, the speaker commands a "boy" to do the work: "Go, boy; go drive the beasts to feed / while he his mind recite" (1.27–28). Or, in Turberville's translation of Mantuan's fourth eclogue, the speaker narrates, "With pennie I a Lad did hire / my little flocke to keepe."[65] These boys could certainly be described as wage laborers if one were to use the terminology of economic historians. In this way, pastoral portrays not one but two occupational possibilities—the owner of sheep and the hireling—and, therefore, a particular labor relationship that matches the new agrarian capitalism. Agrarian capitalism insists on the lord as the sole owner of lands and erases the workers' claims of ownership (on the commons). As Alan Everitt writes, "the larger man was working his way up into the ranks of the husbandmen, and the small peasant was becoming a mere wage-worker."[66] Although the feudal and patriarchal relations between masters and men continued, attitudes were slowly shifting, and laborers were beginning to be viewed as employees.[67]

The independence and self-sufficiency of the shepherd that characterize the pastoral mode are, not surprisingly, positive attributes of ownership. In this way, the pastoral mode rewrites the anxiety that fills the anti-enclosure treatises, namely, that the lords were taking everything into their "own hands." In the pastoral, ownership does not lead to (or stem from) covetousness as it does in the treatises. No one can accuse shepherds of covetousness if they already possess everything that they need.

More importantly, the central fantasy of pastoral, the shepherds' *otium* (leisure), also takes on new meaning when approached from the perspective of the enclosure controversies. *Otium* has, of course, long been considered a necessary, even definitive, aspect of the pastoral mode, but its meaning is typically understood as self-evident. After all, the fantasy of leisure makes a great deal of sense on a personal level: who wouldn't rather lie around in the field and sing songs than dig ditches? It would seem that this is the reason that few scholars have examined leisure in any detail. Those who have done so—Renato Poggioli briefly and Louis Montrose at greater length—draw attention to the relationship between leisure and class, or socioeconomic position. As Poggioli notes of classical pastoral, "the idea of pastoral leisure is after all but an imaginative projection of the classical and humanistic antinomy of mechanical and liberal arts. The former are the natural activities of the slave, the latter, of the freeborn."[68] According to Montrose, when pastoral is translated into Elizabethan culture the leisure of the shepherd becomes a sign of gentility, whereas labor belongs to the "meaner sort."[69] Despite Montrose's greater attention to Elizabethan culture, the presence of *otium* in the pastoral still seems entirely straightforward in its meaning: it is a reflection of a desire not to do work (with all that work means, such as class).

But the desirability of *otium* was not, in fact, self-evident for early pastoralists. The eclogues of Mantuan and Alexander Barclay present somewhat contradictory views of shepherds, who are characterized both by labor and by leisure, as discussed in chapter 2. Their contradictions should remind us that the version of *otium* one finds in the pastoral mode was entirely novel in the sixteenth century. To characterize laborers (even shepherds) solely in terms of their leisure was unheard of in the Middle Ages, unless, of course, laborers were being condemned for their laziness; what defined rural laborers was their labor (on which see chapter 1). Perhaps more importantly, pastoral *otium* implies the denigration of labor, as Poggioli and Montrose make clear, and such a blanket denigration would have been rare in the Middle Ages. Indeed, we must distinguish between the denigration of laborers, or the "meaner sort," and the denigration of labor itself. As much as medieval writers might have shared with their Elizabethan counterparts a distaste and contempt for actual rural laborers, they did not have a contempt for rural labor.[70] Rather, they saw it as both fundamental to the social world and spiritually significant, as demonstrated in the expositions of the parable of the laborers in the vineyard, in which all members of society are considered laborers.

Moreover, a persistent interest in labor characterizes even the "real world" pastoral fantasies of certain gentlemen in the sixteenth century: the Elizabethan gentleman Sir Horatio Palavicino, described by Montrose, "signed letters from his Cambridgeshire estate 'being amongst my shepperds clipping my shepe.'"[71] Palavicino sees himself as a shepherd because he is one, if we understand shepherds less in terms of their leisure than in their ownership of sheep. Palavicino's point of view is echoed in the passage taken from William Harrison's *Description of England*, quoted above, in which he imagines the "men of great port" becoming butchers, tanners, grazers, etc., so that they might have all the gain from their sheep.

Why the representation of *otium* may not have been so straightforward for early pastoralists is suggested by the enclosure treatises, which invite us to read *otium* rather differently than it has been read thus far. That is, theorists of pastoral typically emphasize what leisure is: the sign of gentility and what that might mean in either classical or Elizabethan culture. But it is also useful to think about what it is not: leisure marks the absence of labor. While such a state might seem personally desirable for many, it was certainly not considered so by the writers of the anti-enclosure treatises in the sixteenth century. Rather, it presented an immense social and economic problem: the decay of villages, the end of the old order, and imminent famine (the scarcity of corn). These writings consistently detail the absence of laborers in the countryside and their replacement by sheep: "where tyllage was wont to be, now is it stored wyth greate vmbermente of shepe" (*Certayne Causes*, A4r). For the anti-enclosure polemicists, sheep are as much the sign of labor's absence as for the pastoralist. But in the pastoral that same absence has been transformed into a positive presence: leisure.

In the anti-enclosure treatises, the absence of labor in the countryside (and the presence of sheep) is a sign that many will starve: labor is, therefore, the means by which people earn their "livelihood" (a term repeated throughout). But in the pastoral, the absence of labor, now rewritten as leisure, has no effect on livelihood. In fact, labor is entirely irrelevant, and livelihood (even wealth) is understood specifically in terms of property, whether land or sheep. A compelling example of this transformation can be found in Mantuan's third eclogue, which is quoted here in Turberville's translation:

> For Cattle is the onely wealth
> that Countrymen enioy
> And Pasture ground that subiect is
> to this and like anoy.
> The Citizens haue heaped hoords
> and coffers full of pence.[72]

Cattle (the Latin is "pecus"—a single sheep or head of cattle) are here equated with capital, piles of cash. Keeping cattle is not, therefore, so much an occupation or a means to feed a household (as it is still in Barclay) but a kind of accumulation or saving. From this perspective, shepherds and their leisure demonstrate a shift characteristic of agrarian capitalism: the wealth of the countryside is no longer produced by labor, and, therefore, laborers can have no claim upon it. As the anti-enclosure treatises lament, everything is in the lords' "own hands."

Perhaps the finest example of the compatibility between the pastoral mode and an emergent agrarian capitalism can be found in book 6 of Edmund Spenser's *Faerie Queene*, to which I'll return in more detail in chapter 6. It should suffice to say that this episode has a Golden Age sensibility in that it imagines that food and clothing are produced without labor. Meliboe, the wise old shepherd, tells Calidore, the admiring visitor to the countryside, that "The fields my food, my flocke my rayment breed."[73] One can find here the same sensibility that Williams finds in the country-house poems: "the unworked for providence of nature."[74] Yet, on second glance, this Golden Age reflects less an ideal, or the desire for no economic relations, than the reality of capitalist economic relations. Meliboe does not, in fact, sit lazily by while God or Nature provides for him. Instead, his energies are spent in accumulating:

> The litle that I haue, growes dayly more
> Without my care, but onely to attend it;
> My lambes doe euery yeare increase their score.[75]

Meliboe contradicts the Golden Age mentality in the second line of this quotation: he attends to his sheep. And he is rewarded for this attention, which, significantly, is not described as labor, by the increasing of his flock. In a sense this passage matches Barclay's account of sheep keeping, but it is colored by the optimism of accumulation instead of the threat of "failing."

From the perspective of the anti-enclosure tracts, which insist on the destruction of the countryside, the most disturbing aspect of pastoral might be its capacity to re-imagine a scene of violent expropriation (the enclosure of the commons for the purposes of sheep keeping) as an idyll. This idyllic aspect of pastoral has, of course, long been appreciated as fundamental to the pastoral mode, whether that idyllic aspect is described in terms of the "beautiful relation between rich and poor," to quote Empson, or the simple fact that the pastoral "does not envisage deprivation," as Alpers observes.[76] Both Empson and Alpers hint at what is specifically being mystified: namely, class conflict. This is a conflict made glaringly apparent in writings about the enclosure controversy, which insist that sheep keeping has destroyed not only the traditional way of life (tillage) but the very people (the commons) who depend on the land, as mentioned above. The perceived violence of this process is underlined in Sir Thomas More's famous image of sheep eating people. In contrast, the first writers of the pastoral imagine shepherds to be independent of the traditional social order (the three estates), and, therefore, the countryside is portrayed as free of the exploitations and violent disruptions that threaten this order, including depopulation, the exploitation of peasants, and the potential for rebellion. Even Barclay's shepherds, who complain at length about poverty and the difficulty of laboring, do not complain about their oppression at the hands of lords.

It is difficult to make an argument based on absence, but the significance of this absence will perhaps be more apparent if the pastoral is read in relation to medieval texts and as part of a broader tradition of "writing rural labor." In the medieval period the countryside was certainly a site of violence and exploitation, and, importantly, of class antagonism: the husbandman who complains about taxation in the mid-fourteenth-century *Song of the Husbandman*; the shepherds who complain about the lords in the first and second shepherd plays in the Towneley cycle; the farmer, Peace, who complains about the king's purveyor, Wrong, who steals his livestock, in William Langland's *Piers Plowman*. These texts give a sense, however limited, of the way in which class conflict emerged out of or in terms of thinking about rural life. In this way, they give a hint of the "realities" of rural life: Robert Brenner's famous (and controversial) essay, "Agrarian Class Structure and Economic Development in Pre-Industrial Europe," finds class conflict absolutely definitive of socioeconomic relations between lords and tenants in the late Middle Ages.[77] As the site of class conflict, the countryside is also the site for imagining reform. It is the plowman of Langland's poem and not, say, a cobbler or a craftsman/laborer more closely associated with the town who becomes a figure for social reform in the late medieval period and into the sixteenth century.

Yet, one of the most important pastoral conventions, the contrast between the country and the town, seems to have encouraged early writers of pastoral to assign oppressive labor relations and the potential violence (and inequities) of the social order to the town—in other words, away from the people, the peasants, with whom these concerns (and the solutions to them) had so long been associated. Once again Alexander Barclay's poetry, which depicts the countryside in far less idyllic terms than most, understands the town in terms of wage labor, which ultimately leads to "det and pouertie" (5.24). The shepherd Amintas in the fifth eclogue has tried a variety of jobs before returning home:

> First was he hosteler, and then a wafrer,
> Then a costermonger, and last a tauerner,
> About all London there was no proper prim
> But long time had bene familier with him,
> But when coyne fayled no fauour more had he.
> (5.27–31)

His friend Faustus, in contrast, has always been "content with his estate" as a shepherd (5.34), which is not, importantly, imagined as poverty-stricken, only simple. Part of this idyll in the countryside is, as Barclay suggests, being "content with one's estate." Indeed, the opposite—not being content with one's estate, or social mobility—is in these texts a veiled means to discuss threats to the social order and consistently associated with the town. Barclay's Amintas, although a shepherd, has a "lord's" appetites, and that's why he goes to town. Similarly, Spenser's Meliboe, in book 6 of the *Faerie Queene*, becomes a gardener at court because he wishes to earn money (as discussed further in chapter 6). Assigning economic discontent, which was in this period often the motive for violence in the countryside, to the town allows these writers to re-imagine that countryside as "a pleasant place" (Googe, *Eclogues*, 3.49), a site of "suffisaunce" or contentment.

The writings of the enclosure controversies make clear that the traditional rural laborer, the plowman or Piers, had come in the sixteenth century to stand for a critique of agrarian capitalism, in addition, of course, to his myriad other meanings. In re-imagining the rural laborer anew, as the shepherd of the eclogue, early pastoral both represses that critique and, however indirectly, aligns that shepherd with a capitalist worldview. For that reason we should see the pastoral emerging as a response not only to real rural laborers, or "what the country was really like," but also to the figurative rural laborers of the plowman tradition and the breaking apart of the entire "symbolic universe" of the late Middle Ages.

FOUR | *Transforming Work*

The Reformation and the *Piers Plowman* Tradition

Thus far, this study has argued that the history of pastoral belongs properly to a history of "writing rural labor." Such a history must take into account not only specific changes in how rural laborers might be represented—the distinguishing characteristics of shepherds, for example, which were discussed in chapters 2 and 3—but also shifts in what I've been calling *the symbolic imagination* around rural labor: that is, how and what rural labor can mean. The sixteenth century witnessed a momentous disruption in that symbolic imagination during the Reformation in the struggle over the religious significance of "works," with which rural labor had long been associated. To investigate that struggle, this chapter must momentarily set the pastoral mode aside and concentrate on its alter ego—the *Piers Plowman* tradition—which haunted the English pastoral from the beginning. Nevertheless, an implicit argument about the pastoral guides this reading: that the Reformation redefinition of "works" helped, however indirectly, to make the new pastoral mode intelligible, even possible.

Works played a vital role in Reformation debates: the central doctrine of justification by faith alone meant the subordination of works to faith.[1] Yet the extent to which this shift in doctrine (the meaning of *works*) caused a shift in how labor was viewed (the meaning of *work*) during the sixteenth century is still an open question. Max Weber famously argued that the Puritan position on works had consequences for how we understand work, or "worldly activity," but he located that transformation in the seventeenth century.[2] Scholars of the sixteenth century have, in contrast, typically held religion and labor (indeed most economic questions) separate, claiming that Tudor texts demonstrate a radical religious reformism and a conservative social vision. In his *Religion and the Rise of Capitalism*, R. H. Tawney writes,

> That the problems of a swiftly changing economic environment should have burst on Europe at a moment when it was torn by religious dissensions more acute than ever before, may perhaps be counted as not least among the tragedies of its history. But differences of social theory did not coincide with differences of religious opinion, and the mark of nearly all this body of teaching, alike in Germany and in England, is its conservatism.[3]

More recently, Andrew McRae has noted that sixteenth-century complaint literature, much of it in the "plowman tradition," such as Hugh Latimer's "Sermon on the Plowers," "conflates a radical religious agenda with an essentially conservative socio-economic vision."[4]

Two assumptions guide this perspective: first, that the Protestantism of mid-sixteenth-century texts is entirely uniform and internally consistent, and second, that the direction of influence runs from religious belief to social/economic views and not vice versa. Both assumptions are problematic. First, the Reformation was not a switch, by which Protestant beliefs were "turned on" in a sudden and radical break with the past. One must rather speak of "reformations" or a process of transformation.[5] Second, as Tawney himself noted, the mid-sixteenth century was characterized by a striking simultaneity of changes, making it difficult to sort out causal relationships between religious and social views.[6] In short, we cannot assume that these texts "do" what they say they are doing—whether insisting on the traditional social order or on new religious beliefs.

That the relationship between religious belief and socioeconomic views was complicated in this period is apparent in some of the most popular examples of complaint literature: texts in the *Piers Plowman* tradition. These include editions of William Langland's late-fourteenth-century poem, *Piers Plowman*, which was printed three times by Robert Crowley (1550) and once by Owen Rogers (1561); imitations of Langland, such as "I playne Piers which cannot flatter" (?1547), *Pyers plowmans exhortation, vnto the lordes, knightes and burgoysses of the Parlyamenthouse* (1550), and *A godly dialogue and dysputacyon between Pyers plowman, and a popysh preest* (1550); and finally, the pseudo-Chaucerian *Plowman's Tale* (printed in Thynne's edition of Chaucer's poetry in 1542).[7]

At first glance, these texts fit the pairing described above: social conservatism and Protestantism. That is, all insist upon the traditional three-estate structure and its mutuality; they also align themselves with the "new" religious beliefs or lament that reform is not moving quickly enough. But the oddity of choosing Piers to represent this particular relationship should be noted. Although the Piers of Langland's late-fourteenth-century poem can be read in terms of his social conservatism—that is, his support for the three estates as they work together on the Half-Acre—he is also indebted to a particularly medieval Catholic symbolic imagination in which work is closely associated with works.[8] After all, the majority of the poem, from Passus 8 to the end, is a search for the allegorical figures "Do Well," "Do Better," and "Do Best" around the figure of a plowman. Although Langland's own position on the role of works in salvation has perhaps been overstated and simplified, there is no denying that he saw works as a fundamental element of church teaching at this time and, therefore, a theological matter that deserved careful consideration.[9] More importantly for my argument here, the poem resists at every turn any attempt to distinguish between religious views of work (such as penance) that would for later readers be incompatible with Protestantism, and social views (such as the three estates) that could be compatible with Protestantism. Instead of seeing the popularity of Langland's poem and its plowman in the sixteenth century as "puzzling," as Anne Hudson notes, we might say that it was precisely Piers's special capacity to represent that connection between the religious and the social that made him attractive to writers throughout the Reformation period.[10] This special capacity might well have been appealing in the mid-sixteenth century because of the simultaneous disruptions in both religious beliefs and agrarian practices.[11] As I shall argue here, the figure of Piers allowed writers to investigate the changing relationship of work and works in the wake of Protestantism. This was not, as shall become clear, an easy transformation. Although these mid-sixteenth-century texts are unquestionably Protestant, they reveal a resistance to the kind of transformation that the Reformation supposedly accomplished—in which work, particularly rural labor, is separated from its connections with works. This is a particularly *religious* resistance, a difficulty in accepting those aspects of Protestant doctrine that would affect perceptions of rural labor.

Works Redefined

The Protestant redefinition of works is a fundamental aspect of the Reformation. Protestants distinguish themselves from the medieval tradition with their insistence on "justification by faith alone." As William Tyndale writes in *The Parable of the Wicked Mammon* (1527), "That faith only before all works and without all merits, but Christ's only, justifieth and setteth us at peace with God, is proved by Paul in the first chapter to the Romans."[12] As William Clebsch notes, "Tyndale first, among English writers, gave literary expression to the major theological themes of law, covenant, works, and rewards upon which the Puritan tradition within English-speaking Christianity built."[13] This redefinition has semiotic as well as theological consequences because it necessarily changes how works can be represented. Yet the nature of this new semiotics, and its impact on the language of labor, has not been investigated; indeed, Tawney asserts that labor is a kind of constant in these early Protestant writings, even if the theology around it changes. It is true that, on the surface, these writings tend to be entirely sympathetic to "tradition" in that they uphold the three-estate model and, therefore, assign a value to agricultural work, particularly plowing. Nevertheless, a closer look will demonstrate that the new Protestant semiotics of work ultimately resulted in a kind of devaluing of rural labor and a limiting of its symbolic range. This is what Marshall

Sahlins has called "the functional revaluation of the categories"—that is, "the old names that are still on everyone's lips acquire connotations that are far removed from their original meaning."[14]

As demonstrated in chapter 1, the symbolic imagination around rural labor before the Reformation was shaped at least in part by medieval Catholicism. Indeed, rural labor played a central role in explaining religious beliefs and practices as a metaphor for spiritual works: everyone must work in his/her estate, and everyone must do works (penance, prayers, good deeds) to be saved. This is not to say that works dominated medieval discussions of doctrine, although they were popular material for sermons; but when they do appear, works were commonly represented through rural labor. The efficacy of this metaphor is likely familiar to most readers from the Middle English poem *Pearl*, in the Pearl Maiden's exposition of the parable of the laborers in the vineyard. Her exposition takes up the familiar equation—the laborers are Christians doing works—in order to challenge the dreamer's simplistic view that one can "earn" salvation. One might also turn to late medieval discussions of the passage from James 2:26: "faith without works is dead." After quoting this passage, one medieval sermon gives an extended account of the need to arise from sin and amend:

> Arise þan, for now is tyme of mercy, whils þat þou lyvest here; for more [ty]me þan we gett whilst þat we liff here shall we neuer haue aftur þat we are passed hens, but oure owne werkes shall folowe vs where-euer þat we goye [go]—"*Opera enim illorum secuntur illos.*" And þerfore seis Seynt Poule in is [his] pistell [epistle], "*Dum tempus habemus, operemur bonum ad omnes*—whils we haue tyme, do we good to all men," "*quia ipse reddet vnicuique mercedem secundum suum laborem*—for," þe apostell seis "he shall ʒeue mede [give a reward] to iche [each] man aftur is [his] labour here." And þer-fore as muche mede as þou wilt haue þer, so muche traveyll þou most haue here.... for Seynt Poule seyth, "*Qui parce seminat, parce et metet*;" and also "*Quicquid seminauerit homo, hoc et metet*": "He þat skarsely saweþ, skarsely shall reepe"; and "he þat sawethe in blyssynges, he shall repe euerlastynge liff."[15]

Although this passage certainly takes a more "Pelagian" position than *Pearl* (indeed, *Pearl* might be read at least in part as a correction of this kind of popular simplification), both reveal the illustrative efficacy of rural labor, particularly for a society in which the vast majority of people worked the land. The necessity of rural labor in providing for the entire society helped underline the necessity of works to salvation. Perhaps more importantly, the ubiquity of this metaphor demonstrates the inextricability of the social and economic from the religious and, consequently, gives the lie to Protestant attempts to maintain the traditional social order while changing one of the fundamental ideas with which it was associated and one of the most frequent images with which it was represented.

In early Protestantism works necessarily shift from "means" to "signs," to borrow terminology from Max Weber, who noted the semiotic consequences of a shift from works as "means of attaining salvation" to "signs of election."[16] As the author (perhaps Thomas Cranmer) of the *Homily on Good Works* writes, "In the last Sermon was declared unto you, what the lively and true faith of a Christian man is; that it causeth not a man to be idle, but to be occupied in bringing forth good works."[17] As signs, works are only important insomuch as they reveal the faith within, the motive that gives the work its meaning; the *Homily* continues, "If a heathen man clothe the naked, feed the hungry, and do such other like works; yet, because he doth them not in faith, for the honour and love of God, they be but dead, vain, and fruitless works to him."[18] The lesson for the Christian has changed—the meaning precedes the action; there is no acknowledgment that in doing an action, such as feeding the hungry, one might be trained to feel the charity and faith that go with that action.[19]

Because works themselves no longer matter in and of themselves, the action of "working" (sowing and reaping) tends to disappear from theological discussions. A new metaphor emerges to describe this new view of spiritual work: a tree and its fruit (faith and works, respectively). This metaphor is as ubiquitous as the rural labor (plowing and digging) described in medieval theological writings; it appears in Martin Luther's *Lectures on Galatians* and in the writings of English writers such as Tyndale and John Frith.[20] Tyndale writes,

> Take forth also the similitude that Christ maketh: "A good tree bringeth forth good fruit, and a bad tree bringeth forth bad fruit." There seest thou that the fruit maketh not the tree good, but the tree the fruit; and that the tree must aforehand be good or be made good, ere it can bring forth good fruit. . . . So likewise is this true, and nothing more true, that a man before all good works must first be good; and that it is impossible that works should make him good, if he were not good before, ere he did good works. (*Mammon*, 50)[21]

This metaphor has a biblical precedent in Matthew 7:16–20:

> Ye shall knowe them by there frutes. Do men gaddre grapes of thornes or feggs of bryeres. Even so every good tree bryngeth forth good frute. But a corrupte tree bringeth forth evyll frute. A good tree cannot bringe forth badde frute ner yet a badde tree can bringe forthe good frute. Euery tree that bringeth not forth good frute shal be hewen downe and cast in to the fyre. Wherfore by there frutes ye shall knowe them.[22]

This metaphor underlines the shift to works as signs: the true Christian will be known by his fruits, which indicate whether he is good or bad. It is worth emphasizing the marked shift in symbolic imagination: a spiritual work is now an object, a product of faith when praised or a commodity when condemned, not an action. Spiritual works are thus no longer similar to work (as actions). Even medieval sermons that describe works as things, such as armor or a plow, capture the actions involved in doing a work: one must put on armor, as in the letter to the Ephesians, and one must plow with a plow.[23]

This shift to a new metaphor coupled with the condemnation of Catholic beliefs around works had a particular effect on rural labor. Rural labor had long played an important role in how medieval Catholic theology had been imagined and described, as apparent in both *Pearl* and *Piers Plowman*. That rural labor continued to exert a kind of "Catholic" pull, a symbolic imagination that must be transformed or reformed, is evident in the writings of William Tyndale, who played an important role in redefining works in English. In his *Exposition on*

Matthew, Tyndale offers an illuminating example that contrasts the parent-child relationship with the laborer-employer relationship:

> [Faith] pretendeth not the goodness of her work, but knowledgeth that our works deserve it not, but are crowned and rewarded with the deservings of Christ. Take an ensample of young children, when the father promiseth them a good thing for the doing of some trifle, and when they come for their reward, dallieth with them saying: "What, that thou has done is not worth half so much: should I give thee so great thing for so little a trifle?" they will answer: "Ye did promise me: ye said, I should have it . . . ." But hirelings will pretend their work, and say, "I have deserved it: I have done so much, and so much, and my labour is worth it." (89–90)[24]

This odd analogy opposes the child with the "hireling" and the "doing of some trifle" with "labour." The true believer is, of course, the child who expects to earn a reward and does not (and who is teased, somewhat cruelly, by the father), and the false believer (the Catholic) is the hireling who thinks he deserves his reward. Interestingly enough, Tyndale has already stacked the deck against the laborer even before he claims his reward because he is called a "hireling," a term reserved for those denigrated in the Bible, such as the shepherds who do not watch the sheep in the parable of the good shepherd (John 10:11–18). Even more importantly, the opposition has less to do with the understanding of reward, which should ultimately be the issue, than with terminology. The child's "doing" is only a trifle, whereas the hireling's is work, even though both the child and the worker are motivated to act (that is, work) by the reward, and even though both "workers" act according to a kind of contract between the two parties: the child reminds the father of his promise, and the worker insists that he should be paid for what he has done. While it is clear that Tyndale desires to rewrite the relationship between God and Christian as familial instead of contractual, the analogy ends up endowing the rural laborer with a negative connotation that he had not heretofore possessed in devotional and homiletic literature. There is certainly more to say about the strange ideas about parenting (and power relations) that inform

Tyndale's example. But what I'd like to draw attention to is the ideology of work: Tyndale alters the expected example ("he shall give meed to each man after his labor" ['he shall ʒeue mede to iche man aftur is labour'], in the Middle English translation of Romans 2:6) to condemn labor. Physical labor is no longer analogous to a good deed but tainted by a kind of materialism (the hireling's demand for his wage). Similarly, in *Mammon*, Tyndale rails against the false belief of those who "live well, for heaven's sake or eternal reward": "These are servants that seek gains and vantage, hirelings and day-labourers, which here on earth receive their rewards, as the Pharisees with their prayers and fastings" (63–64).

Indeed, Tyndale's one account of virtuous labor involves a shoemaker, not a rural laborer:

> Faith is the life of man, as it is written, *Justus ex fide vivit*; out of which life the pleasantness of all his works spring. As for an ensample, thou art a shoe-maker; which is a work within the laws of God; and sayest in thine heart, "Lo, God, here I make a shoe as truly as I would for myself, to do my neighbour service, and to get my living in truth with the labour of mine hands, as thou commandest . . ." Lo, now this faith hath made this simple work pleasant in the sight of God. (*Exposition*, 125)

And Tyndale answers the question that such an example demands: How does shoemaking as a work compare with other works, such as Abraham's will to slay Isaac:

> "Yea, but shoe-making is not commanded by God." Yes; and hath the promise of God annexed thereto. For God hath commanded me, for the avoiding of sin, to do my brethren service, and to live thereby, and to choose one estate or other. . . . Now have I God's commandment to work therein truly; and his promise annexed thereto, that he will bless mine occupation, and make it lucky and fruitful, to bring me an honest living. Work I not now at God's commandment, and have his promise that it pleaseth him? (*Exposition*, 125–26)[25]

On the one hand, Tyndale's use of a shoemaker reinforces precisely that view of work that we find in medieval accounts of rural labor (such as the laborers in the vineyard): everyone should work in his "estate." In fact, in *Mammon* Tyndale states this view explicitly: "Now thou that ministerest in the kitchen, and art but a kitchen-page, receivest all things of the hand of God; knowest that God hath put thee in that office; submittest thyself to his will; and servest thy master not as a man, but as Christ himself" (101). On the other hand, this example introduces a new approach to rural labor. Instead of describing all Christians as manual laborers, some of whose labor is read spiritually (the image of laborers cutting vines is read as priests rebuking sin), Tyndale sees every labor in its specificity as fulfilling God's commandment. Manual labor no longer has, therefore, a role to play in imagining or representing a good work or the necessity of work, as it does for the author of *Pearl* or for a writer of the fifteenth-century *Lollard Sermons*: "God, for his grete godnesse, grante vs þoru his grace to wirche so wiseli in þis world oure werkis in þis vyne, eche man in his estaat þat he stant inne, þat we moun like [might please] þe Lord þerwith and be alowed þe peny."[26] For Tyndale, in contrast, rural labor is assigned to a purely literal level: if one is a laborer, then physical labor has a spiritual component (following God's commandment). Otherwise it has no power to explain the Christian's relationship to God, and the necessity of certain actions in this world.

We can find a similar discomfort with the "Catholic" potentialities of rural labor in Hugh Latimer's "Sermon on the Plowers." Although this text has long been read in terms of social complaint and has, therefore, been understood as compatible with and even part of the *Piers Plowman* tradition, it nevertheless demonstrates the way in which a Protestant semiotics tends to devalue (and de-spiritualize) rural labor because of its association with works.[27] It is worth recalling that Langland's poem assigns the plowman a number of spiritual meanings: his holiness, his "kynde knowyng," his capacity to figure Christ. Piers is thus both literal and figurative and always in motion between the two levels. Latimer's sermon, in contrast, marks a clear distinction between literal and figurative levels, controlling the figuration of the plowman—the figurative level being, of course, the more capacious (and therefore more dangerous) level of meaning. For Latimer there are plowmen (literally) and there are preachers who should think of themselves as plowmen: "For preaching of the gospel is one of God's plow works, and the preacher is one of God's plowmen."[28] Such a figuration should not be surprising. After all, there is a long tradition of reading the sower in this parable in terms of Jesus, his disciples, and preachers/prelates.[29] But Latimer explicitly draws our attention to the process of figuration itself by referring to his comparison as a "similitude": "Ye may not be offended with my similitude in that I compare preaching to the labor and work of plowing and the preacher to a plowman," and then, "Ye may not then, I say, be offended with my similitude, forbecause I liken preaching to a plowman's labor and a prelate to a plowman" (*Selected Sermons*, 29–30, 30). Latimer's self-consciousness about the similitude reveals not only his concern with decorum (not offending his audience) but also an attempt to control the plowman figure. Saying that one entity resembles another is not at all the same as saying that it *is* the other. To claim that a plowman has access to knowledge not shared by the clergy, or to make a plowman pope, is to assert a more radical version of holy simplicity (as both Langland and the author of "I playne Piers" surely know). But to make a preacher resemble a plowman reminds us that these categories remain separate; the plowman can only have the literal labor (of digging and threshing) and never the spiritual labor of knowledge or doing well.

Latimer's plowman remains inflected with a medieval meaning—the link between rural labor and the works required of every Christian (penance, good deeds)—although such a focus is not required by the pericope itself. Many preachers, after all, keep themselves to the figurative meaning that Jesus himself gives in the parable: sowing seed is read as preaching the word of God. For Latimer, however, the figurative meaning of works, that is, good deeds and penance, haunts the discussion of rural labor; it is what remains "left over," the meaning that no longer fits once he has adapted this allegorical exposition to Protestantism. Latimer explains that he has likened the preacher to the plowman "for their labor of all seasons of the year" and "for the diversity of works and variety of offices that they have to do" (*Selected Sermons*, 31). And he goes on to set up what promises to be a very traditional symbolization of rural labor in listing the various details that he will allegorize: "For as the plowman first setteth forth his plow, and then tilleth his land and breaketh it in furrows, and sometime ridgeth it up again and at another time harroweth and clotteth it, and sometime dungeth it and hedgeth it, diggeth it and weedeth it, purgeth and maketh it clean, so the prelate, the preacher, hath many diverse offices to do" (*Selected Sermons*, 31). At this point, readers of any medieval sermon would expect the discussion of the preacher's various duties as allegorical labor: for example, cutting branches is read as reproving sin. But if the reader is reminded of the practice of medieval allegory, then so is Latimer. Before telling us the symbolic meanings of rural labor, he interrupts himself with a rant against works:

> He hath first a busy work to bring his parishioners to a right faith, as Paul calleth it, and not to a swerving faith, but to a faith that embraceth Christ and trusteth to His merits; a lively faith, a justifying faith, a faith that maketh a man righteous without respect of works, as ye have it very well declared and set forth in the Homily. He hath then a busy work, I say, to bring his flock to a right faith and then to confirm them in the same faith; now casting them down with the law and with threatenings of God for sin; now ridging them up again with the gospel and with the promises of God's favor; now weeding them by telling them their faults and making them forsake sin; now clotting them by breaking their stony hearts. (*Selected Sermons*, 31)

Latimer's insistence on justification by faith alone (and his interest in distinguishing this faith from a trust in works) interrupts his allegory of rural labor precisely because he is aware, as any audience member would be, that rural labor is traditionally allegorized as spiritual work. That is, rural labor is so strongly correlated with traditional directions to do works that he fears his allegory might be misunderstood as having something to say about the importance of works. Latimer wants to ensure, therefore, that audience members do not confuse the message that preachers must labor with the belief he attributes to Catholics— that is, that all must labor for salvation. For Latimer, work may still have a figurative meaning but only for priests, not as penance for all

Christians: "Then if it be good work, it is work; ye can make but a work of it. It is God's work, God's plow, and that plow God would have still going. Such then as loiter and live idly are not good prelates or ministers" (*Selected Sermons*, 32–33). The repetition of the word *work* here threatens a collapse into a purely figurative meaning, of *works*, but Latimer rescues that figurative meaning by assigning it to God.

Latimer's sermon underlines the plowman's value in a manner that seems entirely compatible with a medieval worldview in which the plowman is the basis of the social world (the three estates). Indeed, one can see here the "conservative social vision" that both insists on the traditional social order and condemns individual profit, as Tawney and others have found in early Protestant texts.[30] This conservative social vision is found throughout Latimer's other sermons, which consistently advocate for the traditional rights of peasants to "common" against the enclosers.[31] But this social conservatism is oddly hermetic; the plowman is a sterile exercise in figuration, not a dynamic figure to address contemporary concerns (both religious and social) as in Langland's poem. Despite Latimer's awareness of agrarian crisis—the enclosures and rack renting that he describes elsewhere—his plowman has a kind of timeless allegorical status. As McRae observes, Latimer's use of the plowman "strengthens the authority of grievances expressed through representatives of the lower orders, yet leaves them powerless substantially to affect or improve their positions."[32] Indeed, the very old-fashionedness of this allegory suggests that the social conservatism of Latimer (and perhaps others) protests too much. It seems motivated at least in part by an awareness that Protestantism itself might indeed alter that social order fundamentally, not only, as was feared at the time, with what seemed to be a potential for agrarian communism, but also by emptying out one of the foundational beliefs of the traditional social order: the value of rural labor in supporting the entire society.

The Piers Plowman Tradition

Tyndale and Latimer suggest the potential for Protestantism to alter how work (as a physical and economic activity) is conceived in relation to spiritual matters, but their texts do not provide the last or only word. Overtly Protestant texts contemporary with Tyndale and Latimer, texts of the *Piers Plowman* tradition, resist this reduction in meaning, and we could argue, therefore, that the transition to a Reformation view of works was contested *precisely because* of the consequences for understanding rural labor. In other words, the *Piers Plowman* tradition can be read as an attempt to keep rural labor linked to a spiritual component, to maintain its spiritual significance in the new semiotics—that is, to suggest that rural labor equals works, which equal faith. This resistance to the limiting trend that I've identified in Tyndale and Latimer is apparent in three post-Reformation responses to Langland's poem: Robert Crowley's edition of *Piers Plowman* (1550); the treatise "I playne Piers which cannot flatter" (?1547); and the ballad "Jack of the North" (ca. 1549).

The texts in the sixteenth-century *Piers Plowman* tradition have long been understood as clearly Protestant in their emphasis. Indeed, it is a scholarly commonplace that later writers did not understand Langland's poem, nor did their imitations reproduce its complexity, and this general inferiority has been attributed to the authors' Protestantism.[33] Such an approach makes a great deal of sense if we understand the later versions as clearly informed by Protestant theology, as John King and James Simpson have argued, or as primarily socioeconomic in their interests, as argued in Andrew McRae's study of the plowman. Either way, work is limited to physical and economic activity, and the rich and ambiguous figuration of medieval Piers becomes inaccessible to Protestants (who can only misread). Later Piers is an "upright, honest labourer," not a figure for Christ, "kynde knowyng," or the Christian embarking on penitence that we find in Langland's poem.[34] But such an approach also suggests "subtraction" instead of a real shift in thinking—post-Reformation Piers is simply less than Langland's Piers, the literal vehicle absent its tenor. From the perspective of most scholars, the Protestantism of the mid-sixteenth century provides a context or background against which one can place the new versions of Piers.[35] I shall argue here, in contrast, that mid-sixteenth-century responses to Langland's poem are not, in fact, merely simple, Protestantized misreadings, nor have they left religious concerns behind. Despite their overt Protestantism, these texts demonstrate the persistence of the "medieval" link between work and works.

Discussions of Robert Crowley's second edition of *Piers Plowman* offer a perfect example of the dominant scholarly approach to this tradition: until recently scholars have focused on Crowley's attempt to harness Langland's poem to Protestantism.[36] One can certainly point to evidence that Crowley read the poem as support for the Reformation view of works as subordinate to faith, but the evidence is not as overwhelming as one might suppose. Instead, as an avowedly Protestant response to Langland's poem, Crowley's marginalia lend particular insight into the kinds of contradictions that characterized the Reformation itself. Although he twice repeats the Protestant "line" on the relationship between faith and works in his summaries of the first and the seventh Passus, a closer look reveals that these are not, in fact, clear endorsements of that position.[37]

For the first Passus, he writes, "[the poet] Declareth that worckes muste sprynge out of our fayeth: and that if wee be liberall to the pore, God wyll be liberal to vs."[38] This gloss is a response to an early (and unambiguous) insistence on the role of good works in salvation in Langland's poem, when Holy Church alludes to James 2:26, *Fides sine operibus mortua est* [Faith without works is dead]: "That fayth without the feate, is right nothing worth / And as deade as dore tree, but if the dedes followe" (B3v).[39] Instead of following Langland's metaphor, which preserves the medieval insistence on action, Crowley alludes to the Reformation emphasis on products: works "spring" like leaves or grapes from a vine. But his sentence seems to change track halfway through. Despite the initial clarity of the Protestant view, the second part of the sentence reinforces precisely the kind of logic that undergirds the medieval position on works: our gifts to the poor will result in God's gift to us. The "if/then" construction gives the priority to a person's actions, the "in quod se est" [what lies within him] that results in God's grace.[40] Finally, it is significant that the "worckes" that Crowley describes are alms, not the pilgrimages, relics, and bells that the Protestant scorn as "things" bought and sold in the marketplace; his condemnation never reaches the level of the polemic authored by his contemporaries, such as Latimer.

Crowley's interest in heavenly rewards (or gifts) can be found elsewhere in his works, not coincidentally in a text about the poor. In his epigram "Of Leasemongers" (1550), Crowley describes the leasemonger's [landlord's] dream as he waits for a preacher, whom he has called to his deathbed. He sees "pore folke" who "are promised rewarde / in the resurrection" by the preacher because they have suffered ("for theyr sufferaunce"), whereas the leasemongers "are sure to haue hell / by ryght inheritaunce."[41] The epigram's layers of irony—the leasemonger's dream, what the preacher said—allow the reader to see this critique as directed as much against the preacher, who tells the poor to suffer their "oppression," as against the leasemonger. Nevertheless, it would seem that Crowley's interest in the poor keeps him attached to the idea of works: the poor benefit from works, such as alms, and they are also defined by the work of penance, their "sufferaunce."

The second reference to works and faith occurs in the summary of the seventh Passus at a critical moment in the poem, when Piers tears the Pardon and gives up plowing. First Crowley describes what happens in the Passus:

> It declareth what pardon is graunted to the plowman and his helpers, What Marchauntes shoulde do, That menne of lawe shoulde take no money, howe menne shoulde geue almes, That patiente Pouertie hathe like pardon with the plowmanne, Howe Pierce reasoned with a blinde prieste, Howe Daniel expoundeth the dreames of Nabugodonosor, Howe Iacob expounded Iosephs dreame.

But the summary ends with what seems to be a Protestant interpretation: "And that to truste for salvation in workes, is but a vayne thing" (¢1r). If we read "workes" here as referring to the pardon itself, then Crowley has merely anticipated what many scholars have offered as a reading of this poem: that in tearing the Pardon, Piers is attacking the economy of the institutional church—the works that have come to dominate the penitential system. In other words, Crowley does not reject penance, which is significantly also a "work," nor does he reject the possibility of the plowing functioning as a work. This relatively narrow reading of "workes" as pardons specifically seems to be supported by the marginalia. Next to the dreamer's musings about the power of the pope to grant pardons that follow the tearing of the Pardon, Crowley has included the following: "Note howe he scorneth the auctority of popes" (K3r). But the lines that distinguish inappropriate works from appropriate works remain unglossed: "And to truste to these trentals, truely me thinketh / Is not so siker for the soule as to do well" (K3r).[42] In other words, Crowley has offered a fairly narrow reading of works to be disparaged: pardons and "trentals," which are triennial masses. Crowley is less interested, then, in attacking "workes" from a perspective that we might identify as Protestant ("justification by faith alone" or predestination) and less interested in defining the proper relationship between works and faith, as Tyndale and Latimer are, than he is in upholding Piers's association with the "right" kind of works: penance. This traditional interest is also reflected in the reference to "patiente Pouertie" in the summary; patient poverty gets the same pardon as the plowman. Even the grammatical structure of the summary emphasizes continuity between Piers's penance/work and Protestant beliefs. After the list of who receives pardon, Crowley introduces his very Protestant-sounding message ("to truste for salvation") with "And," as if there is no necessary disruption between belief in the salvific potential of patient poverty and a rejection of works. In sum, Crowley seems to want to have it both ways: casting Piers as Protestant but retaining his penitential (medieval Catholic) meaning. His summary draws our attention to the very ambiguity of a Protestant reading of Piers's speech: a confidence in its rejection of pardons and a desire to hold onto Langland's compelling formulation—in which Piers rejects plowing for penance—despite the significance of these terms having changed under Protestantism.

Crowley's uncertainty about how Piers might be read as Protestant also accounts for his famous mistake: his conflation of the dreamer with Piers in his summary of Passus 8: "It declareth howe Pierce went to seke Dowel, How he reproueth the Fryers for saying that dowel dwelte wyth them" (¢1r–v).[43] And, after detailing that Wit met with Piers (not the dreamer): "Of whom [Wit, that is] Pierce desired to learne what Dowel, Dobet, and Dobest were" (¢1v). This conflation is so interesting because it comes precisely at the moment at which the poem thematizes "Dowel," what one might describe as the works necessary for salvation. Indeed, the traditional divisions of the poem into the Visio, which ends at the end of Passus 7, and the Vita de Dowel (Dobet and Dobest), which begins at Passus 8, should suggest that readers had long been trained to see this part of the poem in terms of this new and important figure. Crowley does not seem to be a particularly bad reader of Langland's poem, so his strange mistake cannot be attributed to a casual error. Although he does not recognize the dreamer as a significant figure, in that he relegates all his conversations and thoughts to a kind of third-person omniscient voice of the poem, he does recognize the other allegorical figures that appear in the poem, such as Holy Church, Study, and Clergy, and he recognizes Piers when he reappears at the end of the poem. If Crowley has trouble with the dreamer at this point, it is not because allegory is alien to him but because of the particular problem surrounding Dowel. Indeed, it seems that it is Dowel or the figuration of work and the worker that is problematic under Protestantism, not figuration itself. Dowel is, of course, the source of much anxiety for the dreamer, and part of his education involves learning about what Dowel means, namely, that it is not a thing, even an abstract thing (as are Holy Church and Clergy), but an action. As Anne Middleton's important essay, "Two Infinites," reminds us, the dreamer's search for Dowel ends with a strangely confusing grammatical discussion in Passus 13, during which he is told that Dowel is an "infinite":

> For one Pierce the Ploughman hath impugned vs al
> And set al sciences at a Soupe, saue loue onelye
> And no text ne taketh, to maintayne hys cause
> But *Dilige deum*, And *Domine quis habitabit*;
> And sayeth that dowell and dobet, are two infinites
> Which infinites with fayeth, fynde out dobest
> Which shal saue mans soul, thus saith Pierce plowman.
>   (R2v)[44]

Middleton writes, "Dowel, Dobet, and Dobest are not personified or hypostatized abstractions taken from the stock of English common nouns"; rather, they are "the essence of Christian action."[45]

Dowel is, significantly, a figure that embodies works; one must "do well" in order to be saved, a point that has already been made clear by the allegorical figure Thought, in Passus 8 at the beginning of the dreamer's search:

> Dowel, and Dobetter, and Dobest the thirde, quod he
> Are thre fayre vertues, and be not farre to finde.
> Who so is true of hys tonge, and of his two handes,
> And through his labor or his lond, his liuelihood winneth
> And is trusty of his taylyng, taketh but his owne
> And is no drunklewe ne de digious, dowel him foloweth.
> (K4v–L1r)[46]

Although Thought first describes Dowel as an abstraction, a virtue, he then explains it in a series of actions: winning, taking, being, and not being. The dreamer's inability to understand Thought is his own fault (and the dreamer must go on to ask many other figures) and not the fault of the description, which is never proved to be "wrong," only inadequate at this particular moment.

In his summary Crowley has inadvertently assigned the search for Dowel, which details the dreamer's inability to recognize works as actions, to Piers in what seems to be an unconscious but extremely revealing moment. In order to be a good Protestant, to exemplify the cause to which Crowley so desires to recruit him, Piers must have a new meaning, as the seeker of the proper relationship between works and faith; he must see faith as the action from which works spring and, therefore, see works as a product or a sign. Indeed, the mistake demonstrates that Piers is, for Crowley, a far more compelling seeker than the dreamer precisely because he is also a worker and both physically and spiritually active.

Crowley's discussion of Dowel thus reveals a kind of uncertainty about the status of doing well in Protestantism. At first glance, Crowley assigns a kind of "thingness" to Dowel, as if to keep it as a "hypostatized abstraction," in Middleton's terminology. Indeed, "Dowel" continually appears in a list with "Dobet" and "Dobest," with no relation to the actions that define these. In a summary of Passus 10, Crowley itemizes what the Passus teaches, "That we should do good whylse we haue tyme, Howe vaine sciences be, What dowel, dobet and dobest be" (¢2r). The separate units in this list suggest that "doing good" and "what dowel is" are two distinct categories, that the action and the figuration of that action no longer match. Even in the account of Dowel that comes closest to what Langland would describe, in his summary of the twelfth Passus—"That charitie is dowell"—Crowley equates two nouns, reducing Langland's lengthy and anxious exploration to tautology (¢2r). Nevertheless, the first part of the sentence in the summary of Passus 10—"we should do good whylse we haue tyme"—recalls the urgency of the medieval view of works. Needing to do good while on earth implies that one's actions will have some kind of purchase on God, that one will be called to account for one's works—a view central, of course, to Langland's poem. In fact, Crowley does take up Langland's insistence on "redde quod debes" in one of his epigrams that, not coincidentally, concerns rural life, "Of Rente Raysers." While bragging of the way in which he has oppressed his tenants, the owner of the land hears a voice that says "'geue accountes of thy baliwicke.'"[47] In the moral economy of the epigram, there is no faith that justifies and no predestination, there is only justice for the actions one performs during one's lifetime.

The anonymous treatise "I playne Piers which cannot flatter" (?1547) also belongs clearly to that tradition of writers who have appropriated Piers for Protestantism, and, like the scholarship on Crowley, the very limited discussions of this text have tended to understand it more in terms of its Protestantism than in terms of Langland's poem.[48] Despite one direct allusion, "yf euer pore plowman of pope might get the keys," the author seems to have borrowed little from Langland's Piers except for his name.[49] His Piers is significantly more of a "real" plowman and less a figure of Jesus, or penitence, or "kynde knowyng." Indeed, John King describes him as "a shallow device."[50] A more recent discussion argues that the diminishing of Piers's figurative meaning has to do with Protestantism itself—namely, the limiting of the meaning of labor that goes with Protestant theology, particularly justification by faith alone.[51] But on closer look, the Piers of "I playne Piers" is far less univocally "Protestant" and less literal than his explicit support of "trewe Tyndale" or his references to "following ploughe on felde" might at first suggest (E2r and A2r). I shall argue here that the text demonstrates the collision between Piers and Protestantism: the text resists the flattening of Piers's meaning, retaining some of the medieval connotations of his work.

It might be useful to begin by asking exactly where the Protestantism lies in this text. The content is difficult to describe, but it seems mainly to be an extended attack on the clergy and the government for not doing enough for reform; this attack is given in the voice of a plowman character, who begins his tirade by referring to his labor. Included are mentions of specific events—such as the burning of William Tyndale and the case of Richard Hunne—that identify this text as Protestant in its sympathies. Although one of Piers's most basic functions in "I playne Piers" is to attack the clergy, we should remember that anticlericalism is not, in itself, a sign of Protestantism. Many of the following views are found not only in "I playne Piers" but in both Wycliffite and orthodox writings of the late fourteenth and fifteenth centuries: the clergy are bad shepherds; they are entirely devoted to money and material things; they are Sodomites; they gloss the Bible any way that they please; as a result of their abuses people must now return to the primitive church.[52] Even the discussion of the sacraments in this treatise goes over the same ground as the Wycliffites: there are two attacks on transubstantiation (B6r and F1r) and one on penance ["shrift"] (E7v). In all of these, the argument is that sacraments should be based on scripture, not new laws (E7v). The only religious (or doctrinal) interest that marks this text as Protestant and not Wycliffite is one brief mention of "goddes electe" (B7r) and one of justification:

> It is god that saueth and iustyfiethe who is it that condempneth, euery one sayth John that beleueth Jhesu Christ to be come in the flesshe, is borne of god we beleue him to be thus come, as the onely saluation of the world, therfore we nothynge doubte to haue god on our side, and yf god be on our side, who can be against vs . . . it is God that makethe rightuous, who wyll them condempne. (B6v–B7r)

Here the author invokes the language of Romans 8:29–31, thus aligning himself with what one might consider the Protestant position on predestination and justification. At the same time, it is worth noting that despite the use of the Protestant terms "iustyfiethe" and "makethe rightuous," the author does not mention works, nor does he engage in the kind of opposition that motivates his contemporaries in which the mention of justification seems to require a condemnation of works. Indeed, this assertion occurs in the midst of his tirade against transubstantiation, which, he argues, is not supported by scripture. In other words, the emphasis here is on opposing the salvific qualities of scripture with that of the sacrament, not on opposing grace and works: "we be rychely ynoughe saued by the knowledge onely that we haue in his scriptures" (B6v).

The author's very limited interest in Piers's spiritual meanings (the fact that the writer imagines Piers as a literal worker) has less to do with the author's Protestantism than it does with the potential radicalism already within the *Piers Plowman* tradition even before it intersects with Protestantism.[53] This potential is made apparent in the rebels' use of Piers during the Peasants' Revolt of 1381. As Steven Justice noted, Piers Plowman is appropriated by the rebels, who model their "symbolic names" after him: "for the rebels, Piers condensed the theological and political authority that Wyclif conferred on the rural population into a meaningful image of rural labor."[54] As a fellow peasant, Piers authorizes the rebels in their pursuit of "clergie" (the learning reserved for the clergy) and of social re-organization. After all, in Langland's poem a plowman not only organizes the labor on the Half-Acre, he becomes pope at the end of the poem; the peasants of the peasants' revolt were also seeking a shift in the way in which power would be distributed in this world. For the writer of "I playne Piers" as much as the peasants in 1381, emphasizing the literal—that is, rural—labor radicalizes the figure: real plowmen and laborers have a special authority *because* they labor (as discussed in chapter 1). Although the Piers of "I playne Piers" expresses the conventional idea that all (not just those in power) are corrupt ("euery harte frome the highest to the loweste is made carefull and couetous"), he claims that some are more to blame than others: "in the clargy it [covetousness] is so muche the more to be detested and abhorred" (D7r, D7v). Indeed, the text reveals a deep anger against the mutuality of the three-estate structure, under which the laborers labor for the rest of the community. This anger is seen in his remarks about what one can describe as the expropriation of labor: at judgment day, the righteous shall stand against those who "hath taken awaye thyr laboures" (B7r). The sense that the clergy "robbe vs" is not a new one, but it is worth noting that this complaint is explicitly tied to labor: "they of our labours do heape vp gold" (E6v). This is not the traditional form of social complaint, which relies on invoking the mutuality of the three-estate model, particularly the responsibility of each estate to the other and the condemnation of greed. It is, rather, a consciousness that it is the status quo itself that has enabled these abuses, not any deviation from that status quo. Again, this form of radicalism is associated with the figure of Piers from the beginning of the *Piers Plowman* tradition, in the rebels' invocation of him in the Peasants' Revolt of 1381.[55]

Perhaps more importantly, traces of the medieval symbolic meaning of labor (penance and good deeds) persist in this figure. Despite the overt mention of justification, cited above, there is no clarion call for justification by faith alone in the text and no attack on works, even the ambiguous attack offered by Crowley. The author is, rather, relying on the efficacy of Piers as a voice of reform not, paradoxically, because of the "Protestantism" of this figure but because of his close association with a very medieval Catholic idea: that we must repent and pay what we owe (satisfaction). Despite the mention of "goddes electe" (B7r), there is no sense that the saved are already saved and damned already damned. Rather, to read this text is to enter the world of much penitential and homiletic writing of the late medieval period, in which there is hope for change in this world if everyone would repent, particularly those who are in charge—that is, the clergy and the lords. In other words, as much as this is a polemic against abuses, it repeatedly holds out the possibility for amendment, and in this sense, it is absolutely in line with Langland's poem:

> Piers can tel you mykel more
> whiche he kepeth yet in store,
> to se yf you wyll amende,
> eles must here suche maner of gere,

euen to the worldes ende.
Stones sayde the lorde
Shall beare recorde,
yf other wytnes fayle,
you kyll the wytnes trewe,
God sendeth euer newe,
lytle to your aduayle.
                    (E2r)

I have transcribed these lines as verse with line breaks after the words that rhyme, although they appear in the printed text as prose. I have done so in order to show that the author draws the reader's attention very carefully to the Piers of the *Piers Plowman* tradition both in the content (amendment) and in the form, by using poetry, even if it is not alliterative poetry.

This plea for amendment is not just a generalized one; the author suggests that those who do not work will be called to account in an echo of *Redde quod debes* [pay what you owe] (Matthew 18:28): "Consyder o Kynges and Princes dere for you we toile and labour consyder I saye eftsones, nowe your flocke how that ye lede you shall make answere, for al defaultes, lewdenes, and yll honoure" (A4r). Here the speaker alludes to the shepherd's responsibilities as described in the bit of biblical pastoral that precedes the parable of *Redde quod debes* (Matthew 18:12), in which Jesus asks whether or not a shepherd leaves his ninety-nine sheep to go after the one that is lost. It is this responsibility, of shepherd for the sheep, that is echoed in the parable in the lord's responsibility for the servant (and the first servant for the second servant). Like the servant in the parable, kings and princes will be called to "answer" for how they have treated their underlings.[56]

This parable and its traditional explication reinforce the centrality of satisfaction, the final stage in the sacrament of penance, in which penitents must repay what they owe, the "debt" of sin, and restore what they have taken from others. Satisfaction, or *Redde quod debes*, is a central idea in the "re-formation" of the church in Langland's *Piers Plowman*. Near the end of the poem, during the foundation of the church, Christ gives Piers power over penance and absolution:

> And whan þis dede was doon do best he [þouȝte],
> And yaf Piers [pardon, and power] he grauntede hym,
> Myght [men] to assoille of alle manere synne[s],
> To alle maner men, mercy and forȝifnesse
> In couenaunt þat þei come and knewelich[e] to paie
> To Piers pardon þe Plowman *redde quod debes*.
> Thus haþ Piers power, b[e] his pardon paied,
> To bynde and vnbynde boþe here and elli[s],
> And assoille men of alle synnes saue of dette one.[57]

The presence of this command at this foundational moment suggests that satisfaction is absolutely central to Langland's understanding. As James Simpson writes, "A theology of modified justice, freely instituted by Christ, requires an institution for the dispensation of grace; this institution itself produces an egalitarian society whose commitment to spiritual sustenance equally underwrites its commitment to labour in the material world."[58] For Simpson this congruence between theology, ecclesiology, and the social world does not obtain for the later *Piers Plowman* tracts nor for Protestantism in general. Nevertheless, in choosing Piers as his spokesman, one who will call both lords and the clergy to account, the anonymous author of "I playne Piers" suggests that Christians were still saved or damned for their actions in this world—that is, for their work, not only by prior election.

This trace of spiritual works also appears in an allusion to Matthew 25:31–46, the foundation of the medieval church's teaching on the seven works of bodily mercy: Christ's apostles "folowed Christes owne trew trade but oures saye yet that they mai for the honour of the Realme, doo cleane contrary . . . for yf oure realme be Christened right and haue not the name for noughte, we must cal him the best and eke the wysest, whiche with his blod vs bought, and all his workes and wordes also mayntayne obserue and kepe, for therin onelye can we espye the gootes from the shepe" (E4v–E5r). This passage establishes Christ as a laborer with "trew trade" and "workes," and thus a fellow of Piers. From this perspective, this author is certainly aware of the potential of Piers Plowman to represent Christ himself, that Christ will joust in Piers's arms (B18.22). Moreover, the "works" that belong to

Christ, that separate the sheep and the goats, are absolutely traditional: feeding the hungry, clothing the naked, and so on. The view of works shows some evidence of a Protestant semiotics; works are signs, and we can read [espye] in them who is saved and who damned (the sheep and goats). But works are also what make "us" Christian. Moreover, this sentence preserves the same "medieval" logic observed in Crowley's sentence on works, a logic that gives works priority: "we" should observe works so that others will know who is saved and damned, as if it is the works themselves that make us sheep and goats (and this is, in fact, the reading that a medieval sermon writer would provide).

The treatise also uses Piers to generate its own spiritual meanings for rural labor, just as Langland did in his poem. To labor means to know God:

> I haue vttered so mani wordes for to shewe playne, be we neuer so pore yf we labour to knowe God he wyll offer himselfe to vs, and take vs as hys owne, howe can we suffer still to be shut from the knowledge of him, whome, *in so many outwarde sacramentes and in outwarde man* we do professe seyng that to knowe him is euer lastynge lyfe, and to be ignorant of him is the iuste cause of dampnacion. And seynge that no man can worke wythoute the instrument of this occupacyon, nether is he anye man of scyence, that knowethe not the rules belongynge thereunto, why or by what reason can you take from the poore Christen man hys instrument, his rules, yea his buckeler agaynst the fyrye dartes of hys ennemy, his sworde to fyghte agaynst all spirituall powers. (B8r–B8v, emphasis added)

The word "worke" and the phrase "the instrument of this occupacyon" (which could be a plow or any tool of the trade) underline the suitability of a manual laborer knowing God; just as a worker needs his tools, so does a good Christian need his knowledge of Christ. In discussing this "instrument," this author creates precisely the kind of movement between literal and figurative levels that is endemic to medieval homiletics: the tool is first assigned an allegorical meaning (a tool of the trade is knowledge of God), then re-literalized (the knowledge of God is a sword), and then refigured (the sword is not real but used to fight against spiritual powers). The "extra" level (the tool that becomes a sword) is, in some way, defensive, as if the author knows that a plow no longer carries the same kind of allegorical importance or universality; it must become a sword.

This passage also modifies the earlier (Protestant) polemic somewhat because it does not dismiss the sacraments (such as penance) out of hand; it merely assigns them a lesser status. Sacraments have only to do with the exterior, with what we profess, not necessarily with what we know. Indeed, the passage suggests that a greater knowledge of God through Bible reading (which is what this speaker wants) will only underline what the church already demonstrates to be true in the sacraments. The language of labor in this passage implicitly reveals that gaining knowledge of God becomes a spiritual work, one that can replace the sacraments, and this perspective can be found throughout the treatise. For example, the argument that scripture should be available in English invokes the language of labor to describe reading itself: "what hartes haue you to the poore men that with theyr laboures daye and nyghte with great expenses and charges wyth great danger and perelles, dyd first of all open vnto vs the waye of truth, the worde of god" (D3v–D4r). The reference to the poor men who labor recalls Piers himself, but here that labor has to do with disseminating "Christes lawe in our tonge," the actions of the sower in Luke 5:8 (expounded by Latimer) and not the literal plowing of the fields.

That laborers can be sowers of the word of God as well as sowers of real seed distinguishes this text from Latimer's sermon and brings it far closer to Langland, whose Piers is both a plowman and a kind of alternative to the clergy and their knowledge with his "kynde knowyng." This alternative is, interestingly, described as a time in the past when the plowman was a shepherd: "thre yeres paste when I Piers scripture myghte reade . . . to tel forth Christes trade, and trade of oure christenyng . . . then was I syr, then was I father, then was I shepherd" (A6r). Given that this author refers to the clergy throughout as shepherds, whom he attacks for not caring for their sheep, his use of the term *shepherd* is a claim for spiritual authority and knowledge (specifically, access to the scriptures). To be sure, this moment underlines the difference between the reformism of the medieval period and that of the Reformation: when Langland assigns Piers a new role, as pope (in Passus 19, quoted above), he reforms the institution—the church and its practice of penance. The plowman remains a plowman in order to emphasize his continued work. For the author of "I playne Piers," the reform is directed toward the individual layperson; the plowman as shepherd suggests less the reform of the institution than the priesthood of all believers. Nevertheless, the author clearly wishes to preserve a spiritual meaning specifically for rural labor.

That spiritual meaning appears most forcefully in a short piece known as "Jack of the North," which also belongs to the sixteenth-century *Piers Plowman* tradition, at least insofar that it makes use of a character called "Pyrse Plowman." Unlike the two texts discussed previously, it is not an overtly Protestant text. Nevertheless, it insists so strongly on the close relationship between work (rural labor) and good works that it is worth including here as evidence that the figure of Piers Plowman continued to remind writers in the sixteenth century of this relationship even when the writers were not directly concerned with religious matters. The provenance and popularity of the text are difficult to ascertain: it was first printed in the *Annals of Cambridge* following a document concerning complaints about enclosure, and portions of it have been reprinted more recently in *The Penguin Book of Renaissance Verse, 1509–1659*.[59] R. H. Tawney also quotes passages in his *Agrarian Problem*.[60] All of these works follow the *Annals* in dating the poem to 1549, during the reign of Edward VI (*Annals*, 40–42). The *Annals* calls the text a "dialogue in verse," and it is, in brief, a conversation involving ten men whose names indicate their rural status—such as "Jack of the North beyond the style," "Robbyn Clowte," and, most importantly, "Pyrse Plowman"—about the very controversial matter of enclosure. Jack of the North begins by detailing his difficulties with the law (having been falsely accused of murder) and his actions in throwing down enclosures: "Companye be night I take / And with all that I may make / Cast hedge and dyche in the lake" (40). He also states his reasons for doing so: "Thus I Jake do recompense / Ther nawghty slawnderous offense" (40). Jack then turns to each of the other characters for a response to what he has done (and his plans for continuing). All, of course, approve of the actions, including "Pyrse" (Piers), who, like his predecessor, points out the moral failings of their social world: the "covetous nacyon" and "men of no conscyence" who have enclosed the land (41). Although the text is certainly more radical than the anti-enclosure treatises discussed in the previous chapter (because it advocates the violent overthrow of the enclosures), it shares many of the same ideas: the use of Piers Plowman to lament covetousness; the concern that the poor are being oppressed; and the fact that some are taking "other mennes landes" into "ther handes." For these reasons, the text reads as a far more interesting version of the treatise *Pyers plowmans exhortation* because it uses voices of "real" peasants and lends insight into their actual conditions: those who only have "one sealy [pitiable] cowe" will be glad to have the return of the commons (41).[61] Despite its insurrectionary potential (the peasants' rising up to tear down the hedges), then, the text also reveals the "conservative social vision" that is typically associated with the *Piers Plowman* tradition. That is, the commons insist upon their traditional rights, which are being altered by new forces; they do not wish to destroy the traditional order. As Tawney writes, the speakers "are conservatives, not radicals or levelers, and to them it seems that all the trouble arises because the rich have been stealing the property of the poor."[62] In addition, the text seems limited to a social vision; Pyrse is merely one peasant among others, with no particular figurative resonance and only the faintest echo of his past religious significance when he invokes the idea of conscience in his phrase, "men of no conscyence" (41).

Even if the figure of Pyrse himself does not provide a strong link to Langland's poem, the dialogue contains two startling moments that distinguish it from the anti-enclosure polemic and return this "conservative social vision" to the symbolic imagination of works and work associated with the original Piers. When asked for his opinion about tearing down enclosures, about halfway through the dialogue, Buntynge on the Hill states, "Syr, I think that this wyrke / Is gud as to byld a kyrke" (41). Similarly, when asked for his opinion, near the end, Whyp Wylliam says,

> "Bylakyng syr it is a gud dede [good deed]
> As it is to burye the dede [bury the dead]

> Therfor now the lorde ye spede
> And acquyte ye in all your nede."
>
> (42)

In both of these quotations the speakers equate the work of throwing down the hedges and the stakes with good deeds in a recognizably medieval "reformist" manner. That is, physical labor is not just a symbol for reform of the social world (the return to the status quo); it actually is the reform itself because the laborer carries it out. The particular deeds offered by way of comparison are revealing. The first offers what seems to be a paradox: destruction (of the hedge) is the same as construction (of the church). And yet, from the perspective of the "commons" (and not enclosure) this is not a paradox at all: the return of the commons is the construction of a communal space, like a church. The second good deed is one of the seven corporal works of mercy, and its mention comes at a significant moment, after Harry Clowte and Jack of the North have discussed the likelihood that the enclosers will repent of their misdeeds. Burying the dead, like the other works of mercy, is an act of charity to one's neighbor, as is, in this text, the return of the commons to the people who need it. Perhaps most importantly, these comparisons return us to the reformist and even radical possibilities contained in Langland's poem: the value assigned to rural labor, its capacity to represent good deeds, can be appropriated by the worker himself. Indeed, the text hovers on the line between reformism, which desires a return to an idealized status quo (the three-estate structure) and the radicalism of the peasants in 1381, who demanded the overthrow of that structure. The workers only want what was theirs, but in taking it, instead of "suffering" as do the victims of Crowley's landlord in his epigram, they break down the very order to which they desire to return.

That Langland's poem still spoke to readers and writers in the mid-sixteenth century demonstrates that the introduction of what we might consider Protestant beliefs—predestination, justification by faith alone—did not disrupt entirely or replace easily the medieval symbolic imagination of work and works in England. Nor was the yoking of social conservatism and religious reform easy. Indeed, what is striking about Crowley's edition and "I playne Piers," as well as "Jack of the North," is the interest in maintaining the special status of rural labor, its capacity to figure both the bettering of this world and salvation itself. We could then say that the desire of early Protestants to hold onto a medieval understanding of rural labor (that social conservatism long ago identified by Tawney) translates, however ambivalently and contradictorily, into a desire to hold onto some form of spiritual works. From this perspective, the continuing interest in Langland's poem in the sixteenth century might, surprisingly, have less to do with Piers's suitability as a Reformation spokesman, as has long been assumed, than with his capacity to represent and resolve the anxieties about the impact of the new religion on "tradition."[63]

FIVE | *Spenser's* Shepheardes Calender
and a Poetry of Rural Labor

*T*he previous chapters have explored the way in which sixteenth-century pastoral emerged in relation to broader traditions of writing rural labor: the ecclesiastical pastoral, the polemic of the enclosure controversy, and the *Piers Plowman* tradition. Such a broad approach may seem well-suited for the poetry discussed thus far—the eclogues of Alexander Barclay and Barnabe Googe—because for many critics this poetry is not properly pastoral. Barclay and Googe are not included in the influential work of Louis Montrose and Paul Alpers, and those scholars who do discuss them describe them as "medieval" in outlook.[1] For most, the first "proper" pastoral is Edmund Spenser's *Shepheardes Calender* (1579); as Paul Alpers argues, the *Calender* "was the first set of English pastorals in the European tradition."[2] Yet, as this chapter will demonstrate, a broad approach to pastoral as "writing rural labor" can also illuminate Spenser's poem. It is true that scholars have long recognized Spenser's debts to what one might consider a non- (or pre-) pastoral "native tradition," including the *Piers Plowman* tradition and ecclesiastical pastoral. First and most obviously, Spenser uses "an olde name" for his "new worke."[3] That is, the title of his eclogue collection refers to *The Shepherds Kalender*, a text printed by

Thomas Pynson in 1506 (and throughout the sixteenth century), that could be said to be quite "medieval" in its eclectic interests: it includes conventional religious knowledge (the seven sins, for example) alongside information on astrology and, of course, a calendar.[4] Spenser's interest in the "olde" is further attested by the *Calender*'s archaic language and references to Chaucer as Tityrus. Finally, and most importantly for my argument here, the text explicitly aligns itself with the *Piers Plowman* tradition: a character named Piers appears in two of the eclogues (May and October), and the character Diggon Davy, who is drawn either from Langland's poem or another poem written in imitation of *Piers Plowman*, appears in the September eclogue. These traces of medieval literary traditions have not been perceived as in any way complicating Spenser's interest in the "new" eclogue form. Instead, Spenser is typically praised for his skill in fusing or grafting the various traditions.[5]

As the previous chapters have demonstrated, however, these native traditions of "writing rural labor" offer a potentially antagonistic, or at least anxious, relationship with the new eclogue form because they keep us focused on a medieval Christian and feudal (not a classical) understanding of work and works. As such these medieval traces resist assimilation into a Virgilian model. It will not do, therefore, to assign the contradictions or inconsistencies in the *Calender*, particularly those having to do with rural labor and rural laborers, to some vague idea of georgic that Spenser could have inherited from Virgil so that we might retain the focus on classical literature.[6] Whereas Spenser rarely invokes Virgil's *Georgics*, he consistently approaches labor from a "medieval" perspective: through the *Piers Plowman* tradition and the ecclesiastical pastoral.[7] Indeed, the lack of interest in georgic is quite notable not just in Spenser but in the sixteenth century more generally; representations of labor do not follow Virgil's poem.[8] Spenser's use of the medieval tradition underlines a question that should guide our reading of his pastoral: How do the shifts in the symbolic imagination around labor in the wake of the Reformation and the dramatic socioeconomic changes of the sixteenth century (shifts evident in the *Piers Plowman* tradition) intersect with the pastoral mode? I'd like to suggest that the specifically medieval rural laborers in Spenser's poem—Piers and, to a lesser degree, Diggon Davy in the September eclogue—can be seen as a disruption to precisely that aspect of the pastoral so attractive to late-sixteenth-century writers: the capacity of "herdsmen and their lives" to represent a social world that is largely free of class antagonism (and sometimes free of class) and of labor.[9] In invoking an earlier symbolic imagination around labor, Piers and Davy become signs of what needs to be repressed and rewritten for the newly rediscovered pastoral to function. In other words, these figures are a kind of historical unconscious that "haunts" Spenser's poem.[10] From this perspective, Piers and Davy are what Pierre Macherey describes as the "splitting within the work," the conflict that shows us what is behind the novelty of pastoral: the rediscovery of one tradition (the pastoral mode) was only made possible by the emptying out of another. The significance of Spenser's novelty, then, is that it draws attention not so much to his skill as a poet (although no one would deny this skill) but to the shift in the symbolic imagination around labor that made pastoral possible.

The Problem of Figuration

The *Calender* begins by overtly advertising itself as a pastoral in the Virgilian tradition, in which shepherds sing of love and related topics: the figure for Spenser, Immerito, begins the book by addressing it, commanding it to say that "A shepheards swaine . . . did thee sing, / All as his straying flocke he fedde" ("To his Book," 9–10). The first four eclogues develop this image of the singing shepherd. In the March eclogue, for example, the Argument states that "shepheards boyes taking occasion of the season, beginne to make purpose of love and other plesaunce, which to springtime is most agreeable" (p. 57). This broad focus on seasons and young love seems to fit very nicely with Alpers's theory of the pastoral, according to which the eclogues are "representative anecdotes" that use herdsmen and their lives to explore what could be considered to be "universal" human concerns: "literary shepherds are often lovers because their lives are felt to represent some (not all) fundamental aspects of love as a human experience."[11]

Being a shepherd in these first four eclogues seems to be little more than a pose, or a background context, and there is little discussion of shepherding duties. What little there is quickly gives way to other topics. For example, in March, Thomalin's concern for his injured ewe leads to a story that explicitly depicts the shepherds at their leisure: "It was upon a holiday, / When shepheardes groomes han leave to playe" (March, 61–62). In sum, these opening eclogues suggest that the shepherd is a useful figure because, simply put, he lives in the countryside and notices the seasons. This is, after all, a calendar.

But with the May eclogue, Spenser shifts to a new mode: an allegorical pastoral, in which shepherds are figures for priests and the conversation covers church matters (not love). This is a recognizably medieval and reformist mode, and it is no accident that this shift to the medieval (as opposed to classical) inheritance signals his interest in the nature of the shepherd's labor and its potential meanings. To summarize briefly, this eclogue consists of a debate between two shepherds, Piers and Palinode, about the practice of Maying. Piers insists that shepherds should do their jobs and care for the sheep, and Palinode asks why shepherds shouldn't have fun too. Piers has the last word with a fable about a fox tricking a kid (in order to prey upon him) that emphasizes the dangers of priestly negligence: foxes (Catholics) are ready to prey on hapless Protestants (the kid). Given its apparent rejection of Maying and its anti-Catholicism, the eclogue is typically understood within the context of Spenser's Protestantism or even his Puritanism.[12] But it is also a scholarly commonplace to note that Spenser's point of view does not seem to be entirely aligned with Piers's moral voice. As the editor of the Yale edition notes, "In terms of doctrine Piers clearly wins the debate. In terms of the poem's depiction of human experiences, he doesn't" (p. 86). Readers have not wanted to see Piers as the "hero" of this eclogue, and this reluctance makes perfect sense because Piers leaves little room for the leisure that the other eclogues embrace. But if we view this eclogue less as what it tells us about Spenser's religious beliefs and more about what it tells us about pastoral, then we can set aside which perspective (Piers's or Palinode's) is closer to Spenser's.

In turning to an allegorical pastoral familiar from medieval and Reformation discussions of the church (typically called ecclesiastical pastoral), Spenser offers a kind of self-reflexivity about the representation of rural labor in pastoral, and about the appropriation of shepherds. This self-reflexivity is possible first and most obviously because ecclesiastical pastoral functions quite differently than Virgilian pastoral in that it assigns a clear and consistent figurative meaning to shepherds; this is why it is allegorical. The shepherd-speakers of the May eclogue are not supposed to be "real" shepherds, as in the previous eclogues, but priests: "under the persons of two shepheards Piers and Palinodie, be represented two formes of pastoures or Ministers, or the protestant and the Catholique" (p. 87). Second, and more importantly, ecclesiastical pastoral tends to work at cross-purposes with the Virgilian pastoral even when the two are combined; the former is not particularly interested in the details of rural life as such, however idealized these details might be. Instead, the ecclesiastical pastoral is often a mode of anticlerical complaint: a discussion of shepherds is a discussion of what priests should be doing but are not: watching their flocks. Of course, these two forms of pastoral are linked in one of Spenser's models for the *Calender*: Mantuan's eclogues, which were printed in 1498 and appeared in George Turberville's English translation in 1567.[13] But the ecclesiastical pastoral also resonates with a medieval reformist tradition (as discussed in chapter 1) with which Spenser would have been familiar.

Spenser draws our attention (however unwittingly) to the incompatibility of the two modes—Virgilian and ecclesiastical pastoral—in the confused figuration around the shepherds discussed by Piers and Palinode in the May eclogue. Palinode first describes what the shepherds are doing at the opening of the eclogue:

Sicker this morrowe, ne lenger agoe,
I sawe a shole of shepeheardes outgoe,
With singing, and shouting, and jolly chere.
                    (May, 19–21)

He then goes on to describe the "fayre flocke of Faeries" and "a fresh bend / of lovely Nymphs" (32–33). Such language seems to belong to the April eclogue, marking the celebratory gathering of shepherds, and there is no sense that these are anything but "real" shepherds enjoying the countryside. This apparently "literal" mode is all the stranger when we consider that the Argument has already told readers to read shepherds as priests. The reader cannot help but wonder, Are Palinode's singing shepherds also priests? The next eclogue in the *Calender* that uses allegorical pastoral, July, does not have this problem because it stays consistently in the mode of the figurative: we are told in the Argument that the shepherds are pastors, and the debate between them turns not upon the meaning of shepherding but upon the meaning of the hills and valleys. The final eclogue that understands its shepherds as figures for priests, September, also has problems of figuration that will be discussed further below. Of course, Piers's response in May quickly moves us to the realm of the figurative:

> Those faytours little regarden their charge,
> While they letting their sheepe runne at large,
> Passen their time, that should be sparely spent,
> In lustihede and wanton meryment.
> Thilke same bene shepeheards for the Deuils stedde,
> That playen, while their flockes be unfedde.
> Well is it seene, theyr sheepe bene not their owne,
> That letten them runne at randon alone.
> But they bene hyred for little pay
> Of other, that caren as little as they,
> What fallen the flocke, so they han the fleece,
> And get all the gayne, paying but a peece.
> I muse, what account both these will make,
> The one for the hire, which he doth take,
> And thother for leaving his Lords taske,
> When great Pan account of shepeherdes shall aske.
> (May, 39–54)

We now know that these shepherds are, in fact, priests, and the ground has shifted toward what priests should do for their flocks. As a result Palinode's ensuing arguments about shepherdly "leasure" (66) and "felicitie" (155), which rightly belong to the *otium* of classical tradition, take on an extremely negative cast, as arguments against the very virtues extolled by the ecclesiastical pastoral of the medieval tradition: the shepherd-priests' watchfulness and work.

In dramatizing the interpretive shift from "real" to figurative shepherds (as opposed to merely beginning with figurative shepherds, as promised by the Argument), Spenser causes us to reflect on the nature of shepherding. What is striking about the figurative shepherds here is that they are far more closely linked to the actual labors of shepherds than their counterparts in the first four eclogues. In attacking the shepherds who go a-Maying, Piers offers an account of what it is that shepherds are supposed to do, as in the passage quoted above. Obviously, the tasks of feeding and watching their sheep have figurative meanings; priests should preach to and care for their congregations. As Spenser informs us at the beginning of the eclogue, these shepherds are masks ("persons"). Nevertheless, the details of labor remain: we could not understand this eclogue, nor would we understand ecclesiastical pastoral, if we did not know what it is that real shepherds do and why it is that they do it. In this way, the ecclesiastical pastoral seems to offer a compelling meditation on the absence of shepherdly duties in the first four eclogues and, ultimately, in imitations of classical pastoral more generally: in other words, the "real" shepherds of this new literary genre are, in some way, far less defined by their labors than their medieval figurative counterparts.[14] After all, to describe preaching to one's congregation as feeding a flock is to emphasize the priest's labor and thus his connection to the rural laborers in his congregation.

This self-reflexivity around labor is particularly tied to a medieval literary tradition in both the May and September eclogues (the first and the last eclogues to use ecclesiastical pastoral). May includes a shepherd named Piers and September includes Diggon Davy, whom I'll discuss further below. Piers is, of course, a familiar figure, one clearly associated with the representation and the figuration of rural labor in the cultural imagination at this time: he is the plowman of William Langland's poem and of the literary tradition inspired by that poem.[15] But Spenser's version of Piers changes the nature of his labor: he is a shepherd, not a plowman. This change is significant because it alters his figurative potential. Instead of having the capacious (because novel) figuration that characterizes Langland's poem, Piers has the predetermined meaning that goes with ecclesiastical pastoral: he is a priest. To be sure, ecclesiastical pastoral appears in other texts related to and in the *Piers Plowman* tradition, such as the pseudo-Chaucerian *Plowman's Tale*. In those texts, however, the pastoral is only one of many ways to inveigh against the clergy, and Piers remains a plowman. In making Piers a shepherd/priest, Spenser limits his radical potential and draws our attention to the mutability of figuring labor. The laborer in ecclesiastical pastoral *stands for* the priest; laborer and priest are similar only metaphorically. In this way, Spenser underlines that rural labor and rural laborers will not appear in a discussion of church reform or discussions of financial compensation (the concerns of this eclogue) unless these elements are read figuratively within the safe confines of ecclesiastical pastoral. In contrast, the Piers of the *Piers Plowman* tradition provides a much more flexible and ambiguous system of figuration: Piers is a laborer and has access to some kind of spiritual knowledge, his "kynde knowyng." Perhaps most importantly, Piers remains a plowman, and this fact signals that the discussion of both church reform and the ordering of the social world will (and must) take place around rural labor and laborers.

We could say, then, that Spenser's mixing of modes—combining the ecclesiastical pastoral with the eclogue form and the plowman tradition—leads to a kind of historical self-reflexivity about labor: as much as the Virgilian pastoral provides a new language for writing about rural life (whether idealized or not), it also drastically limits the possibilities for meanings of labor even when paired with the more "labor friendly" language of the ecclesiastical pastoral. This limiting is made most apparent in the way in which the May eclogue, which is the first to detail shepherdly labor, systematically detaches the figure Piers from labor. The most obvious sign of not working, or the absence of work, is the eclogue's focus on Maying and recreation, which are defined precisely in the eclogue as a refusal to work. Palinode, the other speaker in this eclogue, enviously notes of the shepherds who've gone out to "make such jouysaunce," "How great sport they gaynen with little swinck" (May, 25 and 36). Although we know (from the Argument) that Piers is supposed to contrast with Palinode, Spenser does not invoke any language of laboring to distinguish them. At the end of Palinode's initial complaint that everybody else has gone out merry-making, he states "But we here sytten as drownd in a dreme" (16). The opposition that begins this eclogue is not, therefore, working and not working (as one might expect from the debate structure) but two kinds of not working—recreating and sitting around (in a dream). One can't help but wonder whether Spenser is referring to the opening of Langland's poem, which also sets together water and dreaming:

> And as I lay and lenede and loked on þe watres
> I slombred into a slepyng, it sweyed so murye.
> Thanne gan I meten a merueillous sweuene.[16]

If Spenser wants to invoke Langland here, he has transformed Piers into the dreamer (the one "drowned"), thus immobilizing him and separating him from one of his defining attributes—labor.

Of course, the discussion of not laboring (recreating) seems, at first glance, to turn to a discussion of work in Piers's speeches, which represent the anti-Maying perspective. But this is an account, once again, of not working, of what shepherds fail to do. In the passage quoted at length above, we hear that shepherds pass their time in leisure instead of caring for their flocks. Such a description is typical of the satirical possibilities of biblical/ecclesiastical pastoral and would not be out of place in Chaucer's description of the Parson or in the pseudo-Chaucerian *Plowman's Tale*. For these texts, the pastoral enables the writer to contrast the "faytours" with the hard-working Parson. But Spenser's Piers does not work; rather, he identifies the ideal for shepherds' work not within himself but within the past:

> The time was once, and may againe retorne,
> (For ought may happen, that hathe bene beforne)
> When shepeheards had none inheritaunce,
> Ne of land, nor fee in sufferaunce:
> But what might arise of the bare sheepe.
> (May, 103–7)

In contrast to Piers's earlier speech, we finally get an account of what good shepherds should do—live off of the "bare sheepe"—but this direction has nothing to do with labor itself, such as watching over the sheep. Instead, it focuses on the payment of shepherds. Moreover, although this description of the ideal early church is clearly reformist and, therefore, apparently in line with the *Piers Plowman* tradition, it locates that reform in terms of the fee structure and inheritance in the church rather than the rural labor of shepherds generally or Piers specifically.

Finally, Piers's separation from labor is made complete in his agreement to tell the story about the Fox and the Kid. In telling this tale, Piers agrees implicitly with Palinode's suggestion that they will turn over their labor (watching the sheep) to another: "Now Piers, of felowship, tell us that saying: / For the Ladde can keep both our flocks from straying" (May, 172–73). Palinode's words come as a startling reminder that Piers is neglecting his own sheep in telling this tale, at the very moment when he becomes a poet himself.

One way to understand this shift in the meaning of Piers, and the meaning of labor, is in terms of the overt Protestantism of Spenser's text, which intersects with the ambiguities that remain in the Protestant *Piers Plowman* tradition. In redefining and limiting Piers's figurative meaning, particularly by detaching him from his labor, the eclogue also disrupts the metaphor, so central to medieval Christianity, that Langland's Piers embodied work as works. Instead of this equation of material with spiritual, the eclogue insists only on the material basis of work, thus underlining a post-Reformation shift in the meaning of labor. For a medieval Christian, plowing a field, saying a prayer, or giving money to a religious order all could earn a spiritual reward, but only one could earn a financial reward. For Protestants, the situation had become far more confused: no labor of any kind could earn a spiritual reward and the popular metaphor of work and works (however problematic) was disrupted. This disruption should be understood as having an impact not only on economic behavior and thinking—as detailed most famously by Max Weber in *The Protestant Ethic and the Spirit of Capitalism*, which takes up the fallout, so to speak, of Calvinism in seventeenth-century England—but on the symbolic imagination, that is, what work could mean when it was represented in a literary text. We see this impact in Spenser's eclogue most clearly, in that the shepherd's work is consistently described in terms of purely financial good (or reward). Instead of detailing the kinds of labor that shepherds will perform, Spenser's Piers returns again and again to the issue of shepherds' pay. In his first rebuke to Palinode, Piers says:

> But they bene hyred for little pay
> Of other, that caren as little as they,
> What fallen the flocke, so they han the fleece,
> And get all the gayne, paying but a peece.
> (May, 47–50)

Here the shepherds' insufficient labor is really greed—the desire for a profit independent of how much they work (or care for their flocks). As noted above, Spenser's view of reform has to do with shepherds' accepting their humble pay, and this is a pay that is imagined in all of its materiality: "Butter enough, honye, milke, and whay" (May, 115). This payment, the "means" of all shepherds, retains its literal significance in an eclogue that otherwise insists on the allegorical meaning of shepherds as pastors.[17] Oddly enough, two of the terms, *honey* and *milk*, have a symbolic meaning associated with them; they are attributes of Israel when it is described as the promised land (Exodus 3:8). But this symbolism is invoked only to be forestalled by their place in a list of things as only things: butter and whey. From this perspective, Piers sounds a bit like Chaucer's Pardoner, whose things suggest a spiritual meaning that the text does not consistently support. What Marshall Leicester writes of the Pardoner's *Prologue* and *Tale* could easily be said of this eclogue: "a spiritual level of meaning is being deliberately and consciously put in play by the speaker," and the text is marked by "a failure or refusal to distinguish carefully and consistently between literal and spiritual levels of meaning and discourse."[18] The materiality of the shepherdly reward for Spenser is a consequence of insisting on the physicality of labor and its relevance within this world. If labor has no spiritual component (it is not a good deed; it does not earn a reward), then it has only a material value.

This meditation on materiality and the work/works equation continues into the allegorical fable told by Piers at the end of the eclogue, which is meant to "warne the protestaunt beware, howe he geveth credit to the unfaythfull Catholique" (105n304). This fable invokes the allegorical pastoral of the medieval tradition only to assert its distance from it. On the most obvious level, it uses a familiar stereotype of predator and prey from a pastoral perspective: a fox and a kid (goat) replace the wolf and sheep. But the difference is not merely that Spenser has changed the animals to alter the reader's reactions: a goat's figurative meaning is certainly negatively inflected (the goats are those damned, after all), and a fox is less frightening than a wolf. More importantly, there is no shepherd and, therefore, no figure laboring to protect the goats from those preying upon them.

In addition, the allegory reinforces the eclogue's new focus on the material, as opposed to spiritual, rewards. It does so within a specific historical context: Protestant vulnerability to Catholic ideas. Piers's emphasis on materiality is disconcertingly prescient, for the lesson of the eclogue has nothing at all to do with being a good worker (as one would assume a lesson in response to not working would be), whether physically or spiritually, but, rather, tells us to be good consumers.[19]

The inset fable concerns a kid left by his mother at home alone (with a warning not to open the door). A fox comes to the door disguised as "a poore pedler . . . / Bearing a trusse of tryfles at hys backe, / As bells, and babes, and glasses in hys packe" (May, 238–40). The Kid opens the door when he becomes "enamored" with a "newell" [new thing], which is, significantly, a mirror, and the Fox seizes him and carries him off (276).[20] E. K.'s gloss to the line quoted above makes clear that the Fox's baubles signify Catholicism: "by such trifles are noted, the reliques and ragges of popish superstition, which put no smal religion in Belles" (104n240). In other words, the "things" he is selling are "works." From this perspective, the allegory underlines the Protestant position on works: they make salvation into a marketplace because they are not, in fact, deeds but commodities. One might only look at the attack on Catholic works in the *Homily on Good Works*: "[they have] marts or markets of merits, being full of their holy relics, images, shrines, and works of overflowing abundance ready to be sold; and all things which they had were called holy, holy cowls, holy girdles, holy pardons, holy beads, holy shoes, holy rules, and all full of holiness."[21]

Works are, of course, typically opposed to faith in Protestant polemic, and E. K.'s glosses make clear that the fable concerns faith: the moral quoted above refers to the "unfaythfull Catholique," and Piers's emblem is translated as "what fayth then is there in the faythless" (p. 105). But Spenser's condemnation of "works" is dependent on narrative not polemic, and his use of the Kid shows less a championing of the alternative to works (faith) than an uncertainty about what will replace them. After all, the Kid's fatal error is not only his inability to recognize a Fox (the old wolf in sheep's clothing) but also the desire for the objects themselves—a consumer's greed for novelty—and his lack of knowledge about their provenance and meaning. As the Kid reveals, it is not some abstract and corrupt Catholic "they" (as in the *Homily* quoted above) who have turned belief into a marketplace with their focus on "works" but rather the specific desires of the believer. Moreover, what should be the alternative to works, faith, seems to participate in the same language of materiality that describes works. Faith is rendered as a kind of object in the explanatory glosses because it is something one has or doesn't have ("the ground of religion" [p. 105]) and not something that one does or says.

What is perhaps most striking in this allegory of the contemporary religious situation is its view of church membership, which is imagined not, as one might expect, in terms of sheep and shepherd (the bad shepherd who leaves his sheep to suffer from wolves) but in terms of a financial transaction between the peddler and his gullible mark. The consequences of this shift for reform seem quite bleak: the believer must navigate a marketplace of choices after being abandoned by his mother, who might otherwise provide some direction.[22] Indeed, the allegory itself is oddly chilling: neither a sheep under the guidance of a shepherd nor a worker in the vineyard of the Lord, the believer is now a vulnerable baby animal filled with unhealthy desires. There are no communal means (such as labor) through which one might know one's new allegiance, no assistance from anyone at all. In abandoning both the plowman tradition (before he has even begun) and the ecclesiastical pastoral (before the end of the eclogue), Spenser's poem suggests that work no longer offers a figurative vocabulary to write about either the pressure on religious belief or the remedy for religious conflict. In the new religious situation all we have are different kinds of not working. We hear this despair in the words with which E. K. concludes his final gloss to the eclogue: "thys is all that they saye" (p. 105).

The September eclogue takes up and reinforces this despair through the lament of another medieval rural laborer, Diggon Davy, underlining what seems to be the end of a particularly powerful medieval tradition: the reformism associated with the rural laborer.[23] Diggon Davy most likely refers to the speaker in the brief poem by Thomas Churchyard, *Davy Dycar's Dreme* (1560), who is based on a character briefly mentioned in William Langland's *Piers Plowman*.[24] In Langland's poem Diggon appears in a prophecy that marks the end of the experiment on the Half-Acre, which has been undermined by the workers' refusal to work. This prophecy promises a famine that will punish the workers, notably "Dawe þe Dykere" who will "deye for hunger":

> Ac I warne yow workmen, wynneþ whil ye mowe
> For hunger hiderward hasteþ hym faste.
> He shal awake [þoruȝ] water wastours to chaste;
> Er fyue [yer] be fulfilled swich famyn shal aryse.
> Thoruȝ flo[od] and foule wedres fruytes shul faille,
> And so sei[þ] Saturne and sent yow to warne.
> Whan ye se þe [mone] amys and two monkes heddes,
> And a mayde haue þe maistrie, and multiplie by eiȝte,
> Thanne shal deeþ wiþdrawe and derþe be Iustice,
> And Dawe þe Dykere deye for hunger
> But [if] god of his goodnesse graunte vs a trewe.[25]

We could say that Diggon Davy is the dark side of the figure Piers: whereas Piers represents the potential of the laborer to reform the world, Diggon Davy represents the laborer who is punished for not working (and for being a waster). Thomas Churchyard takes up this figure, most likely because he was associated with prophecy, and moves him closer to Piers. Most obviously, this poem underlines the dream vision in its title—*Davy Dycar's Dreme*—in homage to Langland.

Moreover, Churchyard uses this figure to imagine a reform in much the same terms (although much more briefly) as Langland: "When Justice ioynes to truth, and law lookes not to meede, / And bribes help not to build fair bowres, nor giftes gret glotons fede."[26] This is a social world free of the corrupting influence of money (and greed). Of course, like Langland's vision of the Half-Acre, this "new order" is not really new but the idealized status quo achieved when "euery wight is well contente, to walke in his estate" (A1r). Nevertheless, Churchyard shifts the emphasis away from the worker and his potential laziness and greed (the wasters in Langland's poem who will be punished by hunger) to how greed has corrupted social relations. In other words, Churchyard's Diggon Davy will most likely die from hunger not through his own greed or laziness (his refusal to "win while he can") but due to the corruption around him.

Spenser's use of Diggon demonstrates his interest in the reformist and prophetic tradition that Langland initiates and Churchyard draws upon.[27] Like the Piers of the May eclogue, Diggon is a shepherd, and, like the account of Piers, this description draws attention to his figurative potential: "Diggon Davie is devised to be a shepheard" (p. 151). Yet that potential is far more ambiguous in this eclogue. Although Spenser clearly invokes ecclesiastical pastoral (Diggon "discourseth at large" about the "loose living of Popish prelates" [p. 151]), the Argument does not say definitively, as in May, that Diggon is a shepherd understood as priest. The word "devised" seems to suggest both that readers are already familiar with the character Diggon Davy (and associate him with a particular occupation, that is, digging) and that his identity here as a shepherd is, therefore, something novel and perhaps strange. If we are meant to see Diggon Davy as a figure for a particular historical person—Bishop Richard Davies, as the editor notes—the figuration is even stranger (p. 149). In "devising" him as a shepherd, Spenser adds another confusing layer to what readers expect from ecclesiastical pastoral: Is the bishop first a ditch-digger and then a shepherd? Or both at once? Whether Diggon refers to the figure drawn from Churchyard and Langland or to the historical bishop (or both), the use of "devised" ensures that this figure preserves his previous existence as laborer and marks that existence as somehow distinct from his new identity as shepherd. The questions that the eclogues have thus far avoided seem to be faced head-on: What does it mean to represent the rural laborer as a shepherd? What does it mean for pastoral to mediate readers' understanding of rural labor?

On the one hand, the eclogue seems to rediscover the radical potential of representing a rural laborer (whether as shepherd or not) within the pastoral. Indeed, some readers have seen Spenser's eclogue in terms of "protest literature" or a critique of "rapidly changing agrarian relations in Elizabethan England."[28] Diggon's complaint to Hobbinol about his experience in "forrein costes" seems to match the dire tone of Churchyard's poem:

> In tho countryes, whereas I have bene,
> No being for those, that truely mene,
> But for such, as of guile maken gayne,
> No such countrye, as there to remaine.
> They setten to sale their shops of shame,
> And maken a Mart of theyr good name.
> The shepheards there robben one another,
> And layen baytes to beguile her brother.
> Or they will buy his sheepe out of the cote,
> Or they will carven the shepheards throte.
> The shepheards swayne you cannot wel ken,
> But it be by his pryde, from other men:
> They looken bigge as Bulls, that bene bate,
> And bearen the cragge so stiffe and so state,
> As cocke on his dunghill, crowing cranck.
> (September, 32–46)

Here greed has corrupted the relations between shepherds and "brothers" just as in Churchyard's poem. Even the alliteration ("so stiffe and so state") echoes the form used by Churchyard and Langland. The object of attack in this eclogue is not only the church, as suggested by the pastoral and its language for describing the familiar failures of shepherds in watching their sheep, but the lords themselves, who are characterized as "bigge Bulles of Basan," which "the leane soules treaden under foote" (September, 124 and 126). For these reasons we can see Diggon as representing a return to a lay, reformist voice, one that desires to return to an idealized status quo in which relations between estates have not been corrupted by greed; in other words, precisely the kind of sentiments that animate the treatises against enclosure written in the plowman's voice.

On the other hand, Spenser's laborer does not entirely fit the mold provided by Churchyard for the reformist worker because he himself is motivated by the greed he condemns: "I wote ne Hobbin how I was bewitcht / With vayne desyre, and hope to be enricht" (September, 74–75).[29] In other words, he wanted to leave his shepherdly status behind. Such a desire should be familiar from Barclay's fifth eclogue, as discussed in chapter 3, in which the shepherd Amintas leaves the countryside behind in order to make his way in the town. But Spenser's poem maps this pastoral desire onto a familiar reformist figure, thus suggesting that his figure is less a victim of others' greed than a willing participant in the economy. Diggon's status as worker does not separate him from the church/clergy and the lords, does not lend him the authority of virtuous rustic simplicity that can be found in the first-person narratives of the *Piers Plowman* tradition and Churchyard's poem. Rather, his status as worker seems to have caused his predicament. Even the emblem and its gloss underline Diggon's responsibility for his own unfortunate circumstances: "*Inopem me copia fecit* [plenty made me poor]" (September, 261). E. K. writes,

> This is the saying of Narcissus in Ovid. For when the foolishe boye by beholding hys face in the brooke, fell in love with his owne likenesse: and not hable to content him selfe with much looking thereon, he cryed out, that plentye made him poore, meaning that much gazing had bereft him of sence. But our Diggon useth it to other purpose, as who that by tryall of many wayes had founde the worst, and through great plentye was fallen into great penurie. (p. 165)

Here the agency is assigned to Diggon himself—who has tried many ways—and his fall into poverty is not the result of others' actions, namely, the greed of lords and the clergy that are described in Churchyard's poem. Indeed, Diggon's life as a worker is, implicitly, entirely untouched by the greed of the outside world until he seeks it out.

This situation is, of course, in direct opposition to the interdependence of rich and poor described by Langland and then Churchyard. In this way, Spenser's eclogue suggests that the greed of clergy and landlords has "trickled down" to the worker, and, as a result, the worker does not maintain the virtues that are necessary to reform even as the worker desires that reform. Perhaps even more depressing is the way in which the emblem reminds us of the hope for change in Churchyard's prophecy only to show its impossibility. The emblem is a half-recollection and seeming inversion of one of Churchyard's prophetic utterances: that the ideal society will be achieved when "plenty please the poore" (A1r). By associating plenty with Narcissus and his self-directed desire, Spenser removes it from the material world that Churchyard defined, suggesting that Diggon needs what we would now call a psychological cure for his poverty (and his desire) instead of a socioeconomic one. In other words, Spenser implies, presciently, that Diggon should change his own inner state, not the material conditions that have determined his situation. Such a perspective resonates quite interestingly with our own cultural moment: people are made responsible for their own prosperity, as if wealth were a function of desire (our personal motivations) and not of particular material conditions that are largely outside our control.

In Diggon Davy, like Piers of the May eclogue, Spenser invokes the prophetic (and reformist) voice of the rural laborer only to empty it of its power. Most obviously, Diggon has lost the sheep that were in his care and, therefore, his authoritative pastoral voice:

My sheepe bene wasted, (wae is me therefore)
The jolly shepheard that was of yore,
Is nowe nor iollye, nor shepehearde more.
     (September, 25–27)

He is, then, a figure of loss who points toward the past, and not a figure who outlines what could be. Moreover, as I've mentioned above, Diggon the laborer has separated himself from the world and its corruption not to call for reform, exactly, but to lament his own descent into poverty. To be sure, the eclogue contains a long description of a virtuous shepherd, Roffy, who does seem to offer a kind of reform:

For thy with shepheard sittes not playe,
Or sleepe, as some doen, all the long day:
But euer liggen in watch and ward,
From soddein force theyr flocks for to gard.
                    (September, 232–35)

But this is the reformism of ecclesiastical pastoral, not the dream vision or prophecy that we associate with Diggon Davy (and Piers); and it pointedly addresses only one of the dangers facing shepherds—the predatory wolves (that is, Jesuits)—and not the danger of greed that Diggon has himself described for much of the eclogue. While there might be hope for the reform of the church, as suggested by the ecclesiastical pastoral, there seems to be little hope for the reform of the social world along with it. The inefficacy of the pastoral in offering an alternative to greed and corruption is underlined by Diggon himself: "all this long tale, / Nought easeth the care, that doth me forhaile" (September, 242–43).

New Figurations

When read next to its medieval and Reformation antecedents, Spenser's poetry registers an important rupture in the language of labor: once rural labor begins to be detached from its medieval, Christian significance (embodied by Piers) and refigured in terms of the pastoral mode, it no longer carries with it the same reformist possibilities that were so central to *Piers Plowman* and its tradition. In the pastoral rural labor is not the language through which one finds Truth, or does well, or establishes a community. Separated from its earlier symbolic range, rural work is freed for other figurative meanings—namely, the writing of poetry. Of course, the laborer as poet has long been considered central to (even definitive of) the pastoral mode. As Alpers writes, "one can derive from the Eclogues the formula which established pastoral as a poetic kind and which at the same time made possible its historical variety. The Virgilian formula is: the poet represents (himself as) a shepherd or shepherds."[30] But the first eclogues by Mantuan, Barclay, and Googe demonstrate that the equation between shepherd and poet is not entirely expected or automatic, certainly not as automatic as the movement between literal and figurative so central to ecclesiastical pastoral—that is, the shepherd who is a priest. Whereas all the early writers of eclogues make use of the shepherd/priest, they do not all embrace the shepherd/poet. Googe is entirely uninterested in examining this figure, and both Mantuan and Barclay detail the difficulty of the shepherd/poet equation: the "real" labor of shepherding gets in the way of poetic labor, as shall be discussed further below.

We should then pay special attention to Spenser's *Calender* because it offers the first self-conscious meditation on the pastoral convention of the shepherd/poet in English. Despite its classical antecedents, Spenser's meditation quite interestingly refers the reader back to a pre-pastoral "native tradition." First and most famously, in the April eclogue, one of the "recreative" eclogues, Hobbinol demonstrates his "skill in poetrie" (Argument, p. 70) in a song that specifically identifies him as a laborer:

> Soone as my younglings cryen for the dam,
> To her will I offer a milkwhite Lamb:
> Shee is my goddesse plaine,
> And I her shepherds swayne,
> Albee forswonck and forswatt I am.
> (April, 95–99)

This appropriation of rural labor to the poet has been persuasively discussed by Louis Montrose in light of its topicality: namely, the poet's participation in the cult of the Virgin Queen.[31] From this perspective, the courtier/poet imagines himself as a rural laborer in order to disguise his desires for advancement; pastoral is "a medium in which well-educated but humbly born young men could gracefully advertise themselves to the courtly establishment."[32]

This appropriation is more complicated than it first appears, however, as the allusion to "native tradition" makes clear. The reference to "forswonck and forswatt" is taken from the anticlerical *Plowman's Tale*, and it is a reference to the plowman himself, who is in this poem, as in the *Piers Plowman* tradition more broadly, a voice calling for the reform of the church and, to a more limited degree, the social order. From this perspective, Hobbinol's work is *already* a figure, not for the poet's labor but for the labor of reform. The oddness of this allusion should be noted. As David Norbrook writes, "To readers familiar with the old prophetic tradition, the clash of discourses would have amounted to an alienation effect."[33] Removed from its reformist and anticlerical context (in which the worker is the voice for reform), the line is simultaneously re-literalized (to refer to a swain's work) and refigured to refer to the poet's labor. In this way, Spenser draws our attention not only to one of the conventions of pastoral but to the consequences of that appropriation. To make the poet the laborer is to replace the older figurative meaning of laborer: the reformer. This line reminds us that there is no natural representation of "herdsmen and their lives" in which they must necessarily "sing and woo."

Spenser explores the consequences of appropriating rural labor for the poet at greater length in the October eclogue, the second eclogue in which Piers appears.[34] Once again, the figuration of the shepherd as poet is imagined in relation to "native tradition," which is here the figure of Piers. The eclogue is framed (in its Argument) with a distinction between poetry and labor—poetry is "a divine gift and heavenly instinct not to bee gotten by labour and learning, but adorned with both" (p. 170)—and it follows a debate structure. For most readers of the eclogue, Cuddie and Piers offer two opposed views of poetry: the practical/worldly and the divine/transcendent, respectively.[35] Cuddie complains that he has not received "good" or "gayne" from his piping (October, 10); in other words, he insists that his poetry is work, even as Piers insists that poetry is its own reward: "The glory eke much greater than the gayne" (October, 20). It is worth noting that the Argument aligns poetry with a "Protestant" understanding of faith and works: poetry is a gift (like grace) that cannot be earned ("gotten") through labor although it should be accompanied by labor, just as faith should produce works.

In debating the relationship between poetry and work Spenser departs from one of his models, Mantuan's fifth eclogue.[36] In Mantuan, as in Barclay, who adapts this eclogue in the fourth of his series, the focus is on patronage and payment, as it is in Spenser as well. But both Mantuan and Barclay portray the shepherd's labors as hindering his poetry. Mantuan's shepherd Silvanus asks (in George Turberville's translation): "Can he [a shepherd] not both attend / his flocke, and otherwhile / At vacant time make Uerses . . . "[37] The answer is a definite "no." Candidus gives a long account of the labors that take up his time:

> No (friend) a Shephierd must
> All laysure time vnto
> his Cattle well implie,
> Trot out in hast, retourne in poast,
> and bout his matters hie:
> Keepe off the barking Woulfe,
> close vp his flocke in folde,
> Buie strawe and fodder to sustaine
> his Beasts from Winter colde.[38]

For these poets, rural labor is not the same as poetry, even figuratively. The shepherds are still characterized by "real" labor even when they are poets, and they have no "laysure" because they are working constantly. For this reason, the recreational activities mentioned by Mantuan and Barclay, such as singing or piping, receive little attention; they are not, therefore, the defining aspects of shepherd life. As Alexander Barclay writes in his fifth eclogue:

> Howe men vplondish on holy dayes rage.
> Nought can them tame, they be a beastly sort,
> In sweate and labour hauing moste chiefe comfort.
> On the holy day assoone as morne is past,
> When all men resteth while all the day doth last,
> They drinke, they banket, they reuell and they iest,
> They leape, they daunce, despising ease and rest.
> If they once heare a bagpipe or a drone,
> Anone to the elme or Oke they be gone.
> There vse they to daunce, to gambolde and to rage,
> Such is the custome and vse of the village.

> When the ground resteth from rake, plough and wheles
> Then moste they it trouble with burthen of their heles.
> To Bacchus they banket, no feast is festiuall,
> They chide and they chat, they vary and they brall,
> They rayle and they route, they reuell and they crye,
> Laughing and leaping, and making cuppes drye.[39]

For Barclay, piping and singing are intimately connected to labor: they are what laborers do as respite from laboring (on the holidays). Indeed, they even resemble labor in that the shepherds refuse "ease and rest" in order to engage in these activities. We are still in the world of the medieval nativity plays and Chaucer's "Former Age," in which writers have a difficult time imagining a rural life without labor. Barclay's text demonstrates that the *otium* of classical tradition has not yet been fused with the "native" recreational traditions that later writers of pastoral see as so closely connected. In other words, the freedom to sing, which Alpers finds definitive of pastoral, is not an entirely familiar or recognizable aspect of shepherding in the early pastorals.

Spenser, in contrast, is quite interested in the figure of the shepherd-poet and, indeed, insists upon the natural relationship between poetry and shepherding. Cuddie is clearly a shepherd; this is the same name used for the shepherd boy in the February eclogue, and in the October eclogue he is described in the Argument as "the perfect paterne of a Poete" (p. 170). Moreover, poetry is an identifiably shepherdly activity, not something extra that certain shepherds do when they have leisure. Indeed, the recreational activities have become constitutive of shepherding and have replaced labor, as made clear in Piers's opening address to Cuddie: "Whilome thou wont the shepheards laddes to leade, / In rymes, in ridles, and in bydding base" (October, 4–5). This is the only reference to shepherding in the entire eclogue, which is otherwise concerned with the rewards of poetry. When read in relation to the earlier eclogues of Mantuan and Barclay, which preserve the shepherds' labor as distinct from poetry and other recreational pursuits, Spenser's eclogue demonstrates the capacity of the pastoral, with its new metaphor (poetry is rural labor), to shift readers' understanding of rural labor: the more that writing poetry is imagined as rural labor, the more rural labor must become like writing poetry (in that it consists of piping and singing).

Given the novelty of using shepherds to imagine the relationship between poetry and labor, at least as far as the English tradition is concerned, the choice of the name *Piers*, which refers the reader back to a medieval and Reformation context, seems surprising. How does this meditation on poetry, so indebted to classical ideas, resonate with the "native tradition" of Langland's poem and its imitations? I'd like to suggest that this sense of dissonance is precisely the point. Spenser can explore poetry through rural laborers only because the medieval symbolic imagination around work (represented here by Piers) has been disrupted by the Reformation. Indeed, both the pastoral and Protestantism require that work be re-literalized, severed from its older associations of shepherd-priests or good works.

It is worth remembering that writing poetry is rarely described in terms of rural labor in the Middle Ages, and Langland's poem, in particular, holds these activities distinct.[40] Instead, Langland is concerned with whether writing poetry is a "good work." If we assume for a moment that Spenser was familiar with Langland's poem, the discussion of poetry and reward in the October eclogue resonates quite interestingly with *Piers Plowman*. Whereas Spenser's shepherds wonder whether poetry is work or not, the dreamer of Langland's poem wonders whether poetry is a good work or not. In Passus 12 of *Piers Plowman*, the figure Ymaginatif castigates the dreamer for writing: "þow medlest þee wiþ makynges and myʒtest go seye þi sauter, / And bidde for hem þat ʒyueth þee breed."[41] In other words, instead of writing the dreamer should do "works" (prayers). The dreamer responds by claiming his writing is a "werk":

> Ac if þer were any wight þat wolde me telle
> What were dowel and dobet and dobest at þe laste,
> Wolde I neuere do werk, but wende to holi chirche
> And þere bidde my bedes but whan ich ete or slepe.[42]

Here his "werk" is the search for Dowel and is thus intimately tied to good works. In this way, the writing of poetry can become a good work although its status as such is uncertain because it is opposed to one of the traditional penitential works: prayer. For Spenser, in contrast, the earthly and the transcendent are no longer linked through the metaphor of work (that physical activity might symbolize a good deed or penance or reform). Instead, his pastoral establishes a binary between the earthly and the transcendent, between that which brings material gain and that which brings "glory."

Whether or not Spenser is invoking Langland's poem or the imitations, the eclogue serves as a kind of valediction to the medieval and Reformation tradition Piers represents. To be sure, the poetic past imagined here is a classical one, as described in Cuddie's speech:

> Indeede the Romish Tityrus, I heare,
> Through his Mecoenas left his Oaten reede,
> Wheron he earst had taught his flocks to feede,
> . . . .
> But ah Mecoenas is yclad in claye,
> And great Augustus long ygoe is dead:
> And all the worthies liggen wrapt in leade.
> (October, 55–63)

But it is worth asking why a figure named *Piers* is necessary to mediate this "new" view of poetry.[43] The conversation between Piers and Cuddie can be understood as the poetic past confronting the poetic present and future, in which the past (of Piers) is definitively abandoned. This abandonment involves a gradual silencing of Piers and the medieval reformist mode that he represents.

The first stage of this abandonment occurs when Piers urges Cuddie to change the topics for his poetry from rural to martial interests: "Abandon then the base and viler clowne, / Lyft up they selfe out of the lowly dust: / And sing of bloody Mars, of wars, of giusts" (October, 37–39). This is, of course, a reference to Virgil's career—his movement from pastoral to epic—but the wording is ambiguous. "Clowne" might refer to either the subject matter (the pastoral) or the audience (or both).[44] If the word refers to the audience, then Cuddie must abandon a poetry written *for* the "clowne." A poetry for "clowns" (rustics, plowmen, shepherds) would be a poetry with aims similar to Langland's; it would be a reformist text, whereas a poetry *about* clowns could be reformist but more likely would be written for a "non-clown," that is, elite, audience.[45] In choosing the ambiguous wording as well as an ambiguous spokesperson (we still don't know what Piers represents here), Spenser ensures that we read this advice on at least two levels: Cuddie should move from pastoral to epic (following Virgil), and Cuddie must set aside the reformist poetic tradition he shares with Piers, a tradition that takes the "clowne" as both subject matter and potential audience. Piers's pun on his name functions similarly, separating him from the future of English poetry:

> O pierlesse Poesye, where is then thy place?
> If nor in Princes pallace thou doe sitt:
> (And yet is Princes pallace the most fitt)
> Ne brest of baser birth doth thee embrace.
> (October, 79–82)

The future of poetry lies at the court, which is not at all interested in a poetry that a Piers might produce.

The abandonment of Piers is complete at the end of the eclogue when Piers disappears from the poem in silence, without an emblem. It is worth noting that in all of the other debate eclogues, each speaker gets an emblem that reinforces his position in the debate. In those eclogues in which only one speaker has an emblem (such as March, June, or September), E. K. does not interpret the silence of the other speaker. For Piers E. K. glosses silence as approbation: "Hereby is meant, as also in the whole course of this Aeglogue, that Poetry is a divine instinct and unnatural rage passing the reache of comen reason. Whom Piers answereth Epiphonematicos as admiring the excellencye of the skyll whereof in Cuddie hee hadde alreadye hadde a taste" (p. 183). If poetry passes "comen reason," then it certainly is beyond the capacity of the plowman. Having facilitated his own removal from the realm of poetry, Piers must finally be quiet.

The Piers of the October eclogue recalls in some sense the Piers of the May eclogue, in that both become spokesmen for the problematics of figuring labor, whether of priests or of poets. In this way, they invoke the medieval and Reformation heritage, but they do so by asserting a certain distance from it. This distance might seem to be an obvious consequence of the pastoral mode as it is inherited from the classical tradition: the pastoral is about having the leisure to sing and implicitly or explicitly denigrates labor. But we cannot forget that Spenser stood in a different relation to pastoral than we do, at the beginning of a trend rather than at the end. For Spenser, there still was a poetry of rural labor that was not pastoral, a poetry of how to do well through work and one whose relationship to the "new," Virgilian pastoral had not yet been determined. But this is the poetry that he sets aside: Piers's transcendent view makes a poetry about work impossible. If poetry is an "immortall mirrhor" (October, 93), then it is certainly not a tool to shape reality, nor is it a means to do well. Indeed, the mirror cannot help but underline the self-reflective, even self-indulgent, nature of pastoral poetry. As Roland Greene writes,

> Spenser's reply to the aesthetic of Gascoigne, Googe, Turberville and the *Mirror for Magistrates*—to the commonplace, stagnant by the late 1570s, that poetry properly reflects reality—is to insist on showing that relation gone awry in the case of a poet who has lost his referential priority to his world and has become, in fact, its object. If poetry mirrors reality, the implicit argument goes, reality may just as easily be seen as forestalling poetry.[46]

The final words of the October eclogue underline the sense that poetry can no longer "fix" what has gone awry. Even Cuddie accepts Piers's account of poetry's role; he merely finds it too difficult: "it is all to weak and wanne, / So high to sore" (85–86).

Readers of the *Calender* have long identified therein a kind of uncertainty or instability.[47] And it would seem that this instability is due, at least in part, to the incompatibility of the Langlandian tradition with the eclogue. On the one hand, this incompatibility is a sign of loss; the symbolic imagination around rural labor had been radically altered by agrarian controversy and the redefinition of works in Protestantism. On the other hand, it suggests the possibilities of the new, not just the newly rediscovered pastoral as such but the intersection between pastoral and Protestantism. Pastoral, according to the Virgilian model, requires the literalization of the shepherd (he is supposed to be a "real" shepherd, not just a figure for a priest, as in medieval ecclesiastical pastoral), and Protestantism requires a kind of literalization of work because works can no longer have a spiritual reward.

SIX | *Reading Pastoral in Book 6 of Spenser's* Faerie Queene

In book 6 of his Faerie Queene *(1596) Spenser returns to* the pastoral mode, but this is a far more self-consciously courtly version that seems to have little or nothing to do with the broader traditions of writing rural labor that helped to shape the *Calender*. Indeed, the defining feature of this pastoral episode is the life of ease, *otium*, which appears only inconsistently and sometimes contradictorily in the English eclogues written before Spenser's pastorals. As Calidore, the knight around whom this episode turns, observes to the old shepherd, Meliboe, "How much (sayd he) more happie is the state, / In which ye father here doe dwell *at ease*."[1] Spenser's new emphasis on *otium* is, of course, directly related to a heightened interest in what scholars call Arcadian or "art" pastoral, whose defining features are not only leisure but also the idyllic landscape and the piping and singing of shepherds. The Arcadian pastoral has long been defined by its contrast to the Mantuanesque pastoral, the "moral" tradition that informs the *Calender*.[2] If the *Calender* still holds out the possibility that the eclogue tradition and, therefore, the pastoral might at least intermittently depict "ordinary life," the real shepherds in the English countryside, or the reformist tradition associated with "writing rural labor," the *Faerie Queene* seems far more interested in the "enamelled world," to use Raymond Williams's famous phrase[3]—or as Spenser writes, "the happy peace" and "perfect pleasures, which doe grow / Amongst poore hyndes" (6.10.3.4, 5–6). Spenser's choice of Arcadianism in the *Faerie Queene*, and thus his implicit rejection of the broader tradition of "writing rural labor," has, of course, a larger cultural resonance. As a brief glance at later pastoral, such as Shakespeare's *As You Like It* or *Winter's Tale*, makes clear, the future of pastoral looks more like the *Faerie Queene* than the *Calender*.[4] If the function (however unwitting) of the early eclogues of Barclay, Googe, and, most importantly, Spenser himself was at least in part to empty the rural laborer of his labor and, therefore, his potentially reformist and anticapitalist associations, then the *Faerie Queene* demonstrates the success of those attempts. Indeed, its pastoral episode signals the changed role of rural labor with its opening, when the speaker appropriates plowing to figure his own writing:

> Now turne againe my teme thou iolly swayne,
> Backe to the furrow which I lately left;
> I lately left a furrow, one or twayne
> Vnplough'd, the which my coulter hath not cleft:
> Yet seem'd the soyle both fayre and frutefull eft,
> As I it past, that were too great a shame,
> That so rich frute should be from vs bereft;
> Besides the great dishonour and defame,
> Which should befall to Calidores immortall name.
> (6.9.1.1–9)[5]

Scholars have long understood this passage as a "georgic moment."[6] While *georgic* is usually broadly intended, meaning quite simply a reference to rural labor and not to Virgil's *Georgics* specifically, its use, perhaps inadvertently, underlines Spenser's neoclassicism.[7] From this perspective, Spenser's reference to plowing in a book concerned with pastoral grows out of a kind of Virgilianism and is, therefore, hardly surprising: plowing is the same as shepherding, a figure for poetry. But to focus on the similarity of these figures (plowing and shepherding) is to ignore Spenser's own past. After all, Spenser's previous pastoral, the *Calender*, bears the traces of medieval and Reformation texts, such as the pseudo-Chaucerian *Plowman's Tale*, in which plowmen are most certainly not indebted to the *Georgics*. Moreover, these medieval and Reformation plowmen exist in a potentially antagonistic relationship to the pastoral quite simply because of their association with rural labor and, therefore, with medieval Christianity and social and religious reform. If we approach the *Faerie Queene*, then, from the perspective of the *Calender*, the appearance of plowing in the *Faerie Queene* has less to do with following Virgil and more with Spenser's desire to resolve the antagonism between these figures, to make them the same. To do so is, of course, to remove "real" rural labor entirely from the field of representation; it is only a figure that informs the reader's understanding of poetry.

Despite redirecting his pastoral toward the Arcadian tradition and its rejection of labor, Spenser prevents the reader from fully embracing this new "enamelled world." If this is the future of pastoral, and, therefore, of writing about rural laborers, then it is one that causes Spenser some trepidation, a vague and nightmarish anxiety about the consequences of representing the countryside as "labor-free." Simply put, the episode demonstrates the potentially dangerous effects of reading the Arcadian version of pastoral, both on the courtly readers who demand it and on the rural laborers it claims to represent, as I shall argue in this chapter. These effects are demonstrated first and most obviously through the knight Calidore, who is, of course, the courtly reader in the text.[8] Calidore is a famous misreader of the pastoral world; he represses not only "what the country was really like"[9]—a repression that is surely typical for the pastoral—but also even familiar pastoral conventions that have the potential to threaten the idealization of this life. This repression is shown to be quite harmful, although not, importantly, for the reader Calidore, who survives the pastoral episode and gains what he most desires (Pastorella); the harm is experienced by the shepherd world itself, which ends violently and abruptly when the shepherds are captured to be sold into slavery and then massacred. In this way, Spenser demonstrates that the logical consequence of embracing the idealized pastoral is, paradoxically, the end of the "real" pastoral world—that is, the life of the free laborer in the English countryside. The particular nature of this end is, as I shall demonstrate, significant. In imagining the shepherds as slaves, Spenser's episode reminds the reader of what the "new" neoclassical pastoral must repress: the kind of labor and labor relations that make *otium* both possible and desirable.

Before I begin my analysis, a brief summary might be useful, especially since part of my argument depends on the trajectory of the narrative. The episode begins when the knight Calidore gives up his pursuit of the Blatant Beast to live as a shepherd. He falls in love with a shepherdess named Pastorella and receives a vision of poetry when he stumbles upon (and eavesdrops on) Colin Clout and the dancing Graces on Mount Acidale. While Calidore is away hunting, the pastoral retreat is violently interrupted when brigands capture the shepherds to sell them into slavery. When the brigands offer the shepherds to certain merchants as slaves, disagreements over Pastorella lead to a massacre in which all of the shepherds are killed by the brigands, except Pastorella and one other shepherd, Coridon. Finally, Calidore rescues Pastorella from the brigands and takes her to court, leaving the shepherd world, now reduced to one shepherd (Coridon), entirely behind.[10]

Calidore's Version of Pastoral

The opening of the pastoral episode makes clear that it is the convention of shepherdly *otium* more than any other that generates Calidore's readerly desire:

> He chaunst to spy a sort of shepheard groomes,
> Playing on pypes and caroling apace,
> The whyles their beasts there in the budded broomes
> Beside them fed, and nipt the tender bloomes:
> For other worldly wealth they cared nought
> To whom Sir Calidore yet sweating comes.
> (6.9.5.2–7)

The reader here "sees" the shepherds through Calidore's eyes. This voyeurism should remind us of reading: Calidore watches activities (the piping and the caroling) that are, of course, familiar from books, even from Spenser's own eclogues in the *Calender*. Calidore's distance from the shepherds, as watcher, underlines that we (the readers outside the text) see leisure not only as a characteristic of shepherds, as we did in the eclogues, but as precisely that element that distinguishes them from their "readers." While the shepherds revel, Calidore labors (because he is sweating). Even the shepherds' "beasts," who do not require labor because they feed peacefully beside the shepherds, are an odd echo of Calidore's beast (the Blatant Beast), who is, in contrast, making him labor. From this perspective, shepherdly leisure is not just "out there" waiting to be portrayed; it is produced in relation to a reader, in this case, by the demands of the quest. Indeed, it is as if Calidore needs the shepherds to be leisurely because he needs a break from his quest.

Even more importantly, Calidore's desire for *otium* renders its meaning fluid: as he converses with Meliboe, he shifts the emphasis from a simple freedom from labor, and the leisure to dance and pipe that initially attracted him, to a freedom from care, which is far more generally defined:

> How much (sayd he) more happie is the state,
> In which ye father here doe dwell at ease,
> Leading a life so free and fortunate,
> From all the tempests of these worldly seas,
> Which tosse the rest in daungerous disease?
> Where warres, and wreckes, and wicked enmitie
> Doe them afflict, which no man can appease,
> That certes I your happinesse enuie,
> And wish my lot were plast in such felicitie.
> (6.9.19.1–9)

Calidore's first mention of "ease" refers back to the shepherds at their leisure. But as he proceeds in describing that "ease," it becomes clear that this is not primarily a freedom from labor relations and from the demands of the market economy. He sees both of these freedoms when he first encounters the shepherds, who care nothing for "worldly wealth." These are conventional freedoms in pastorals, but Calidore is more interested in a kind of psychological freedom from the figurative tempests and seas and from a state of "disease"—here, clearly, the absence of ease. In other words, the shepherds' happiness is a result of their distance from the world ("worldly seas") to which Calidore belongs, a world that we assume to be the court. This particular reading of leisure, as having the implicit advantages of the court (no labor) without the disadvantages (figurative storms), is entirely self-interested. Spenser makes that self-interest clear in Calidore's choice of metaphor (the storms) for the worldly cares that affect all who are not shepherds. The metaphor relies on the reader's understanding that "real" storms can do serious damage that certainly would affect the shepherd world (if not the courtly world). That literal storms also occur in the shepherd world is made clear in Mantuan's third eclogue, which begins with a description of a terrible storm. The shepherd Faustus states (in Turberville's translation of 1567):

> The hayle (my friend) from Baldus mount
> that yesterdaye did fall
> (We thank the Gods, that saue our corn)
> anoyde vs nought at all.
> But Harculus reported hath
> and bruted here a fame:
> That in the coast was much a doe
> from whence he lately came.
> Verona fieldes were pestred sore,
> the cattell with the folde:
> The Shepecots and the Barnes the haile
> (as he half weeping tolde)
> Hath ouerwhelmde and layd on ground,
> and in such sorte defast:
> As all good hope that husbands had
> is quite berefte and past.[11]

Mantuan's passage approaches a kind of realism about the vulnerability of the shepherd's existence: the storm has destroyed the crops and livestock and, therefore, the hopes of the farmers for prosperity or even for subsistence. The realism of these shepherds is underlined by the references to actual locations—Baldus mount and Verona's fields. Spenser echoes Mantuan's passage, not only because Calidore refers to storms but also because he suggests their destructive potential for agriculture in using the word *tempest*, which is particularly associated with hail.[12] But, of course, Calidore's storms are not real, and, therefore, Spenser reminds us of what he is repressing (shepherds' vulnerability) even as he represses it. Perhaps more importantly, Calidore's metaphor demonstrates how a "truth" of pastoral—that shepherds are safe from the machinations of the court—leads to a lie, or at least a kind of mystification—that they are safe from all harm. Paradoxically, this lie is generated out of the very real conditions of shepherd existence.

The consequences of the desire generated by the pastoral become clear at the end of Calidore's conversation with Meliboe. This is not a desire for more knowledge about the details of shepherd life but a desire to affirm what Calidore already believes (or needs to believe) to be true.[13] In other words, pastoral is primarily narcissistic, leading back to the reader, not outward toward the shepherds. At the end of Meliboe's account of shepherd life, Spenser describes Calidore's response:

> Whylest thus he talkt, the knight with greedy eare
> Hong still vpon his melting mouth attent;
> Whose sensefull words empierst his hart so neare,
> That he was rapt with double rauishment,
> Both of his speach that wrought him great content,
> And also of the obiect of his vew,
> On which his hungry eye was alwayes bent;
> That twixt his pleasing tongue, and her faire hew,
> He lost himselfe, and like one halfe entraunced grew.
> (6.9.26.1–9)

This description makes Calidore's readerly desire clear, not only because it describes his ear as "greedy" but also because listening has the same effect upon him as the sight of Pastorella. Both Meliboe's words and Pastorella's image cause him to "lose" himself. It is no accident that both the words and the image amount to the same thing:

that is, the pastoral world. But this pastoral world is not the same one that Meliboe has described. Although Calidore has "hong" on every word, he has not necessarily heard them, or at least all of them. Instead of responding to Meliboe's emphasis on accepting one's station in life (on which more below), Calidore repeats his initial position on the freedom from figurative storms at the end:

> Yet to occasion meanes, to worke his mind,
> And to insinuate his harts desire,
> He thus replyde; Now surely syre, I find,
> That all this worlds gay showes, which we admire,
> Be but vaine shadowes to this safe retyre
> Of life, which here in lowlinesse ye lead,
> Fearelesse of foes, or fortunes wrackfull yre,
> Which tosseth states, and vnder foot doth tread
> The mightie ones, affrayd of euery chaunges dread.
> (6.9.27.1–9)

This praise of pastoral life is now explicitly motivated by desire, here his "harts desire," although this phrase is ambiguous. Either he wants to insinuate, as in "worm his way," into Pastorella's heart (she is his "harts desire") or he wants to insinuate, as in suggest, his "harts desire" to the others (his "harts desire" would then be a desire to stay in the pastoral world). Either way, pastoral life is now more emphatically "safe"—free of "foes" and of the kind of disasters that afflict "the mighty"—than it was in Calidore's opening speech. This misreading is even more chilling than the first. The first fantasy of the shepherds' freedom was a response to their leisure (their ease), in which Calidore read leisure as a freedom from care, from tempests, and from labor. Now, in contrast, he claims that it is their "lowliness" (Meliboe's topic) and not their leisure that makes the shepherds safe. Here the claim of pastoral *otium*—that poor people are happy because they have time to recreate (or as Alpers would have it, that "poor, humble, and deprived people are simply free to sing and woo")—has a sinister effect. Pastoral makes readers think that poor people are happy *because* they are poor.[14]

This disturbing consequence of reading pastoral is further emphasized by the most famous example of Calidore's "self-deception" in the conclusion to his exchange with Meliboe.[15] Meliboe makes the quite conventional claim that "It is the mynd, that maketh good or ill, / That maketh wretch or happie, rich or poore" (6.9.30.1–2). As the editor of the Penguin edition notes, "Meliboe's advice is the traditional Christian precept about earthly fortune: one must use what God has given us and not look for more."[16] In other words, Meliboe merely repeats the position with which he began, that his happiness rests in being content with his lot. Rich and poor are, significantly, not described in terms of material goods but as a state of mind. Those who want more, no matter what they already have, consider themselves poor. Calidore misreads Meliboe's statement, however, as describing a kind of freedom from actual social conditions—from rich and poor as "real" states—not a freedom from material desires or from the ambition that makes one unhappy with one's fated social condition (as Meliboe has suggested):

> Since then in each mans self (said Calidore)
> It is, to fashion his owne lyfes *estate*,
> Giue leaue awhile, good father, in this shore
> To rest my barcke, which hath bene beaten late
> With stormes of fortune and tempestuous fate.
> (6.9.31.1–5, emphasis added)

The word *estate* is, of course, significant, for it means both "state" (as in psychological situation) and class position. For Calidore, then, the pastoral world allows him to believe that he can escape the social structures, such as class, that obtain in the outside world by exerting control over them. This control is expressed in the final metaphor of the ship, which may be tossed about by fortune but is still directed by Calidore (as opposed to the "rudderless" ship of romance).

If Calidore's speech insists that the shepherds' leisure is a freedom from the existing social order, with all of its figurative storms, then Meliboe's speech reads as a kind of correction, an insistence on the intractability of labor, and consequently class, even within a recognizably "literary" pastoral world. The reader knows that this pastoral world is literary because of Meliboe's name (Meliboeus, which is taken from Virgil), but also because Spenser is borrowing some (if not a great deal) of this speech from Torquato Tasso's *Gerusalemme Liberata*.[17] It would be a mistake, of course, to see Meliboe as the voice of "what the country was really like" or of alternative traditions for writing rural labor. Nevertheless, Meliboe's version of rustic simplicity insists upon the social world that Calidore desires to dismiss. For Meliboe the poor are happy because they accept their station in life, not because they are leisurely or free from worldly care, the two pastoral conventions that so interest Calidore. Indeed, the "pastoral" aspects to Meliboe's speech are presented in such a way as to discourage Calidore's identification and to insist upon the class difference between them. What looks like a description of the Golden Age and the ease of rural life that might appeal to all turns out, instead, to be a statement about Meliboe specifically—his poverty in relation to others:[18]

> Surely my sonne (then answer'd he againe)
> If happie, then it is in this intent,
> That hauing small, yet doe I not complaine
> Of want, ne wish for more it to augment,
> But doe my selfe, with that I haue, content;
> So taught of nature, which doth litle need
> Of forreine helpes to lifes due nourishment:
> The fields my food, my flocke my rayment breed;
> No better doe I weare, no better doe I feed.
> (6.9.20.1–9)

As in the Golden Age, nature provides what he needs. Meliboe does not need to labor: the fields and flocks do all the work. But the context of the statement is not, as one might expect, nature's bounty or Golden Age prosperity, even though Meliboe goes on in the following stanza to describe living in a bountiful version of nature where he can hunt, fish, and drink from streams. It is rather the independence of his "nourishment" from "forreine helpes"; the fields and flocks are all that he has. Knowledge of his ownership ("my food" and "my flocke") is informed at least in part by the fact that others have more. He drives this point home with the repetition of "better" in the last line: he does not look for better because that would bring him outside his station.

Perhaps more importantly, Meliboe's version of another familiar pastoral convention—the contrast between the town and the country—underlines the shepherd's status as rural laborer, and in this way returns briefly to the "realism" associated with the early eclogues of Mantuan and Barclay:

> The time was once, in my first prime of yeares,
> When pride of youth forth pricked my desire,
> That I disdain'd amongst mine equall peares
> To follow sheepe, and shepheards base attire:
> For further fortune then I would inquire.
> And leauing home, to roiall court I sought;
> Where I did sell my selfe for yearely hire,
> And in the Princes gardin daily wrought:
> There I beheld such vainenesse, as I neuer thought.
> (6.9.24.1–9)

In this passage the shepherd life is characterized both by "baseness" and the labor of "equall peares" in following sheep, and the court, in contrast, is characterized by a desire for advancement: his "pride." This conventional contrast typically serves to condemn the life of the court by associating it with pride and greed, and this is how Meliboe intends it to work: he ends up missing the "lowly quiet life" and returns to the shepherd world (6.9.25.9). But this contrast does little to promote the countryside or the shepherd life. Its inefficacy has to do with the instability of the contrast between "sweet peace" and "vainenesse" as attributes of the country and court respectively, an instability that characterizes the eclogues of Alexander Barclay as well. If the countryside is so perfect, why then do shepherds long to leave it? Like Coridon, in Barclay's first eclogue, Meliboe has an ambition generated by the experience of the shepherd world, specifically the baseness of labor. In other words, his knowledge of his class position among "equall peares" (but peers in laboring) is the problem. Only further knowledge of what that class position means, a period of service as a waged laborer (a gardener) who cannot rise up the social ladder (his efforts are "in vaine"), causes him to accept his original "estate," whose inescapability is made clear because it is one that he "inherits" (6.10.25.4, 9).

While this pastoral convention is certainly familiar, it appears here in a new context. This is not, as in Barclay and Mantuan, a dialogue between shepherds but a dialogue between a shepherd and a courtier who desires to join the pastoral world. In this context, the speech indirectly draws our attention to the particular blindness to class that makes the courtly version of pastoral possible. If Calidore were paying attention, he would see that he could not possibly identify with Meliboe or take on the role of shepherd. Spenser suggests that impossibility by drawing our attention to a potential parallel that, rather paradoxically, cannot be one. That is, Meliboe's journey at first glance resembles Calidore's in reverse: instead of the courtier coming to the countryside, the shepherd goes to the court. But on closer look, these journeys have nothing in common: a courtier in the countryside might be a shepherd, but a shepherd at court is a wage laborer. Moreover, Spenser highlights Calidore's own failure of logic. If to be a shepherd is to accept one's class position, then Calidore's donning of the shepherd disguise (his rejection of his own class) ensures that he is, in fact, not one.

Consequences of Reading Pastoral

Perhaps the most obvious consequence of reading (or misreading) the pastoral is the desire to live a shepherd life, and Spenser describes Calidore's transformation in great detail:

> And doffing his bright armes, himselfe addrest
> In shepheards weed, and in his hand he tooke,
> In stead of steelehead speare, a shepherds hooke,
> That who had seene him then, would haue bethought
> On Phrygian Paris by Plexippus brooke,
> When he the loue of fayre Oenone sought,
> What time the golden apple was vnto him brought.
>
> (6.9.36.3–9)

Calidore puts on the shepherd clothes and becomes a figure in neoclassical pastoral. He looks like Paris, not a laborer nor even Meliboe nor the other shepherds he has encountered. As Alpers writes, this is a "glamorous form of pastoralism."[19] Calidore's appropriation, which stands for the courtier's appropriation, at first seems harmless enough, misguided and self-deluding as it is; Spenser at this point seems to want us to view Calidore with some distance but not necessarily condemn his escapism.[20]

But Calidore's embrace of the pastoral life and his insistence that it is a retreat from the violence of the world are shown to be fantasy when the brigands attack. Perhaps more compellingly, the attack offers a kind of perverse parallel to Calidore's appropriation; it is the dark underside of Calidore's "capture" of shepherd identity.[21] This parallel between Calidore and the brigands emerges first and most obviously in the structure of the narrative: from the perspective of the reader it is only because Calidore has joined the shepherd world (has decided to live his fantasy) that the brigands attack. This logic appears in the Argument to canto 10, in which Spenser links the climax of the pastoral moment (Calidore's vision of Colin Clout) with the attack on the shepherds:[22]

> Calidore sees the Graces daunce,
> To Colins melody:
> The whiles his Pastorell is led,
> Into captiuity.
>
> (p. 988)

Of course, this argument does not exactly match what happens. Calidore returns from his encounter with Colin Clout, then he goes off again to hunt and only at that moment is Pastorella carried off. Nevertheless, readers are forced to see the two events as conjoined ("the whiles"): first Colin Clout and the Dance of the Graces, then the captivity of the shepherds.

That the Dance of the Graces is a kind of culmination of the pastoral cannot be doubted, but to view it only as such is to neglect why Spenser juxtaposed it with the brigands' attack. It is true that the Dance of the Graces offers a transcendent vision of poetry, and in

184 *Transforming Work*

this sense its value to Calidore is clear. But the episode also demonstrates that it is precisely this transcendence that endangers the shepherds.[23] This episode replays Calidore's first vision of the shepherd world, but this is an echo that reduces (or elides) what is distinctly shepherdly about that world. As in the initial encounter with the shepherds, Calidore comes upon a shepherd piping and people dancing (6.10.10–12). Both episodes place a beautiful woman, who represents more than just a woman, at the center of the circle. Once again, Calidore desires to hear a shepherd, here Colin Clout, explain what he has seen. Finally, Calidore has the same reaction to his vision; he wants to join the world that he sees before him:

> And with delight his greedy fancy fed,
> Both of his words, which he with reason red;
> And also of the place, whose pleasures rare
> With such regard his sences rauished,
> That thence, he had no will away to fare,
> But wisht, that with that shepheard he mote dwelling share.
> (6.10.30.4–9)

With the final line of the stanza, Calidore insists upon Colin as a shepherd, but what has been omitted in this echo of the first vision of the shepherds is the sheep, precisely that aspect that would make Colin a laborer (as well as a poet, as in the eclogue form). In other words, pastoral has been refined to a particular version that Alpers identifies as "silvestris," with its emphasis on songs and a mythical landscape (in contrast to the aspect of pastoral concerned with everyday life—"agrestis").[24] But Calidore does not recognize this moment as myth, and his desire, his "greedy fancy," demonstrates how bizarrely he has understood that myth to be a reality in which he could live: where "he mote dwelling share." In this way, Spenser makes clear that the particular problem with pastoral is that the reader desires to live in the world that he reads about, even if that world does not actually exist.

That the reader should understand Calidore (and his particular misreading) as causing the brigands' attack is underlined by the reappearance of his favored metaphor for describing the safety of the shepherd world in contrast to the dangers of the outside world: storms. Immediately before the attack, Calidore finally wins Pastorella:

> And ioyed long in close felicity:
> Till fortune fraught with malice, blinde, and brute,
> That enuies louers long prosperity,
> Blew vp a bitter storme of foule aduersity.
> (6.10.38.6–9)

In this context this passage is entirely conventional, yet it also echoes Calidore's conversation with Meliboe, in which he insists (three times) that the shepherd world is safe from storms. As that conversation demonstrates, Calidore's (and therefore the courtly reader's) view of the storms reveals a misreading of the pastoral world and an insistence on a grossly exaggerated version of *otium*, in which the shepherds are free of both labor and the dangers of the outside world. For this reason, this figurative storm (the attack of the brigands) reads less as punishment for love of a woman than punishment for love of the pastoral world. Of course, the text suggests these two loves are inseparable: this version of pastoral is synonymous with Pastorella herself.

Otium informed the pastoral episode, and the attack of the brigands offers a kind of perversion of *otium*: the brigands, like Calidore, desire leisure. This is not the happy leisure that Calidore sees in the shepherd world—the piping and dancing, the lack of concern for worldly wealth. Rather, it is violent and parasitic, hardly "ease" at all. It is, nevertheless, characterized by an absence of labor, specifically agricultural labor:[25]

> It fortuned one day, when Calidore
> Was hunting in the woods (as was his trade)
> A lawlesse people, Brigants hight of yore,
> That neuer vsde to liue by plough nor spade,
> But fed on spoile and booty, which they made
> Vpon their neighbours, which did nigh them border,
> The dwelling of these shepheards did inuade,

And spoyld their houses, and them selues did murder;
And droue away their flocks, with other much disorder.
(6.10.39.1–9)

So that we see the parallels between the brigands and the shepherds, the passage offers a kind of inversion (or perversion) of Calidore's first vision of the shepherdly world at the beginning of canto 9. In both cases Calidore is a laborer whereas the others are not: his hunt of the Blatant Beast is described as a kind of labor, since he is sweating, and here he is hunting again, an activity described as "his trade." In addition, wealth is not produced by labor: the shepherds see their worldly wealth only in terms of their sheep (who graze without their having to attend to them), and the brigands live off of booty (or thieving). Perhaps most importantly, this version of *otium* demonstrates what has been repressed in the portrait of happy shepherds who do not work but still have wealth: someone must work for others to live. Those who do not work (those who have leisure), then, must by definition exploit those who do.

This link between *otium* and the exploitation of others is underlined by the plans the brigands have to sell the shepherds into slavery:[26]

Meaning so soone, as they conuenient may,
For slaues to sell them, for no small reward,
To merchants, which them kept in bondage hard
Or sold againe. . . .
(6.10.43.3–6)

Here the shepherds are re-imagined as slave laborers: "in bondage hard." And Spenser insists upon their new status as slaves four times in two stanzas: the merchants are looking for "bondmen" and "slaues" and "bondslaues" (6.11.9.3, 6; 6.11.10.2) to buy, and the shepherds are ultimately referred to as "slaues" who are to be "sold for most aduantage" (6.11.10.8–9). They have thus altered drastically from nonlaborers (in Calidore's view), caroling and piping in Golden Age prosperity, to forced laborers. What has disappeared in their trajectory, although it emerges by contrast with the brigands, is their status as free laborers, those who live by plough and spade.

In imagining slavery as a kind of consequence (or the necessary dark side) of the Arcadian pastoral, Spenser uncovers the ideology of labor that informs the classical pastoral: that *otium* emerges out of a material reality, the concrete and inescapable fact that Romans used slaves and the "derogatory attitudes toward work" that were produced out of this association between slavery and manual labor.[27] We cannot know for certain what exactly Spenser knew about slavery in the classical period. Slavery does appear in the most authoritative pastoral text known to Spenser; Virgil's first eclogue begins with an account of how Tityrus has freed himself from "servitio," which was rendered as "bondage" in the first translation of Virgil's *Eclogues* in 1575.[28] In addition, the sixteenth century witnessed a growing interest in Roman treatises on agriculture, such as those by Cato, Varro, and Columella, which were first printed on the Continent and then made their way to England.[29] In these treatises rural labor in particular is associated with slaves.[30] But none of these texts offers an extended account of Roman slavery or labor relations more generally, and Spenser could hardly have understood, as we do now, that Rome was a "slave society."[31] Nevertheless, we can assume that his reading of classical pastoral could have reached the same conclusion as modern pastoral theorists—namely, that these texts insist on the superiority of leisure to labor.[32] While many theorists of pastoral see this superiority as natural and, therefore, not worth investigating further, Spenser's violent juxtaposition of leisure and slavery suggests that he does not.

The strangeness of Spenser's juxtaposition has not been appreciated, most likely because of assumptions that Spenser is merely following his sources in introducing slavery into the pastoral romance. It is true that what seems to be the closest analogue, Longus's Greek pastoral romance *Daphnis and Chloe*, which was translated from the French and published in England in 1587, has provided Spenser with a number of plot elements for the pastoral episode.[33] Both Pastorella and Chloe are nobly born, abandoned as infants, raised by herdsmen, and violently separated from their lovers when they are captured. But it is Daphnis (the youth) and not Chloe who is captured by pirates, and neither he nor Chloe is threatened with being sold into slavery.[34] In short, Spenser might have taken both pastoral leisure and the brigands from Longus but the specific link between pastoral and slavery is new to him. One other important source, Ludovico Ariosto's *Orlando Furioso* (1516; 1532), might have provided some of the material concerning slavery (especially "white slavery"), but this text does not connect slavery with shepherds.[35] Like Pastorella, Isabella in the *Furioso* is captured, held in a cave, and will be sold (although not to merchants but to a sultan).[36] It is also worth noting that while Pastorella is indebted to both Chloe and Isabella, Spenser distinguishes her victimhood from each of these texts. Pastorella is not the only victim of the brigands in the *Faerie Queene*. In the initial account of the attack, the emphasis is on the shepherds as a group and their fate as "bondmen."

Another assumption that seems to have blinded critics, particularly theorists of pastoral, to the strangeness of Spenser's juxtaposition of leisure and violence is that the *otium* of classical pastoral was taken over unquestioningly in the Elizabethan period. Louis Montrose's influential historicist reading of Elizabethan pastoral finds that "the derogatory attitudes" of classical pastoral were entirely compatible with ideas about laborers circulating in Elizabethan England: "the culture of the Elizabethan elite stigmatized the varied tasks of manual labor," and "celebrations of pastoral otium conventionalize the relative *ease* of the shepherd's labors."[37] But such a perspective assumes that the "stigmatizing" of rural labor precedes the pastoral and makes its *otium* both understandable and attractive to Elizabethan readers, not that the pastoral helped to generate *for the first time* a particular kind of condemnation of labor. There is a great difference between "stigmatizing rural labor," which, I would like to suggest, is new to depictions of the countryside at this time, and "stigmatizing rural laborers," which is not new (either in this period or any other). As discussed in previous chapters, the medieval and Reformation literary tradition, with which Spenser was quite familiar, valued rural labor highly, whether this labor was "real" or a figure for other kinds of labor. Even the early eclogues by Barclay, Mantuan, and Spenser himself do not uniformly embrace *otium*, as discussed in previous chapters. However much Elizabethans might have seen manual labor as the marker of a lower class (the peasants), they still paid lip service to the traditional three-estate model in which laborers are praised for their necessary role in supporting the commonwealth. Such a value did not, could not, die away so quickly even in the face of the new emphasis on leisure that Montrose finds in the Elizabethan period. Indeed, Andrew McRae finds a pervasive interest in an "agrarian sense of national identity" during this time; Robert Cecil's remark to Parliament in 1601 is perhaps typical: "I do not dwell in the Country, I am not acquainted with the Plough: But I think that whosoever doth not maintain the Plough destroys this Kingdom."[38] In sum, we should not assume that the *otium* of classical pastoral, which emerged from a culture of slavery, was so easily accepted, that it might not, in fact, have been perceived as both alien and a threat.

The threatening and alien nature of slavery, of the particular fate that Calidore has brought down on the shepherds, is underlined by the topicality of Spenser's brigands. These are indebted to the Barbary Coast pirates who sold European captives into slavery in Turkey and North Africa during this time period.[39] Like the Britons captured by Barbary pirates, Spenser's shepherds belong to an English landscape, however much it is imagined as "Faerie"; they are, therefore, "white slaves" captured by outsiders. Spenser's brigands are a markedly foreign threat. As Nabil Matar points out in his introduction to *Piracy, Slavery, and Redemption: Barbary Captivity Narratives from Early Modern England*, the English were familiar with this form of slavery since they themselves were at times victims of it: between 1577 and 1704, twenty-three captivity accounts were published in England.[40] The first captivity narrative of an Englishman was published in 1589, seven years before book 6 of the *Faerie Queene*, in Richard Hakluyt's *Principal Navigations*. It concerns a John Fox, who was captured by the Turks and held in Alexandria in the 1560s and 1570s before he escaped and returned to England. It is important to note that Fox did indeed consider himself to be a slave, not just a prisoner: his account refers twice to being delivered from "thralldom and bondage" when he escapes.[41]

More specifically, Spenser's brigands, like their Barbary counterparts, enjoy a close relationship with merchants, to whom they intend to sell the shepherds. On the Barbary Coast, slavery also co-existed with other commercial exchanges and could be seen as part of the spectrum of international trade.[42] Finally, Spenser specifically invokes the name *Barbary* in his description of the brigands when the captain looks at Pastorella:

> At sight whereof his *barbarous* heart was fired,
> And inly burnt with flames most raging whot
> That her alone he for his part desired.
> (6.11.4.1–3; emphasis added)

During the late sixteenth century, *barbarous* and *Barbary* were interchangeable words for heathens, Saracens, and the uncivilized; they thus represent a non-Christian foreignness. At the same time, however, the odd parallels—between Calidore's and the captain's desire for Pastorella and between Calidore's and the brigands' desire for *otium*—suggest that the brigands' foreignness is only an extreme version of Calidore's, who is in the position of being outside the shepherd community and looking in.

Spenser's allusion to the non-Christian, barbarous aspect of the brigands raises a question about the relationship between the pastoral and Christianity. Does the contrast between the brigands and the shepherds, whom the reader is surely intended to see as native Englishmen and women, indicate that the shepherds are Christians as well? This implication emerges only by contrast, in the same way that the shepherds' status as rural laborers is evident only when they are under attack. There are, of course, no direct references to Christianity in the pastoral episode, but this absence makes the appearance of potentially Muslim pirates more confusing, not less. It is as if those non-Christian aspects of Arcadian pastoral that cannot be easily assimilated to Spenser's own contemporary world—its imbrication with slavery, its parasitic desire for *otium*—have been excised from the episode and then imagined symbolically as a threat. Of course, it is difficult to make arguments about the absence of Christianity, which is certainly not expected in Arcadian pastoral, but Spenser's previous pastoral, the *Calender*, moves continuously (even if contradictorily or choppily) between Christian and neoclassical modes, as did the early eclogues of Googe and Barclay.

The enslavement of the shepherds is never realized in the text, but this does not mean that the shepherds are rescued from the fate that Calidore has brought down upon them: all the shepherds except Coridon and Pastorella die in the crossfire between the brigands and the merchants who are to buy the shepherds. In other words, the shepherd world associated with Meliboe (indeed Meliboe himself) comes to a definite and violent end. Calidore's claims for the ease and safety of the shepherd life are shown, in the most dramatic fashion, to be very mistaken. This massacre is not, however, quite the end of the pastoral for Calidore, and his final "version" of pastoral underlines the material realities of shepherding, reversing and revising the initial Arcadianism of his sojourn. First, when Calidore begins his search for Pastorella with Coridon, "[b]oth [are] clad in shepheards weeds agreeably" (6.11.36.2). This stanza explicitly echoes the first time Calidore embraces the shepherd identity by dressing up, which also occurs at stanza 36 (of canto 9) but with an important difference. Now the shepherd clothes are merely a disguise for Calidore, who is "armed priuily" underneath his shepherd clothing (6.11.36.4).

Similarly, his first sight of the shepherds reprises his first encounter with the shepherd world in canto 9, when he views the sheep and shepherds from a distance: "They chaunst, vpon a hill not farre away, / Some flockes of sheepe and shepheards to espy" (6.11.36.6–7). Again, this reprise revises our understanding of the shepherd world to emphasize its material reality. Whereas Calidore's first encounter thematized the shepherds' *otium*, both their happy piping and dancing and their freedom from concerns about "worldly wealth," this encounter emphasizes labor. When the brigands ask Calidore and Coridon who they are,

> they answer'd, as did appertaine,
> That they were poore heardgroomes, the which whylere
> Had from their maisters fled, and now sought hyre elsewhere.
> (6.11.39.7–9)

In this version, *otium* has disappeared entirely. Shepherds are now "poore" and oppressed by "maisters." They are part of (not separate from) contemporary labor relations, a point made clear in the repetition of "hyre" in stanza 40: the thieves immediately make an offer to "hyre them well," and Spenser adds that the men "earnest tooke, / To keepe their flockes for litle hyre and chepe" (6.11.40.2, 6–7). Instead of independent owners, whose sheep are their only but prized possession, shepherds are waged laborers in a precarious position, the same as gardeners at court. Indeed, the use of *hire* should remind us of Meliboe's stint as a gardener. It would seem, then, that the destruction of the pastoral world has enabled Calidore to see the material realities that his fantasy had previously occluded.

This brief interlude, of acting like a "real shepherd," is not the beginning of another version of pastoral but the end of the episode. After rescuing Pastorella, Calidore takes her back to the court, and the reader discovers that Pastorella is not a shepherdess at all but a member of the nobility. The pastoral that she symbolizes is, fittingly, a product of the court, not of the countryside. As the future of pastoral quite simply because she is a survivor of the pastoral episode, Pastorella represents a mode that not only does not need the countryside, a fact that is hardly surprising for readers of pastoral, but is positively dangerous to it, even the cause of its destruction. At this point, one might ask, what of Coridon? After all, his survival would seem to indicate the continuity of the world that Calidore first encounters. In the final lines of the canto, Calidore gives all the sheep to Coridon:

> And also all those flockes, which they before
> Had reft from Meliboe and from his make,
> He did them all to Coridon restore.
> (6.11.51.6–8)

With the word *restore* the reader can here imagine that Coridon begins the shepherd world again, and this is, indeed, how one critic has read this moment; it is a kind of restoration of the pastoral.[43]

But this world could hardly match what has been lost: despite receiving his sheep, Coridon is no Meliboe. Indeed, Coridon's status as a shepherd is somewhat uncertain since he is the one shepherd who has been called a "cowherd" (6.10.35.3). This word is an alternate spelling of *coward* but one that associates cowardice with a particular rustic occupation.[44] His "cowherdize" changes his pastoral status, first and foremost because it introduces a distinction between kinds of shepherds (6.10.37.3). Coridon is not, tellingly, described as a shepherd but as "fit to keepe sheepe" (6.10.37.4). Second, his "cowherdize" ultimately renders him a waged laborer. That is, he refuses to help Calidore rescue Pastorella until he has been paid:

> But he, whose hart through feare was late fordonne,
> Would not for ought be drawne to former drede,
> But by all meanes the daunger knowne did shonne:
> Yet Calidore so well him wrought with meed,
> And faire bespoke with words, that he at last agreed.
> (6.11.35.5–9)[45]

In thus distinguishing Coridon from the other shepherds, Spenser seems to anticipates W. W. Greg's argument that "pastoral literature must not be confounded with that which has for its subject the lives, the ideas, and the emotions of simple and unsophisticated mankind, far from the centres of our complex civilization."[46] Pastorella and Meliboe belong to "pastoral literature" and Coridon to "simple and unsophisticated mankind." But Spenser locates both groups within his pastoral episode, thus initially "confounding" them, and the distinction between them is ultimately produced by the pastoral itself. That is, part of the work of pastoral literature is first to invoke "keeping sheepe" as particularly desirable (as in Calidore's first vision of the shepherds) and then to dismiss it with contempt. In this way, Spenser both draws our attention to the "real" rural laborer, with whom he engaged at far greater length in his *Calender*, and underlines his unsuitability for the pastoral mode.

The bleakness of the *Faerie Queene*'s pastoral episode demonstrates the dangers posed by the pastoral mode for the individual, dangers that have long been appreciated. As Calidore's experience makes clear, the pastoral can be a trap, an escape from duty that must be renounced for the "quest" to continue. But the dangers of pastoral are also social, as Spenser takes pains to reveal. In offering readers happy, piping shepherds, instead of hardworking laborers or laborers vulnerable to storms, oppressions, or poverty itself, the pastoral radically alters the framework through which the elite might see the "real" laborers in their midst.

Afterword

The Secret History of Pastoral

The Renaissance has long been understood as a beginning: of the individual, of historical consciousness, of new literary forms. Although medievalists have tried to modify this defining characteristic by pushing these beginnings back to the Middle Ages, it still remains to be seen whether the Renaissance can ever shake its associations with beginnings or even with modernity itself, an association inherent in the newer term *early modern*.[1] The persistence of the Renaissance's special status, its distinctness vis-à-vis the Middle Ages, might have something to do with the way the discipline of literature is organized. After all, jobs in English departments still tend to follow traditional period divisions. But it may also be the case that this special status persists because of early modern writers' own insistence on novelty, as made clear in E. K.'s dedicatory epistle to Edmund Spenser's *Shepheardes Calender*, which he describes as a "new worke" by a "new Poete."[2] Readers can hardly fail to be influenced by repeated claims that the material they are reading is new, even if they might suspect at times that it is not.

The pastoral provides compelling evidence for the novelty of the early modern period, at least in terms of literary forms and modes, but on some reflection this novelty should appear to be less a statement of fact than a desire. It has, therefore, been the goal of this study to investigate the nature of that desire by asking what the "new" would set aside or occlude. That is, this study has been interested in uncovering a kind of secret history for pastoral in precisely those kinds of texts from which pastoral writing seeks to distance itself, at least according to most theorists of pastoral: not just "what the country was really like," a realism that may well have been impossible at the time, but the religious polemic of the Reformation and the outraged rhetoric of the enclosure treatises. My contention has been that this secret history should be read alongside the standard literary histories: the well-known and much-studied rediscovery of Virgil's *Eclogues* as well as what is typically, and often dismissively, called the "native tradition" of medieval plowman writings and ecclesiastical pastoral. To read these histories together is to tie pastoral much more closely both to its medieval past and to the rural labor that it so often seems to set aside. These histories are not so much secret because the pastorals themselves repress them but because they have been largely ignored and neglected by theorists who would prefer to see a universal appeal to pastoral, one that transcends time and place. For Paul Alpers, the leading theorist of pastoral, what defines pastoral is precisely the representative quality of shepherds, that they are a kind of disguise that remains consistent in its meaning: the universal concerns of love or the unchanging vulnerability of the humble to the people in power.[3] In keeping our focus on the disguise, we always ask what it means for the courtier or poet to dress up as a shepherd; we rarely ask what it means (or could have meant) for the "real" shepherd that others desire to use him as a disguise. Perhaps we cannot do otherwise, but we should at least be aware of what it is we are doing when we see pastoral as its own hermetic literary tradition, set apart from other kinds of writing rural labor. As John Barrell reminds us in describing the landscape painting of the eighteenth and nineteenth centuries,

> we should ask ourselves whether we do not still, in the ways we admire Gainsborough, Stubbs, and Constable, identify with the interests of their customers and against the poor they portray. I am not suggesting that we should do anything else, merely that we should ask what it is that we do; to identify with the exhausted and underfed labourers is impossible for us, and would be insulting if it were not.[4]

It is still worth noting that even those pastorals that seem most committed to universalizing and generalizing the shepherd, to celebrating the disguise he affords, can offer a meditation on what is at stake in their own invention and on the relationship between the various literary histories that produced this disguise. I'd like to conclude, therefore, with a brief meditation on a text that has often been understood to embrace fully the new pastoral mode: Shakespeare's *As You Like It*. Although there is critical disagreement on how escapist this pastoral might be, there is no disagreement on (or even discussion of) the provenance of this version of pastoral.[5] Unlike the eclogues discussed in this study, which have long been understood to include "medieval elements," this pastoral can be (and is) explained purely in relation to the rediscovery of Virgil and the popularity of pastoral modes at the end of the sixteenth century. After all, whatever social criticism the play offers in its pastoral is largely mediated through the contrast between the city/court and the country, a contrast central to Virgil and then taken up by sixteenth-century pastoral writers. Even the topical allusions that link the play to "what the country was really like" in the sixteenth century—that is, to enclosure and outlawry—are here easily assimilated to that contrast. They do not work at cross-purposes or remind us of alternative literary traditions.[6] The reference to Robin Hood, for example, which might suggest a mode of representing the countryside indebted to outlawry instead of pastoral, is assimilated to Virgil's Golden Age. Perhaps more importantly, there are no plowmen or shepherd-priests who haunt this pastoral with the particular kind of reformism with which they had long been associated.

For these reasons, this play could be said to represent the early modern pastoral in a way that the eclogues of Googe, Barclay, and Spenser do not, and it is no mistake that Alpers discusses the play at length in his study *What Is Pastoral?*[7] It is as if pastoral has consumed or colonized all other modes for representing rural life. Nevertheless, the play includes a surprising and lucid moment in which it reflects on the process of transformation by which the medieval laborer becomes the shepherd and by which his reformist potential is undercut. That transformation is imagined precisely in terms of the secret history outlined here—the association of shepherds with agrarian capitalism and the separation of good works from rural labor. When

Rosalind, who is disguised as Ganymede, enters the Forest of Arden with Celia, she asks the old shepherd Corin for help with food and lodging. Corin replies,

> Fair sir, I pity her [Celia],
> And wish, for her sake more than for mine own,
> My fortunes were more able to relieve her.
> But I am shepherd to another man,
> And do not shear the fleeces that I graze.
> My master is of churlish disposition,
> And little recks to find the way to heaven
> By doing deeds of hospitality.[8]

This description of the shepherd's life stands out because it is one of the few moments in which the characters address what, specifically, shepherds do—that is, their labor. Elsewhere the shepherds are defined primarily through the Virgilian tradition of singing and wooing. Indeed, this scene has introduced the audience to the two shepherds, Corin and Silvius, as they enter conversing about love, thus suggesting that the play will understand their "shepherdliness" largely in those terms. In directing us away from love to the economics of shepherd life, the passage offers a startling reminder of the association between shepherds and agrarian capitalism, not from the idealizing perspective of many eclogues but from the critical perspective of the anti-enclosure tracts, from the plowman himself.[9] That is, Corin is a wage laborer who does not own his own sheep and is, therefore, impoverished. He cannot share even the simple fare that appears in the pastoral meals described in earlier eclogues, for example, the chestnuts, cheese, and whey in Googe's third eclogue (3.169–70). Moreover, Corin describes the sheep not as sheep per se but as commodities, the fleeces that are sheared for the master to sell (presumably). A sense of loss (of what Corin wants to do for Rosalind and Celia but cannot) thus pervades the passage. The nature of that loss is fully realized in the final lines, when Corin invokes the language of good deeds. Not only are these deeds not done (by the master), they cannot be. The symbolic world of medieval Christianity, in which the worker is associated with good works, has been interrupted and destroyed by the master's greed and, more implicitly, by the Reformation itself: the master will not get to heaven by doing good deeds, but neither can anyone else.

The singularity of Corin's speech within the play should be noted. All other characterizations of the shepherd world are entirely positive. Indeed, in the next act, Corin seems to correct the bleak vision of his situation with which he started. In his conversation with Touchstone about shepherd life he states, "Sir, I am a true labourer. I earn that I eat, get that I wear; owe no man hate, envy no man's happiness; glad of other men's good, content with my harm; and the greatest of my pride is to see my ewes graze and my lambs suck."[10] In revising his earlier speech, Corin links the virtuous rural laborer of the medieval and Reformation tradition to the new pastoral: he exemplifies both the "trewe swynkere" of Chaucer's Plowman and the simple, self-sufficient life described by Spenser's Meliboe in book 6 of the *Faerie Queene*. But the earlier speech should enable us to read the pause between the first statement and the second as a gap: between the plowman, whose manual labor benefits his neighbor and therefore constitutes acts of charity, and the shepherd, who labors only for himself and whose self-sufficiency may be admirable but is in fact lacking in Christian charity. Corin is here glad of others' good and does not envy his neighbor, but he does not actively contribute to his neighbor's good nor does he love him. The gap between these two symbolic worlds, of work and works on the one hand, and shepherdly self-sufficiency on the other, grows wider with each version of pastoral, but for Corin, and perhaps for Shakespeare himself, these worlds remain tenuously linked, and the "true labourer" provides a distant echo of the special capacity of the rural laborer to reform the social world.

NOTES

Introduction

1. This list can only be partial given the great number of studies of pastoral. For the first category, see William Empson, *Some Versions of Pastoral* (New York: New Directions, 1974); Patrick Cullen, *Spenser, Marvell, and Renaissance Pastoral* (Cambridge, MA: Harvard University Press, 1970); the essays by Louis Montrose (on which see note 3); and Susan Snyder, *Pastoral Process: Spenser, Marvell, Milton* (Stanford: Stanford University Press, 1998). For the second, see Paul Alpers, *What Is Pastoral?* (Chicago: University of Chicago Press, 1996) and Judith Haber, *Pastoral and the Poetics of Self-Contradiction* (Cambridge: Cambridge University Press, 1994). Two studies move relatively seamlessly between classical and Renaissance poets: Renato Poggioli, *The Oaten Flute: Essays on Pastoral Poetry and the Pastoral Ideal* (Cambridge, MA: Harvard University Press, 1975) and Andrew Ettin, *Literature and Pastoral* (New Haven, CT: Yale University Press, 1984), thus obscuring the absence of the medieval period. Both Annabel Patterson's *Pastoral and Ideology: Virgil to Valéry* (Berkeley: University of California Press, 1987) and W. W. Greg's *Pastoral Poetry and Pastoral Drama* (London: Bullen, 1906) claim to address the medieval period, but the focus is on Petrarch (Patterson) or Petrarch, Boccaccio, and Mantuan (Greg) rather than on English texts. Helen Cooper's *Pastoral: Mediaeval into Renaissance* (Ipswich: Brewer, 1977) is, of course, an exception, and I will discuss it further below.

2. Paul Alpers, "Pastoral and the Domain of Lyric in Spenser's *Shepheardes Calender*," *Representations* 12 (1983): 83–100.

3. See Louis Montrose, "'The perfect paterne of a Poete': The Poetics of Courtship in *The Shepheardes Calender*," *Texas Studies in Literature and Language* 21(1979): 34–67; "'Eliza, Queene of shepheardes,' and the Pastoral of Power," *English Literary Renaissance* 10 (1980): 153–82; and "Of Gentlemen and Shepherds: The Politics of Elizabethan Pastoral Form" *ELH: English Literary History* 50 (1983): 415–59.

4. For the first printings of Virgil, see *Bucolica Virgilii* (London, 1512; STC 24813) and (London, 1514; STC 24814). For the popularity of Mantuan and the use of his eclogues as a school text, see the introduction to the edition by Wilfred P. Mustard, ed., *The Eclogues of Baptista Mantuanus* (Baltimore, MD: Johns Hopkins University Press, 1911), 35–40. See also Lee Piepho, *Holofernes' Mantuan: Italian Humanism in Early Modern England* (New York: Peter Lang, 2001), 45–92.

5. Cooper, *Pastoral*, 8. The appendix included by Christopher Baswell in his study of the *Aeneid* in England indicates that the *Eclogues* survive along with the *Aeneid* in quite a number of manuscripts (*Virgil in Medieval England* [Cambridge: Cambridge University Press, 1995], 285–308). And yet, they seem to have generated little interest among writers in the vernacular. Baswell notes that the *Eclogues* did not have "topical appeal" for medieval writers (5).

6. Greg, *Pastoral Poetry*, 18. Indeed, Cooper includes very few examples of a "vernacular pastoral tradition" in English: "*bergerie* is thinly scattered among lyrics and poetic homilies, and even the great literary flowering of the reign of Richard II produced little apart from the metrical romance of *King Edward and the Shepherd*. English *bergerie* reaches its perfection, however, in the mystery plays, and in the work of the Wakefield Master in particular, whose shepherds represent the very best of the native English part of the tradition" (49). In other words, her claim for a medieval pastoral in England rests on essentially one play of uncertain date.

7. Cooper, *Pastoral,* 48–49.

8. Montrose quite briefly compares the late medieval shepherd plays to Elizabethan pastorals but finds them to be entirely at odds: "the social milieu and informing spirit of the Nativity pageants are alien to Elizabethan pastorals" (Montrose, "'Eliza, Queene of Shepheardes,'" 161).

9. Although Cooper begins by claiming that "the foundations of the great achievements of Renaissance pastoral were laid" in the Middle Ages (100), she later notes that the Italian, Arcadian version of pastoral "came to displace the mediaeval traditions almost entirely" (105) and consistently points out the novelty of Italian pastoral.

10. Alexander Barclay, *The Eclogues of Alexander Barclay from the Original Edition by John Cawood*, ed. Beatrice White, Early English Text Society, original series, vol. 175 (1928; repr., London: Oxford University Press, 1960), lxii–lxiii; Cooper, *Pastoral*, 124–25; Edmund Spenser, *The Shepheardes Calen-*

der, in *The Yale Edition of the Shorter Poems of Edmund Spenser*, ed. William A. Oram, Einar Bjorvand, Ronald Bond, Thomas H. Cain, Alexander Dunlop, and Richard Schell (New Haven, CT: Yale University Press, 1989), 5. See also Michael Murrin, "Mantuan and the English Eclogue" (Ph.D. diss., Yale University, 1965), who observes that "the English eclogue begins on a distinctly non-classical basis" (108).

11. *General Prologue* to the *Canterbury Tales*, in *The Riverside Chaucer*, ed. Larry D. Benson (Boston: Houghton Mifflin, 1987), 1.514. Hereafter all references to the *Canterbury Tales* will appear parenthetically in the text and will refer to the fragment and line numbers.

12. Greg, *Pastoral Poetry*, 21–22.

13. Mantuan was not the first author to fuse ecclesiastical pastoral with the eclogue form, but he was the most influential. Neither Petrarch's nor Boccaccio's eclogues, which share this characteristic, were as influential in England as Mantuan's. See Greg, *Pastoral Poetry*, 24–27. On Boccaccio's eclogues, see Murrin, "Mantuan and the English Eclogue," 40–52.

14. Cullen, *Spenser, Marvell*, 2–3.

15. See, similarly, Alpers, who sees the classical pastoral as the primary mode, to which the ecclesiastical is later grafted without much difficulty: "most modifications in the depiction of shepherds involve the ways in which it is claimed that they are representative. The biblical metaphor of the good shepherd enters pastoral for this reason" (*What Is Pastoral?*, 27).

16. Poggioli, *The Oaten Flute*, 122.

17. For Spenser, see A. C. Hamilton, "Spenser and Langland," *Studies in Philology* 55 (1958): 533–48; and, more briefly, Robert Lane, *Shepheards Devises: Edmund Spenser's "Shepheardes Calender" and the Institutions of Elizabethan Society* (Athens: University of Georgia Press, 1993), 86–88; and David Norbrook, *Poetry and Politics in the English Renaissance*, rev. ed. (Oxford: Oxford University Press, 2002), 53–54. For Barclay, see Cooper, *Pastoral*, 119; and Sukanta Chaudhuri, *Renaissance Pastoral and Its English Developments* (Oxford: Clarendon Press, 1989), 117, 119–23.

18. Langland includes a short section of ecclesiastical pastoral in the C-text (C9.257–70), which I discuss at greater length in chapter 1.

19. For a brief overview of the manuscripts, see William Langland, *Piers Plowman: The C-text*, ed. Derek Pearsall (1978; repr., Exeter: University of Exeter Press, 1994), 20–24; and *Piers Plowman: The B Version*, ed. George Kane and E. Talbot Donaldson (London: Athlone Press, 1975), 1–15. For the "afterlife" of *Piers* in the sixteenth century, see Anne Hudson, "Epilogue: The Legacy of *Piers Plowman*," in *A Companion to "Piers Plowman*," ed. John A. Alford (Berkeley: University of California Press, 1988), 251–66; Mike Rodman Jones, *Radical Pastoral, 1381–1594: Appropriation and the Writing of Religious Controversy* (Burlington, VT: Ashgate, 2011), 85–131; Sarah Kelen, *Langland's*

Early Modern Identities (New York: Palgrave Macmillan, 2007), 43–76; and John King, *English Reformation Literature: The Tudor Origins of the Protestant Tradition* (Princeton, NJ: Princeton University Press, 1982), 322–39.

20. *The Towneley Plays*, ed. Martin Stevens and A. C. Cawley, Early English Text Society, supplementary series, vols. 13 and 14 (Oxford: Oxford University Press, 1994), 1:xv.

21. "I playne Piers which cannot flatter" (London, ?1547; STC 19903a). Although Jones uses the term "pastoral" in his study, he confines it to the plowman texts and sets aside the relationship between what he calls "radical pastoral" and the more mainstream version of pastoral discussed here (*Radical Pastoral*, 2–3).

22. Three studies propose a kind of continuity between representations of medieval and early modern rural laborers (plowmen and shepherds): Andrew Hadfield, "Foresters, Ploughmen, and Shepherds: Versions of Tudor Pastoral," in *The Oxford Handbook of Tudor Literature, 1485–1603*, ed. Mike Pincombe and Cathy Shrank (New York: Oxford University Press, 2009), 537–54, provides a useful survey that claims Tudor representations of rural laborers were an "authentic link to a past that was disappearing" (538). Ordelle G. Hill, *The Manor, the Plowman, and the Shepherd: Agrarian Themes and Imagery in Late Medieval and Early Renaissance English Literature* (Cranbury, NJ: Associated University Presses, 1993), makes a broad argument about the transition from plowman to shepherd but does little more than survey the texts that contain these figures. The most comprehensive study is that by Andrew McRae, *God Speed the Plough: The Representation of Agrarian England, 1500–1660* (Cambridge: Cambridge University Press, 1996); chapter 1 looks at the way in which commonwealth literature took up the medieval complaint tradition regarding agrarian matters.

23. See Montrose, "'Eliza, Queene of shepheardes,'" 172; Poggioli, *Oaten Flute*, 1; and Cullen, *Spenser, Marvell*, 2, respectively.

24. Greg, *Pastoral Poetry*, 3.

25. Alpers insists that the "representative anecdote" of pastoral is "herdsmen and their lives" (*What Is Pastoral?*, x), and Montrose writes, "as far as Elizabethan writers were concerned, pastorals were indeed poems about shepherds" ("Of Gentlemen and Shepherds," 416).

26. Annabel Patterson, *Pastoral and Ideology*, 134. See also Murrin, who distinguishes between the "*otium* of Arcadia in later tradition" and the "pause in the work of the rustic world" that one finds in Virgil; "the presence of labor is generally recognized in the eclogues [of the Latin tradition]" ("Mantuan and the English Eclogue," 35–36).

27. *Rambler* 37, July 24, 1750, in *The Works of Samuel Johnson*, ed. Arthur Murphy (London: J. Haddon, 1820), 4:239–40, 239.

28. McRae's study, *God Speed the Plough*, persuasively links together a wide range of texts about rural life and rural laborers: complaint, ser-

mons, books of husbandry, chorography, and pastoral. I am sympathetic to his argument about the transition from the "manorial community" to agrarian capitalism in the sixteenth century, as will become clearer below, but I am more interested in the role of medieval literature in shaping the pastoral mode.

29. Alastair Fowler, "Georgic and Pastoral: Laws of Genre in the Seventeenth Century," in *Culture and Cultivation in Early Modern England: Writing and the Land*, ed. Michael Leslie and Timothy Raylor (Leicester: Leicester University Press, 1992), 84.

30. Mantuanus, *Eclogues of Baptista Mantuanus*, 122n45.

31. Mantuanus, *The eglogs of the poet B. Mantuan Carmelitan*, trans. George Turberville (London, 1567; STC 22990), B1v–B2r.

32. Alpers, *What Is Pastoral?*, 175.

33. Anthony Low, *The Georgic Revolution* (Princeton, NJ: Princeton University Press, 1985).

34. Fowler, "Georgic and Pastoral," 85.

35. On the introduction of georgic, see, for example, Alastair Fowler, "The Beginnings of English Georgic," in *Renaissance Genres: Essays on Theory, History, and Interpretation*, ed. Barbara Kiefer Lewalski (Cambridge, MA: Harvard University Press, 1986), 105–25. Fowler does see some influence in Spenser's poetry (112–13) but argues throughout that the conception of georgic in the sixteenth and seventeenth centuries was much looser than it later became. Fowler sees this generic fluidity as a result of Hesiod's influence.

36. Low, *Georgic Revolution*, 8.

37. See, for example, Greg, *Pastoral Poetry*, 71; John King, *Spenser's Poetry and the Reformation Tradition* (Princeton, NJ: Princeton University Press, 1990), 15 and throughout chapter 1.

38. I have been influenced in my thinking about the representation of rural laborers by John Barrell, *The Dark Side of the Landscape: The Rural Poor in English Painting, 1730–1840* (New York: Cambridge University Press, 1980). Although this study takes up a later period, its account of the ideology guiding the representation of the rural poor and of the intersection of pastoral and more "realistic" accounts is illuminating.

39. Peter L. Berger and Thomas Luckmann, *The Social Construction of Reality: A Treatise in the Sociology of Knowledge* (Garden City, NY: Anchor Books, 1967), 96, 99.

40. Marshall Sahlins, *Islands of History* (Chicago: University of Chicago Press, 1985), vii.

41. Ibid., ix.

42. R. H. Tawney, *The Agrarian Problem in the Sixteenth Century* (1912; repr., New York: Harper and Row, 1967).

43. Raymond Williams, *The Country and the City* (New York: Oxford University Press, 1973), 18.

Chapter 1. Medieval Traditions of Writing Rural Labor

1. Alpers, *What Is Pastoral?*, x; and Montrose, "Of Gentlemen and Shepherds," 416.

2. Patrick Cullen, *Spenser, Marvell*, 3; and Alpers, *What Is Pastoral?*, 22.

3. Alpers lists the agreed-upon features of pastoral as "idyllic landscape, landscape as a setting for song, an atmosphere of *otium*, a conscious attention to art and nature, herdsmen as singers, and, in the account of gifts, herdsmen as herdsmen" (*What Is Pastoral?*, 22).

4. See *Song of the Husbandman*, in *Medieval English Political Writings*, ed. James M. Dean (Kalamazoo, MI: Medieval Institute Publications, 1996), 251–53.

5. On this history, see Paul Freedman, *Images of the Medieval Peasant* (Stanford: Stanford University Press, 1999), 16–55.

6. Cooper discusses "shepherd revels" only in terms of a French tradition and provides little evidence that this aspect of the "realistic" account of shepherdly activities that she calls *bergerie* entered the English tradition (*Pastoral*, 57, 62, 68). Indeed, she acknowledges that the English tradition was more narrowly defined and more religious in its outlook (48). My approach to the plays has been informed by readings that link them to Langland's poem and its influences: Elizabeth Salter, "The Annunciation of the Shepherds in Later Medieval Art and Drama," in *English and International: Studies in the Literature, Art and Patronage of Medieval England*, ed. Derek Pearsall and Nicolette Zeeman (Cambridge: Cambridge University Press, 1988), 272–92; and Ruth Nisse, *Defining Acts: Drama and the Politics of Interpretation in Late Medieval England* (Notre Dame, IN: University of Notre Dame Press, 2005), 75–94. Salter notes that the shepherd plays reflect two (somewhat conflicting) interests: the older exegetical approach inherited from liturgical drama, and the newer devotional approach associated with Cistercian and Franciscan spirituality, which emphasizes the humanity of Christ (282).

7. Alpers describes pastoral in terms of the "pretense that poor, humble, and deprived people are simply free to sing and woo" (*What Is Pastoral?*, 6).

8. Montrose, "Of Gentlemen and Shepherds," 427.

9. Martin Stevens, *Four Middle English Mystery Cycles: Textual, Contextual, and Critical Interpretations* (Princeton, NJ: Princeton University Press, 1987), 95, 116–17; Robert Mayer Lumiansky and David Mills, eds., *The Chester Mystery Cycle: Essays and Documents* (Chapel Hill: University of North Carolina Press, 1983), 169, 174. For a discussion of the Towneley manuscript and its dating and provenance, see Stevens and Cawley, eds., *The Towneley Plays*, 1:xvi–xxii.

10. Stevens, *Four Middle English Mystery Cycles*, 109–12.

11. Cooper, *Pastoral*, 47 and chapter 2 more fully.

12. All quotations from the Chester plays are from R. M. Lumiansky and David Mills, eds., *The Chester Mystery Cycle*, 2 vols., Early English Text Society, supplementary series, vols. 3 and 9 (London: Oxford University Press, 1974, 1986). References to the Chester plays will appear parenthetically in the text and will refer to the play title and line numbers. In this quotation and all others from primary sources, the author has spelled out any abbreviations (e.g., "&") used in the original.

13. All quotations from the Towneley plays are from Stevens and Cawley, eds., *The Towneley Plays*. References to the Towneley plays will appear parenthetically in the text and will refer to the play title and line numbers.

14. Nicola Masciandaro argues that medieval views of work are informed by a dialogue between two positions on work, one of which is an idealization of the laborlessness of the Golden Age (*The Voice of the Hammer: The Meaning of Work in Middle English Literature* [Notre Dame, IN: University of Notre Dame Press, 2007], 68). He does not, however, provide any evidence for the popularity of this view, and his only example is Chaucer's "Former Age." Elsewhere he apparently contradicts himself by acknowledging that medieval views of the Golden Age do not consistently exclude work (66). Nevertheless, his claim that this poem isn't just nostalgic, but also a critique of the kind of nostalgia that goes with Golden Age thinking, is certainly compatible with my argument here—that Chaucer has a very difficult time imagining the "Golden Age" in the positive terms we find in his sources (112).

15. V. J. Scattergood, "The Short Poems," in *Oxford Guides to Chaucer: The Shorter Poems*, by A. J. Minnis with V. J. Scattergood and J. J. Smith (New York: Oxford University Press, 1995), 487.

16. See the notes to "The Former Age" in *The Riverside Chaucer*, 1083–84. Scattergood also suggests Virgil's Fourth Eclogue as a possible source ("The Short Poems," 486).

17. *Boece*, book 2, metrum 5, lines 1–3, in *The Riverside Chaucer*, 415.

18. "The Former Age," lines 9–10, in *The Riverside Chaucer*, 650–51. Hereafter all references to this poem will appear parenthetically in the text.

19. Virgil, *The Eclogues*, trans. Guy Lee (New York: Penguin, 1980), p. 57, 4.18–19, 29.

20. A. V. C. Schmidt, "Chaucer's Golden Age," *Essays in Criticism* 26 (1976): 103.

21. Jean de Meun and Guillame de Lorris, *The Romance of the Rose*, trans. Charles Dahlberg (Hanover, NH: University Press of New England, 1983), p. 330, lines 20115 ff. Hereafter all references will appear parenthetically in the text and will refer to line numbers.

22. On the association between "gnodden" and gnawing, see Andrew Galloway, "Chaucer's 'Former Age' and the Fourteenth-Century

Anthropology of Craft: The Social Logic of a Premodernist Lyric," *ELH: English Literary History* 63 (1996): 539.

23. Virgil, *The Eclogues*, p. 57, 4.21–22.

24. Masciandaro divides the stanzas into three groupings, 3–2–3, with the first and last group of three stanzas describing the former age, and the middle group describing the transition to now (*Voice of the Hammer*, 107). This structure doesn't give a good sense of how the poem skips around, because even within the descriptions of the former age the negations keep us focused on the "now," as does the end of the poem.

25. Galloway, "Chaucer's 'Former Age,'" 545.

26. Stephen Knight describes the process by which the voices of rural laborers are "redirected by the religious positioning of the bulk of the authors" as "clericization" in his essay, "The Voice of Labour in Fourteenth-Century Literature," in *The Problem of Labour in Fourteenth-Century England*, ed. James Bothwell, P. J. P. Goldberg, and W. M. Ormrod (Rochester, NY: Boydell and Brewer, 2000), 102.

27. Stephen Barney, "The Plowshare of the Tongue: The Progress of a Symbol from the Bible to *Piers Plowman*," *Mediaeval Studies* 35 (1973): 261. The most famous practitioner of exegetical criticism was D. W. Robertson Jr. See, for example, his *A Preface to Chaucer: Studies in Medieval Perspectives* (Princeton, NJ: Princeton University Press, 1962).

28. G. R. Owst, *Literature and Pulpit in Medieval England* (Cambridge: Cambridge University Press, 1933), 554.

29. There are a few medieval husbandry manuals with brief descriptions of rural laborers and their "offices." The most popular are collected in Dorothea Oschinsky, ed., *Walter of Henley and Other Treatises of Estate Management* (Oxford: Clarendon Press, 1971). On sixteenth-century husbandry manuals, see McRae, *God Speed the Plough*, 135–68, and Joan Thirsk, "Making a Fresh Start: Sixteenth Century Agriculture and the Classical Inspiration," in *Culture and Cultivation in Early Modern England: Writing and the Land*, ed. Michael Leslie and Timothy Raylor (Leicester: University of Leicester Press, 1992), 15–34.

30. Lee Patterson, *Negotiating the Past* (Madison: University of Wisconsin Press, 1987), 3–39; David Aers, *Piers Plowman and Christian Allegory* (London: Edward Arnold, 1975), 2–6.

31. H. Marshall Leicester Jr., *The Disenchanted Self: Representing the Subject in the Canterbury Tales* (Berkeley: University of California Press, 1990), 36.

32. The scholarship here is vast. See, for example, David Aers, *Faith, Ethics, and Church: Writing in England, 1360–1409* (Rochester, NY: Boydell and Brewer, 1999); Sarah Beckwith, *Christ's Body: Identity, Culture, and Society in Late Medieval Writing* (London: Routledge, 1993); James Simpson, *1350–1547: Reform and Cultural Revolution*, vol. 2 of *The Oxford English Literary History*

(Oxford: Oxford University Press, 2002); and Nicholas Watson, "Censorship and Cultural Change in Late-Medieval England: Vernacular Theology, the Oxford Translation Debate, and Arundel's Constitutions of 1409," *Speculum* 70 (1995): 822–64.

33. Fredric Jameson, *The Political Unconscious: Narrative as a Socially Symbolic Act* (Ithaca, NY: Cornell University Press, 1981), 30.

34. Ibid.

35. See Knight, "The Voice of Labour," 103. For similar discussions on how visual representations of labor are ideological, see the following two studies on the Luttrell Psalter, famous for its images of peasants working: Michael Camille, *Mirror in Parchment: The Luttrell Psalter and the Making of Medieval England* (Chicago: University of Chicago Press, 1998); and Richard K. Emmerson and P. J. P. Goldberg, "'The Lord Geoffrey had me made': Lordship and Labour in the Luttrell Psalter," in *The Problem of Labour in Fourteenth-Century England*, ed. James Bothwell, P. J. P. Goldberg, and W. M. Ormrod (Rochester, NY: Boydell and Brewer, 2000), 43–63.

36. What is happening with "real" rural labor in this period is far too large a topic to address here. I am more interested in the way in which these medieval representations intersect with pastoral than in their intersections with the real historical conditions of the rural laborer. For an introduction to labor in this period, see the essays collected in *The Problem of Labour*. For the intersections between historical records and literary representations, see Kellie Robertson, *The Laborer's Two Bodies: Labor and the "Work" of the Text in Medieval Britain, 1350–1500* (New York: Palgrave Macmillan, 2006).

37. *John Mirk's Festial*, ed. Susan Powell, 2 vols., Early English Text Society, original series, vol. 334 (New York: Oxford University Press, 2009), 1:63, lines 105–13.

38. Ibid., 1:65, lines 205–9.

39. Thomas Wimbledon, *Redde Rationem Vilicationis Tue: A Middle English Sermon of the Fourteenth Century*, ed. Ione K. Knight (Pittsburgh, PA: Duquesne University Press, 1967), 67, lines 98–100.

40. Ibid., 123, lines 1021–26.

41. Barney, "The Plowshare of the Tongue," 261; Langland, *Piers Plowman: The B Version*, 5.542. Hereafter all references will appear parenthetically in the text and will refer to the Passus and line numbers. I use the B-text in this discussion but will refer to the C-text when it diverges.

42. D. W. Robertson Jr. and Bernard F. Huppé, *Piers Plowman and Scriptural Tradition* (Princeton, NJ: Princeton University Press, 1951), 6–7.

43. Here I am drawing particularly on the work of David Aers, *Piers Plowman and Christian Allegory* and *Community, Gender, and Individual Identity* (New York: Routledge, 1988); Elizabeth Kirk, "Langland's Plowman and the Recreation of Fourteenth-Century Religious Metaphor," *Yearbook of Langland*

Studies 2 (1988): 1–21; and Anne Middleton, "Acts of Vagrancy: The C Version 'Autobiography' and the Statute of 1388," in *Written Work: Langland, Labor, and Authorship*, ed. Steven Justice and Kathryn Kerby-Fulton (Philadelphia: University of Pennsylvania Press, 1997), 208–317. All of these critics have discussed the poem's complicated view of labor and the laborer.

44. Paul Freedman describes the value assigned to peasant labor in terms of "three types of peasant virtue": "first, their labor is valuable because all of society depends on it; second their suffering confers a spiritual merit that will be rewarded; and third, their labor is virtuous in itself and emblematic of divine labor and sacrifice" (*Images of the Medieval Peasant*, 229).

45. Larry Scanlon, "Langland, Apocalypse, and the Early Modern Editor," in *Reading the Medieval in Early Modern England*, ed. Gordon McMullan and David Matthews (Cambridge: Cambridge University Press, 2007), 54–55.

46. Woodburn O. Ross, ed., *Middle English Sermons*, Early English Text Society, original series, vol. 209 (London: Humphrey Milford, Oxford University Press, 1960), 224.

47. See James Simpson, "Spirituality and Economics in Passus 1–7 of the B Text," *Yearbook of Langland Studies* 1 (1987): 83–103.

48. Although see David Aers, who writes, "The Passus begins by reaffirming the traditional social model [of the three estates] in the face of the challenges it has had to sustain, in the poem and in the poet's society. Here the knight so loves the peasant that he offers to share his manual labour and the peasant so loves maintaining the knightly class in its power and privilege that he quickly rejects the offer in favor of the status quo" (*Community, Gender*, 41).

49. Simpson, *Reform and Cultural Revolution*, 363.

50. On the Statute of Laborers that informs this episode, see Middleton, "Acts of Vagrancy," and Lawrence Clopper, "Need Men and Women Labor? Langland's Wanderer and the Labor Ordinances," in *Chaucer's England: Literature in Historical Context*, ed. Barbara Hanawalt (Minneapolis: University of Minnesota Press, 1992), 110–29.

51. Although Simpson argues that labor is not "purely spiritual" here; see *Reform and Cultural Revolution*, 364.

52. Aers, *Community, Gender*, 54.

53. See J. A. Burrow, "The Action of Langland's Second Vision," *Essays in Criticism* 15 (1965): 247–68.

54. A great amount of scholarly attention has been devoted to why, exactly, Piers tears the Pardon. See, most recently, Emily Steiner, *Documentary Culture and the Making of Medieval English Literature* (Cambridge: Cambridge University Press, 2003), 121–42.

55. In using "bely ioye," I am following an alternate reading for line 123. The Kane-Donaldson edition has "bilyue" but notes that "bely ioye" is a variant in a large number of manuscripts (377n123). It is also worth noting that this speech is deleted from the C-text. Nevertheless, the C-text does at-

tempt to spiritualize Piers's meaning in his next appearance: the Banquet with Pacience. Piers is now affiliated with Pacience and begins his mysterious speech with "*Pacientes vincunt*" (C15.138).

56. Aers, *Community, Gender*, 54–55.

57. Ross, *Middle English Sermons*, 15.

58. See, for example, *English Wycliffite Sermons*, 5 vols., ed. Anne Hudson and Pamela Gradon (Oxford: Oxford University Press, 1983–96), vol. 1, sermon 11, lines 52–61.

59. James Dean, ed., *Piers the Plowman's Crede*, in *Six Ecclesiastical Satires* (Kalamazoo, MI: Medieval Institute Publications, 1991), 1.

60. Ibid., 5–8.

61. Kirk mentions "holy simplicity" as a tradition that the figure Piers taps into ("Langland's Plowman," 16).

62. The quotation is taken from Augustine's *Confessions*. Here I follow the translation in William Langland, *The Vision of Piers Plowman*, 2nd edition, ed. A. V. C. Schmidt (London: J. M. Dent, 1995), 164n455.

63. See William Langland, *Piers Plowman: The A Version*, ed. George Kane (Berkeley: University of California Press, 1988), 11.307–13. This poem ends, significantly, with a slightly different version of what is here line 470: "Wiþoute penaunce at here partyng, into þe heiȝe blisse" (A11:313).

64. In C the passage is somewhat revised:

"Haue me excused," quod Clergie, "be Crist, but in scole,
Shal no such motyef be meued for me, bote þere,
For Peres loue þe palmare ȝent, þat inpugnede ones
Alle kyne connynges and alle kyne craftes,
Saue loue and leute and lowenesse of herte,
And no tixst ne taketh to preue this for trewe
Bote *dilige deum et proximum*, and *domine quis habitabit*,
And preueth by puyre skile inparfyt alle thynges,
Nemo bonus,
Bote lele loue and treuthe, that loth is to be founde."
(C15.129–36)

65. On this dual meaning of "clergie" in the poem, see Fiona Somerset, *Clerical Discourse and Lay Audience in Late Medieval England* (Cambridge: Cambridge University Press, 1998), 13, 22–61.

66. The C-text is quite similar, C21.182–90.

67. Simpson also finds penance—repayment and labor—fundamental to this church (*Reform and Cultural Revolution*, 362–63).

68. The most comprehensive study on the relationship between Langland's poem and the Peasants' Revolt remains Steven Justice, *Writing and Rebellion: England in 1381* (Berkeley: University of California Press, 1996), 102–39.

212   Notes to Pages 37–42

69. Thomas Walsingham, *The St. Albans Chronicle: The Chronica Maiora of Thomas Walsingham*, 2 vols., ed. John Taylor, Wendy R. Childs, and Leslie Watkins (New York: Oxford University Press, 2003), 1:547–48. Also quoted by Justice, *Writing and Rebellion*, 110.

70. Justice, *Writing and Rebellion*, 111. As this quotation suggests, Justice claims that Wyclif's calls for disendowment and valorization of the poor were central in giving peasants a language to appropriate for themselves. This argument is certainly compelling, but it seems difficult to prove that "the people" had access to Wyclif's language. They did, however, have access to the symbolic imagination around work, which was central to homiletics; R. F. Green argues that the letters were part of "the world of the popular preacher" ("John Ball's Letters: Literary History and Historical Literature," in *Chaucer's England: Literature in Historical Context*, ed. Barbara Hanawalt [Minneapolis: University of Minnesota Press, 1992], 187).

71. See the chapter "Social Concepts in the English Rising of 1381," Rodney Hilton, in *Class Conflict and the Crisis of Feudalism: Essays in Medieval Social History* (London: Hambledon Press, 1985), 225.

72. Brinton writes, "Reuerendi patres et domini: Inter cetera que spectant ad officium pastorale tria sunt precipue perimplenda: primo quod pastor oues erroneas et dispersas laboriose querere studeat et vnire; secundo quod oues vnitas studiose regere satagat et cum debita vigilancia custodire; tercio quod ouibus custoditis si tempestas immineat mortem debet animose perpeti et subire." See Thomas Brinton, *The Sermons of Thomas Brinton, Bishop of Rochester (1373–1389)*, 2 vols., ed. Sister Mary Aquinas Devlin, Camden Society 3rd Series, vols. 85–86 (London: Offices of the Royal Historical Society, 1954), 33.

73. Ibid., 33. See similarly Karlfried Froehlich, ed., *Biblia Latina cum Glossa Ordinaria*, vol. 4 (Turnhout: Brepols, 1992) on John 10:1–18.

74. Hudson and Gradon, eds., *English Wycliffite Sermons*, vol. 1, sermon 48, lines 87–89.

75. Jill Mann, *Chaucer and Medieval Estates Satire* (Cambridge: Cambridge University Press, 1973), 55–58.

76. John Gower, *Confessio Amantis*, in *John Gower's English Works*, 2 vols., ed. G. C. Macaulay, Early English Text Society, extra series, vols. 81 and 82 (London: Kegan Paul, 1900–1901), vol. 1, Prol. 390–95.

77. Hudson and Gradon, eds., *English Wycliffite Sermons*, vol. 1, sermon 48, lines 1–2.

78. See *The Plowman's Tale*, in *Six Ecclesiastical Satires*, ed. James Dean (Kalamazoo, MI: Medieval Institute Publications, 1991). See also Andrew N. Wawn, "The Genesis of *The Plowman's Tale*," *Yearbook of English Studies* 2 (1972): 21–40.

79. Salter, "The Annunciation," 280; Nisse, *Defining Acts*, 77. But Nisse sees the Towneley plays as atypical, to a certain degree, as commentary on

the other shepherd plays, an attempt to bring them closer to the ideology of Langland's poem concerning poverty and prophecy (77 ff).

80. Salter, "The Annunciation," 277.

81. Their attention to the literal brings them much closer to the definition of pastoral that goes with the early modern period, a focus on herdsmen and their lives (Alpers, *What Is Pastoral?*, x).

82. The plays are, thus, more interested in representing language politics, the boundary between clergy and laity, than they are in the shepherds' capacity to provide a foil for something else (the court or the corruption of the church), as pastoral is taken to do in the early modern period.

83. Nisse, *Defining Acts*, 81–82.

84. Cooper, *Pastoral*, 76; and Salter, "The Annunciation," 278, respectively.

85. See Nisse, *Defining Acts*, 89–92, on the shepherds as exegetes.

86. Ibid., 79.

87. Stevens and Cawley, eds., *The Towneley Plays*, 2:121n660.

Chapter 2. The Invention of the English Eclogue

1. Cooper, *Pastoral*, 8. See also the appendix of Virgil manuscripts compiled by Baswell in *Virgil in Medieval England*, 285–308.

2. *The Eclogues of Baptista Mantuanus*, 35. For Virgil's eclogues, see *Bucolica Virgilii* (London, 1512; STC 24813). These were printed again by de Worde in 1514 and 1522 and translated by Abraham Fleming in 1575 as *The bucolikes of Publius Virgilius Maro* (London, 1575; STC 24816).

3. "To my dearly loved friend, Henry Reynolds, Esq. of Poets and Poesy," in *The Poetical Works of Michael Drayton, Esq.* (Edinburgh, 1793), 548, quoted in *Eclogues of Baptista Mantuanus*, 40. On the use of Mantuan in schools, see 36–40.

4. Spenser, "Generall Argument" of *The Shepheardes Calender*, line 4, p. 22.

5. Alpers claims that Spenser was the first writer of eclogues in "Pastoral and the Domain of Lyric," 83. Even Sukanta Chaudhuri, who includes Alexander Barclay in his study, claims that the *Calender* "virtually inaugurates English Renaissance pastoral" (*Renaissance Pastoral*, 5).

6. On Barclay, see Chaudhuri, *Renaissance Pastoral*, 116–25; Cooper, *Pastoral*, 118–23; and Murrin, "Mantuan and the English Eclogue," 108–10. Each of these scholars emphasizes Barclay's inferiority to Spenser. For Cooper, Barclay is still writing *bergerie* (the medieval traditions for writing shepherds) and does not find the "dynamic solutions" of the Elizabethans to the problems of writing pastoral (118–19). For Chaudhuri, Spenser is superior because

he moves away from Barclay's satiric model (123). For Murrin, Barclay is "a-pastoral" (108).

7. Alpers, in *What Is Pastoral?*, skips from Virgil to Spenser. See Louis Montrose, "'The perfect paterne of a Poete,'" "'Eliza, Queene of shepheardes,'" and "Of Gentlemen and Shepherds."

8. Cooper and Chaudhuri do, of course, include both authors, but neither of them is particularly interested in describing a theory of a mode: they take the mode largely as a given.

9. Alpers sees the herdsmen and their lives as a kind of representative anecdote (*What Is Pastoral?*, 24). Other studies of pastoral also emphasize the centrality of shepherds to the pastoral in order to limit a definition that had come to include almost any depiction of the countryside. See Montrose, "Of Gentlemen and Shepherds," 425, and Cooper, *Pastoral*, 2.

10. Jameson, *The Political Unconscious*, 99. See further on the "ideology of form," 98–100.

11. For both Cooper and Chaudhuri, Barclay's shepherds are "English peasants" who are linked with plowmen in "demotic literature" (*Pastoral*, 119; *Renaissance Pastoral*, 121, respectively). Googe, in contrast, does not raise these questions for critics because he is entirely uninterested in "native tradition" (*Pastoral*, 124) and does not have "any consistent conception of the pastoral" (*Renaissance Pastoral*, 131), although, as I shall demonstrate below, he is more troubled by "English peasants" than his work might at first appear.

12. See Jones, *Radical Pastoral*, 4 and more fully 85–131 on the shifting anticlericalism of the plowman figure.

13. Chaudhuri sees Barclay as far more sympathetic to the peasant. He claims that Barclay's eclogues "emphasize the poverty and hardship of the shepherd's life" and that Barclay was influenced by the *Piers Plowman* tradition in writing his shepherds (*Renaissance Pastoral*, 117, 119–23).

14. Pierre Macherey, *A Theory of Literary Production*, trans. Geoffrey Wall (1978; repr., London: Routledge and Kegan Paul, 2006), 106.

15. Barclay, *Eclogues of Alexander Barclay*, lxii–lxiii. Hereafter all references will appear parenthetically in the text and will refer to eclogue and line numbers.

16. Spenser, *The Shepheardes Calender*, Epistle, lines 177 and 178, p. 19.

17. Barclay's adaptations and revisions are discussed by John Richie Schultz in "The Method of Barclay's Eclogues," *Journal of English and Germanic Philology* 32 (1933): 549–71.

18. This is the terminology used by Murrin, who identifies two kinds of eclogues: the moral (indebted to Mantuan) that influences Barclay and the idealized (Virgilian) ("Mantuan and the English Eclogue," 108, 112). Such a division is conventional: the editors of Spenser's *Shepheardes Calender* use "Mantuanesque" (critical) and "Arcadian" (idyllic) following Cullen's study, *Spenser, Marvell*, 5.

19. Dean, ed., *Piers the Plowman's Crede*, 421.
20. Williams, *The Country and the City*, 16. See also Annabel Patterson, *Pastoral and Ideology*, 134.
21. *The eglogs of the poet B. Mantuan Carmelitan*, A3v. Hereafter all references will appear parenthetically in the text and will refer to this edition.
22. Empson, *Some Versions of Pastoral*, 22.
23. See, for example, Montrose, "Of Gentlemen and Shepherds," 427, and Poggioli, *The Oaten Flute*, 6.
24. "The Clerk's Tale," in *The Riverside Chaucer*, 4.1162.
25. John Gower, *Vox Clamantis*, in *The Complete Works of John Gower: Latin Works*, ed. G. C. Macaulay (London: Oxford University Press, 1902), vol. 4, book 5, lines 651–52; translated by Eric Stockton in *The Major Latin Works of John Gower* (Seattle: University of Washington Press, 1962), 210.
26. Paul Freedman claims that the majority of images were negative but "favorable images gained currency" in the Middle Ages (*Images of the Medieval Peasant*, 2). On peasants as animals, see 53–54, 139–40.
27. John Gower, *Confessio Amantis*, vol. 1, book 4, lines 2226, 2229.
28. *The Eclogues of Mantuan*, trans. George Turberville, ed. Douglas Bush (New York: Scholars' Facsimiles and Reprints, 1977), ii.
29. Freedman, *Images of the Medieval Peasant*, 63.
30. See Walsingham, *St. Albans Chronicle*, 1:547–48. Both Nicola Masciandaro and Paul Freedman discuss the circulation of the proverb and its ambiguity: it could be used to demand social change or not; see *Voice of the Hammer*, 59–65, and *Images of the Medieval Peasant*, 60–66, respectively. For discussion of the sermon more generally, see Justice, *Writing and Rebellion*, 102–3 and 108–9. For other medieval appearances of this proverb, see Bartlett Jere Whiting, ed., *Proverbs, Sentences, and Proverbial Phrases from English Writings Mainly Before 1500* (Cambridge, MA: Harvard University Press, 1968), A38, p. 4.
31. Walsingham, *St. Albans Chronicle*, 1:547–48.
32. From "The Tree of Common Wealth: A Treatise by Edmonde Dudlay," excerpt printed in R. H. Tawney and Eileen Power, eds., *Tudor Economic Documents*, 3 vols. (London: Longmans, 1924), 3:15–16.
33. What is striking is that Mantuan includes this same distinction in the seventh eclogue, but it occurs in an entirely different context. That eclogue specifically has to do with a shepherd's conversion, and, therefore, it invokes the association between shepherds and priests. Galbula states, in Turberville's translation,

> As Sages sayde, when God
> eche creature gan to make,
> (No trifles I will tell, but such
> of yore as Vmber spake)

> Both Clownish countrey wights
> and Shephierdes he ordainde:
> The Tylman tough, vnmilde, in ci-
> uill nurture neuer trainde,
> Much like the lumpish clay
> that Culter doth controll:
> The Shephierd of a softer kinde
> a sielly hurtlesse soule.
> As simple as the Sheepe,
> deuoide of wrathfull gall.
>
> (K2r)

34. Barnabe Googe, *Eclogues, Epitaphs, and Sonnets*, ed. Judith M. Kennedy (Toronto: University of Toronto Press, 1989), 1.25–28. Hereafter all references to the eclogues will appear parenthetically in the text and will refer to eclogue and line numbers. References to the editor's commentary will appear in the notes and use page numbers.

35. Chaudhuri finds in it the "art-pastoral" that is indebted to the Italian model (*Renaissance Pastoral*, 130). Yet Chaudhuri and Cooper see Googe as inconsistent; he is still indebted to medieval traditions, although by "medieval" they mean merely that he uses moral allegory. See Cooper, *Pastoral*, 124–25.

36. Montrose, "Of Gentlemen and Shepherds," 421.

37. Inquiries concerning the image may be made to ProQuest, 789 E. Eisenhower Parkway, Box 1346, Ann Arbor, MI 48106-1346; telephone: 734.761.4700; email: *info@proquest.com*; webpage: *http://www.proquest.com*.

38. Googe, *Eclogues*, 198–99.

39. Montrose, "Of Gentlemen and Shepherds," 421–33.

40. The editor writes, "neither he [Neville in his preface] nor Googe shows any consciousness of breaking new ground" (Googe, *Eclogues*, 17).

41. Empson, *Some Versions of Pastoral*, 11.

42. For the confession, see Walsingham, *St. Albans Chronicle*, 1:498–500.

43. Hilton, *Class Conflict*, 222 and 225.

44. Googe, *Eclogues*, 154.

45. Ibid., 19.

46. Andy Wood, *The 1549 Rebellions and the Making of Early Modern England* (Cambridge: Cambridge University Press, 2007), 1.

47. The commissions established by Protector Somerset to investigate enclosure "stimulated popular opposition to the gentry" (Wood, *The 1549 Rebellions*, 40). See also Stephen K. Land, *Kett's Rebellion: The Norfolk Rising of 1549* (Ipswich: Boydell, 1977), 9–10; Tawney, *Agrarian Problem*, 331–33; and Joan Thirsk, "Enclosing and Engrossing," in *The Agrarian History of England and Wales*, ed. Joan Thirsk (Cambridge: Cambridge University Press, 1967), 4:200–255. I'll return to enclosure in the next chapter.

Notes to Pages 80–85   217

48. Googe, *Eclogues*, 79–80.
49. The editor also notes the link between this poem and eclogue 3 (*Eclogues*, 158).
50. Gower, *Vox Clamantis*, book 1, lines 395 and 421–22; translated by Stockton, *Major Latin Works*, 59.
51. On the vernacular in Gower's *Vox*, see Justice, *Writing and Rebellion*, 212–13, who discusses the vernacular interruptions of Latin as "noise," or the rebels' lack of articulate speech.
52. Annabel Patterson's *Pastoral and Ideology* is centrally concerned with the ideology of pastoral: "what people think of Virgil's *Eclogues* is a key to their own cultural assumptions, because the text was so structured as to provoke, consciously or unconsciously, an ideological response" (7). But her focus is on "the intellectual's dilemma" (10), not on the ideology of labor.

Chapter 3. The Pastoral Mode and Agrarian Capitalism

1. This is in contrast, for example, to the rediscovery of classical writers on agriculture in the sixteenth century, such as Columella, a rediscovery that generated new farming practices. See Thirsk, "Making a Fresh Start."
2. Tawney, *Agrarian Problem*, 315. See also Thirsk, "Enclosing and Engrossing."
3. Karl Marx, "So-Called Primitive Accumulation," in *Capital*, vol. 1, trans. Ben Fowkes (New York: Random House, 1976), 878–79.
4. Thirsk, "Enclosing and Engrossing," 221.
5. Williams, *The Country and the City*, 18.
6. Ibid., 18.
7. Ibid., 21.
8. Montrose, "'Eliza, Queene of Shepheardes'" and "Of Gentlemen and Shepherds."
9. Montrose, "Of Gentlemen and Shepherds," 425, 427.
10. Ibid., 416, 418. McRae's study, *God Speed the Plough*, has a more materialist focus than Montrose's, but McRae's discussion of pastoral in chapter 9 largely follows Montrose in emphasizing the mystification of the countryside: "pastoral was widely exploited as a mode peculiarly suited to the idealized representation of rural conditions from the perspective of the landed gentry and nobility" (263).
11. Montrose, "Of Gentlemen and Shepherds," 456n27.
12. Thirsk, "Enclosing and Engrossing," 227–28.
13. See Tawney and Power, *Tudor Economic Documents*, 3:80–81. These are reprinted from *The Poems, English and Latin, of the Rev. Thomas Bastard*, ed. A. B. Grosart (Manchester: C. E. Simms, 1880), 37, 49, 72. See Robert Wilkinson, "A sermon preached at North-Hampton . . ." (London 1607; STC

25662), which is briefly discussed in Helen White, *Social Criticism in Popular Religious Literature* (New York: Macmillan, 1944), 171–72.

14. Montrose's remark about the "crudeness" of other historical readings seems anxious, as if he thinks it "scandalous" to assert that actual events might affect literary forms. Fredric Jameson is instructive here: "what is scandalous is not this way of thinking about a given formal change, but rather the objective event itself, the very nature of cultural change.... [T]he scandal of the extrinsic comes as a salutary reminder of the ultimately material base of cultural production and of the 'determination of consciousness by social being'" (*The Political Unconscious*, 26).

15. That the various rural laborers are linked together in this period implicitly guides Hadfield's survey in "Foresters, Ploughmen, and Shepherds."

16. Marx writes that "the methods of primitive accumulation are anything but idyllic"; they consisted of "conquest, enslavement, robbery, murder, in short, force" ("So-Called Primitive Accumulation," 874).

17. Robert Allen, *Enclosure and the Yeoman* (Oxford: Clarendon Press, 1992), 14, 30–36, 45–55.

18. Sir Thomas More, *Utopia*, trans. Ralphe Robynson, ed. J. Rawson Lumby (Cambridge: Cambridge University Press, 1908), 32. *Utopia* was first published in 1516 and translated by Ralphe Robynson in 1556.

19. McRae writes, "the anti-enclosure tirade became something of an independent subgenre of agrarian complaint, impelled by widespread anxiety surrounding the rise of great sheepmasters in the early decades of the sixteenth century" (*God Speed the Plough*, 43).

20. Williams acknowledges that the "new order" of agrarian capitalism began in the medieval period and was developing for two centuries before the Restoration (*The Country and the City*, 39). Nevertheless, he locates the important stage of this process in the seventeenth and eighteenth centuries.

21. Although Marx located the transition from feudalism to capitalism at a kind of watershed moment in the sixteenth century, more recent historians have argued for a much longer development, one that began in the late fourteenth century and continued up through the eighteenth century and beyond. A useful account of the various theories on the nature of that transition can be found in the essays collected in *The Brenner Debate: Agrarian Class Structure and Economic Development in Pre-Industrial Europe*, ed. T. H. Aston and C. H. E. Philpin (New York: Cambridge University Press, 1985).

22. Allen, *Enclosure and the Yeoman*, 21.

23. Wood, *1549 Rebellions*, 16.

24. James Holstun, "The Giant's Faction: Spenser, Heywood, and the Mid-Tudor Crisis," *Journal of Medieval and Early Modern Studies* 37 (2007): 336.

25. Jane Whittle, *The Development of Agrarian Capitalism: Land and Labour in Norfolk, 1440–1580* (Oxford: Oxford University Press, 2000), 9. In her con-

clusion, she assigns the bulk of the changes to before and after the sixteenth century (305, 315).

26. Tawney, *Agrarian Problem*, 402.

27. Holstun, "The Giant's Faction," 336. McRae also notes the significant relationship between shepherds and plowmen: "the polemics of the mid-Tudor period (examined in chapter 1) preempt a bifurcation of the respective modal significance of these two rural figures. Indeed, the Elizabethan pastoral myth of social fixity and natural gentility was formed in part *against* the powerful contemporary discourses of complaint" (*God Speed the Plough*, 268), but he does not discuss this relationship in any greater detail.

28. Langland, *Piers Plowman: The B Version*, 10.463–71.

29. *The Angels and the Shepherds* in *York Plays*, ed. Lucy Toulmin Smith (Oxford: Clarendon Press, 1885), lines 51, 52.

30. Ibid., line 128.

31. *First Shepherds' Play*, in Stevens and Cawley, *The Towneley Plays*, lines 42–47.

32. *Seneschaucie*, in Oschinsky, *Walter of Henley*, 113–17.

33. Ibid., 115.

34. Alan Everitt, "Farm Labourers," in *The Agrarian History of England and Wales*, vol. 4, ed. Joan Thirsk (Cambridge: Cambridge University Press, 1967), 4:414; Montrose, "Of Gentlemen and Shepherds," 422.

35. *General Prologue*, in *The Riverside Chaucer*, 1.533–35.

36. Gower, *Confessio Amantis*, in *John Gower's English Works*, vol. 1, Prol.1065–68.

37. Dean, ed., *Song of the Husbandman*, 1–8.

38. The Towneley play of the murder of Abel opposes the plowman and the shepherd in order to glorify the latter. But this glorification is hardly similar to the pastoral mode; Abel is obedient to God, and Cain is a bad plowman. See *Murder of Abel*, in Stevens and Cawley, eds., *The Towneley Plays*. In fact, Cain fits Gower's description of the greedy, grasping plowman in his *Vox Clamantis*.

39. Hugh Latimer, *Sermons by Hugh Latimer, Sometime Bishop of Worcester* (London: Dent, 1906), 85.

40. Ibid., 85.

41. Thirsk, "Enclosing and Engrossing," 219.

42. Tawney, *Agrarian Problem*, 318–19.

43. *Certayne Causes gathered together . . .* (London, 1552; STC 9980), A4r. Hereafter all references will appear parenthetically in the text.

44. *Pyers plowmans exhortation, vnto the lordes, knightes and burgoysses of the Parlyamenthouse* (London, 1550; STC 19905). Hereafter all references will appear parenthetically in the text. On the plowman figure in this text, see Jones, *Radical Pastoral*, 114–16.

45. See Aers, *Community, Gender*, 41.

46. Whittle, *Development of Agrarian Capitalism*, 12.

47. Robert Crowley, *The Way to Wealth* (London, 1550; STC 6096), A1r, A3r–A3v. Quoted by Helen White in *Social Criticism*, 47. For other examples, see Bernard Gilpin, *A Godly Sermon preached in . . . 1552* (London, 1630; STC 11898), 32–33, 36–37; Thomas Lever's sermon preached in 1550; the opening of the ballad "Vox Populi Vox Dei" (1547–48); and William Harrison's *Description of England* (1587) (the last three texts printed in Tawney and Power, *Tudor Economic Documents*, 3:47, 26, and 72, respectively).

48. Thirsk, "Making a Fresh Start," 15–16. Her answer is the rediscovery of classical writings on husbandry.

49. Tawney, *Agrarian Problem*, 350.

50. In Tawney and Power, *Tudor Economic Documents*, 3:67.

51. As Andrew McRae writes, enclosure is the "preeminent manifestation of covetousness in the countryside" (*God Speed the Plough*, 42).

52. More, *Utopia*, 33.

53. *The Riverside Chaucer*, 1.531.

54. Harrison, *Description of England*, in Tawney and Power, *Tudor Economic Documents*, 3:72.

55. See similarly, "Vox Populi Vox Dei":

> And thus the woyse doth mvltyplye
> amownges your grasis commynalte:
> they are in such grette penvry
> that they can nether sell ner bye,
> Such ys there extreme powertey.
> experyenes dothe it veryfye,
> as trwthe yt selfe dothe testyfye,
> this is a mervellvis mesirie
> for grasiares, and Regrateres,
> with soe many shepe-maisteres
> that of erabell grounde make pasteres,
> are they that be these wasters
> that wyll vndoe this Lande,
> yf thay contyniv and stande;
> as ye shall vnderstonnde
> by this lytell bowke.
>
> (Tawney and Power, *Tudor Economic Documents*, 3:27)

56. "Nowe a Dayes" (ca. 1520), in *Ballads from Manuscripts*, ed. F. J. Furnivall (1868–72), 93. Extract printed in Tawney and Power, *Tudor Economic Documents*, 3:18.

57. Thirsk, "Enclosing and Engrossing."

58. "Vox Populi Vox Dei," in Tawney and Power, *Tudor Economic Documents*, 3:35.

59. Thirsk, "Enclosing and Engrossing," 255.

60. Alan Everitt notes that the percentage of landless laborers grew from between one-quarter to one-third of the laboring population in the sixteenth century to almost half by the seventeenth ("Farm Labourers," 399).

61. Macherey, *A Theory of Literary Production*, 103. He writes, "the investigation into the conditions of the possibility of the work is accomplished in the answer to an explicit question, but it will not be able to seek the conditions of those conditions, nor will it be able to see that this answer constitutes a question. . . . It is this second question which, for us, defines the space of history: it reveals the work in so far as it entertains a specific but undisguised (which does not mean innocent) relation with history. We must show, through the study of an effort of expression, how it is possible to render visible the conditions of this effort—conditions of which it has no awareness, though this does not mean that it does not apprehend them: the work encounters the question of questions as an obstacle; it is only aware of the conditions which it adopts or utilises. We could account for this latent knowledge . . . by recourse to *the unconscious of the work*" (103; emphasis in the original).

62. Jameson, *The Political Unconscious*, 20.

63. Alpers, *What Is Pastoral?*, 6.

64. Pastoral is not necessarily hostile to economic considerations. In Virgil's First Eclogue, Tityrus observes that they often drive their lambs to Mantua to the market (lines 25 ff). In addition, the eclogue gives us a clear sense of the socioeconomic status of shepherds, namely, slave or free.

65. *The eglogs of the poet B. Mantuan Carmelitan*, E5r.

66. Everitt, "Farm Labourers," 418.

67. Ibid., 438–41.

68. Poggioli, *The Oaten Flute*, 23.

69. Montrose, "Of Gentlemen and Shepherds," 428.

70. The complicated views of peasants and labor are persuasively presented in Freedman, *Images of the Medieval Peasant*, 133–73 (on negative representations of peasants) and 24–39 (on labor).

71. Montrose, "Of Gentlemen and Shepherds," 423.

72. *The eglogs of the poet B. Mantuan Carmelitan*, C5v.

73. Edmund Spenser, *The Faerie Queene*, ed. Thomas P. Roche (New York: Penguin, 1978), 6.9.20.8. All references to this work refer to book, canto, stanza, and line numbers.

74. Williams, *The Country and the City*, 25.

75. *Faerie Queene*, 6.9.21.5–7.

76. Empson, *Some Versions of Pastoral*, 11; Alpers, *What Is Pastoral?*, 7.

77. Robert Brenner, "Agrarian Class Structure and Economic Development in Pre-Industrial Europe," *Past & Present* 70 (1976): 30–75. Reprinted in Aston and Philpin, *The Brenner Debate*, 10–63; see also the essays collected therein.

Chapter 4. Transforming Work

1. There is some disagreement about the role of works in early English Protestantism, particularly in the writings of William Tyndale. William Clebsch sees "theological confusion" in early Protestantism, especially in Tyndale, who, he argues, modified his earlier (more Lutheran) position on justification to embrace a "theology of contract," in which works played some role (*England's Earliest Protestants, 1520–1535* [New Haven, CT: Yale University Press, 1964], 258, 184). Carl Trueman also finds variety in English theologians' views but argues for greater consistency in Tyndale. See *Luther's Legacy: Salvation and English Reformers, 1525–1556* (New York: Oxford University Press, 1994), 83–120. Trueman agrees that works were important to Tyndale, but "justification by faith" remained "the foundation of Christian salvation" for him (197) and works were an "outward sign" (102).

2. Max Weber, *The Protestant Ethic and the Spirit of Capitalism*, trans. Talcott Parsons (New York: Scribner's, 1958), 121.

3. R. H. Tawney, *Religion and the Rise of Capitalism* (1926; repr., New Brunswick, NJ: Transaction, 1998), 82.

4. McRae, *God Speed the Plough*, 31. The most recent study of the plowman tradition in the sixteenth century acknowledges that "the strictures of this portrait [religious reformism and social conservatism] sometimes seem rather strained" (Jones, *Radical Pastoral*, 5). Jones understands the religious reformism of these Tudor texts largely in terms of anticlericalism and not, as I do, in terms of doctrinal matters; see further, 85–131.

5. See, for example, the essays in *The Beginnings of English Protestantism*, ed. Peter Marshall and Alec Ryrie (Cambridge: Cambridge University Press, 2002) and Ethan Shagan, *Popular Politics and the English Reformation* (Cambridge: Cambridge University Press, 2003).

6. Tawney, *Religion*, 82.

7. On these texts, see Jones, *Radical Pastoral*, 33–47; 85–131; Kelen, *Langland's Early Modern Identities*, 43–76; Simpson, *Reform and Cultural Revolution*, 333; and Dean, *Six Ecclesiastical Satires*. On Crowley's edition see R. Carter Hailey, "'Geuying Light to the Reader': Robert Crowley's Editions of *Piers Plowman* (1550)," *Papers of the Bibliographical Society of America* 95 (2001): 483–502; and "Robert Crowley and the Editing of *Piers Plowman* (1550)," *Yearbook of Langland Studies* 21 (2007): 143–70.

8. On Langland's commitment to the social ideology of his time as well as his potential questioning of it, see Aers, *Community, Gender*, 20–72. On the way in which Langland is typically read as socially conservative and why such an approach may be misguided, see Scanlon, "Langland, Apocalypse."

9. The scholarly consensus has been that Langland is a "semi-Pelagian." For the clearest articulation of this view, see Robert Adams, "Langland's

Theology," in *A Companion to "Piers Plowman,"* ed. John A. Alford (Berkeley: University of California Press, 1988), 95–98. Aers has recently and persuasively challenged this dominant account of Langland's theology in *Salvation and Sin: Augustine, Langland, and Fourteenth-Century Theology* (Notre Dame, IN: University of Notre Dame Press, 2009), 83–131.

10. Hudson, "Epilogue," 259. Jones argues, as I do, that Langland's poem resonated with sixteenth-century writers, although he sees its legacy in terms of its polemical language of rusticity: its mode of "imagining the politicized divide between country and city" and its anticlericalism (*Radical Pastoral*, 2, 4). In other words, he follows the scholarly consensus in seeing Langland's plowman as easily assimilable to Protestant writings.

11. On the simultaneity of the social and religious crises, at least in terms of legitimating ideas and social order, see Wood, *1549 Rebellions*, 26–30.

12. William Tyndale, *The Parable of the Wicked Mammon* in *Doctrinal Treatises and Introductions to Different Portions of the Holy Scriptures*, ed. Henry Walter (Cambridge: Cambridge University Press, 1848), 46–47. Hereafter all citations will appear parenthetically in the text. This view is repeated throughout Tyndale's works. See, for example, the prologue to his *Exposition of Matthew* (1532): "And thus ye see that faith is the thing that is affirmed to justify, of all parties. For faith in Christ's blood (which is God's promise) quieteth the conscience of the true believers: and a false faith, or trust in works (which is their own feigning), beguileth the blind hypocrites for a season; till God for the greatness of their sin, when it is full, openeth their eyes, and then they despair" (*Expositions and Notes on Sundry Portions of Holy Scriptures Together with the Practice of Prelates*, ed. Rev. Henry Walter [Cambridge: Cambridge University Press, 1896], 11). Hereafter all citations will appear parenthetically in the text. For discussions of Tyndale, see Clebsch, *England's Earliest Protestants*, 137–204, and Trueman, *Luther's Legacy*, 83–120.

13. Clebsch, *England's Earliest Protestants*, 199.

14. Sahlins, *Islands of History*, ix.

15. Ross, *Middle English Sermons*, 111–12.

16. Weber, *Protestant Ethic*, 115. Weber is, of course, discussing seventeenth-century Protestantism, but his interest in "signs" is useful here.

17. *Of Good Works* in *Certain Sermons or Homilies Appointed to Be Read in Churches in the Time of the Late Queen Elizabeth* (Oxford: Oxford University Press, 1840), 41.

18. Ibid., 42. See also Martin Luther, who writes, "Now everyone can notice and feel for himself when he does what is good and what is not good. If he finds his heart confident that it pleases God, then the work is good, even if it were so small a thing as picking up a straw. If the confidence is not there, or if he has any doubt about it, then the work is not good, even if the

work were to raise all the dead." And "A heathen, a Jew, a Turk, a sinner may also do all other works; but to trust firmly that he pleases God is possible only for a Christian who is enlightened and strengthened by grace" ("Treatise on Good Works," in *Works*, vol. 4, ed. Jaroslav Pelikan [Saint Louis: Concordia, 1955–1986], 25).

19. Hence the idea of assurance: works are signs that a person is saved. As Tyndale writes, "Thou canst never know or be sure of thy faith, but by the works" (*Mammon*, 60).

20. See Trueman, *Luther's Legacy*, 64, 90, 125.

21. See also Tyndale, *Mammon*, 108–9.

22. Edward Arber, ed., *The First Printed English New Testament*, trans. William Tyndale (London: Selwood Printing Works, 1871), [viiir] 29.

23. A medieval author commands, "clothe þe as þe apostell techeþ þe with þe armour of God. What is þis armour but þe werkes of light, penaunce, holy bedes and almes dedis" (Ross, *Middle English Sermons*, 112). Similarly, John Wyclif describes the nets that Jesus fishes with as the seven works of spiritual mercy; implicit in this object is the action of catching the audience. See sermon 38 in *Sermones*, ed. Johann Loserth (London: Wyclif Society, 1887), 1:247–48.

24. See also Tyndale, *Mammon*, 107. Trueman sees this use of the father/son (instead of laborer/lord) relationship as indicating that it is "founded upon love, not commercial considerations" (*Luther's Legacy*, 116). Nevertheless, one might contrast Tyndale's version of love with Martin Luther's, who does not seem to be haunted by the laborer and his hire. Luther's example of a man confident in his faith is a husband confident in the love of his wife. This confidence is contrasted with "he who is not at one with God, or is in a state of doubt, worries, and starts looking about for ways and means to do enough and to influence God with his many good works. He runs off to St. James, to Rome, to Jerusalem, hither and thither; he prays St. Bridget's prayer, this prayer and that prayer; he fasts on this day and that day; he makes confession here and makes confession there; he questions this man and that man, and yet finds no peace" ("Treatise," 27).

25. Here Tyndale seems to be responding to the Epistle of Saint James, especially 2:14–19, the source of "Faith without works is dead," which emphasizes the importance of deeds using the example of Abraham, who agreed to slay Isaac.

26. Gloria Cigman, ed., *Lollard Sermons*, Early English Text Society, original series, vol. 294 (Oxford: Oxford University Press, 1989), sermon 8, lines 428–31.

27. King, *English Reformation Literature*, 142–43.

28. Hugh Latimer, *Selected Sermons of Hugh Latimer* (Washington, DC: Folger Shakespeare Library; Charlottesville: University of Virginia Press, 1968), 30. Hereafter all references will appear parenthetically in the text.

29. See, for example, Karlfried Froehlich, ed., *Biblia Latina cum Glossa Ordinaria*, vol. 4 (Turnhout: Brepols, 1992) on Luke 8:5–8; and Stephen Wailes, *Medieval Allegories of Jesus' Parables: An Introduction* (Berkeley: University of California Press, 1987), 96–102.

30. This is Tawney's argument, and it has recently been taken up and expanded in McRae, *God Speed the Plough*, 32, and James Holstun, "The Giant's Faction."

31. See, for example, the "First Sermon before Edward VI," in which he discusses his father, the yeoman (Latimer, *Selected Sermons*, 67–68).

32. McRae, *God Speed the Plough*, 32.

33. For this perspective, see Hudson, "Epilogue," 258; King, *English Reformation Literature*, 323–24; and Simpson, *Reform and Cultural Revolution*, 368–69. Part of the problem for these scholars is that Reformation appropriations are propagandistic and not "literary." That does not mean, however, that they are not complicated. See Jones, who argues for "a figure who is often a great deal more ambivalent and various than one might expect" by surveying the various appearances of the plowman figure in the first part of the sixteenth century and his transformation into a Reformation polemicist (*Radical Pastoral*, 49–131). For more sympathetic perspectives on why Reformation writers found Langland's poem appealing, see Kelen, *Langland's Early Modern Identities*, 48; and Norbrook, *Poetry and Politics*, 36.

34. Hudson, "Epilogue," 258.

35. I borrow the idea of subtraction from Charles Taylor, who writes, "The rise of modernity isn't just a story of loss, of subtraction" (*A Secular Age* [Cambridge, MA: Harvard University Press, 2007], 26).

36. King's account of Crowley's Protestantism is the standard one (*English Reformation Literature*, 326–39). Scholars have begun to take issue with this account: see, for example, Larry Scanlon's recent essay, "Langland, Apocalypse," in which he argues for a common ground between Crowley and Langland, particularly in terms of the "apocalyptic vision" and the "penitential orientation" of both authors (54). Hailey's recent essay on Crowley's edition argues that his editorial practice is not at all ideologically informed ("Robert Crowley," 147). Finally, Jones argues that Crowley's aim is less Protestant propaganda than an attempt to create "an institutionalized, high-kudos vernacular literary classic" (*Radical Pastoral*, 118).

37. For a discussion of similar conflict in writings by Crowley, see Kenneth J. E. Graham, "Distributive Measures: Theology and Economics in the Writings of Robert Crowley," *Criticism* 47 (2006): 137–58. Graham notes that "in Crowley's works, the idea of salvation as payment for good works sits uneasily next to a belief in salvation as unmerited grace" (145).

38. William Langland, *The vision of pierce Plowman nowe the second time imprinted by Roberte Crowlye* ([London, 1550]; STC 19907), ¥3v. Hereafter all citations to this work will appear parenthetically in the text.

39. In the Kane-Donaldson edition, the passage reads, "That Feiþ withouten feet is [feblere þan nouȝt] / And as deed as a dore[nail] but if þe ded[e] folwe" (*Piers Plowman: The B Version*, 1.186–87).

40. For an explanation of this phrase and its importance to late medieval Catholicism, see Alister McGrath, *Iustitia Dei: A History of the Christian Doctrine of Justification*, 3rd ed. (Cambridge: Cambridge University Press, 2005), 83.

41. In *Select Works of Robert Crowley*, ed. J. M. Cowper, Early English Text Society, extra series, vol. 15 (London: Trübner, 1872), 40–41, lines 1180, 1187–88, 1191–92. Printed in Tawney and Power, *Tudor Economic Documents*, 3:61–62.

42. "Ac to truste [on] þise triennals, trewely, me þynketh / [It] is noȝt so siker for þe soule, certes, as is dowel" (*Piers Plowman: The B Version*, B7.185–86).

43. Scanlon does not see this as a casual error either; he writes, "the displacement of Will by Piers underlines the commitment in Langland's poem to social action, a commitment which many of his otherwise most sensitive and accomplished modern readers have underplayed or missed" ("Langland, Apocalypse," 68).

44. For oon Piers þe Plowman haþ impugned vs alle,
And set all sciences at a sop saue loue one;
And no text ne takeþ to mayntene his cause
But *Dilige deum* and *Domine quis habitabit*;
And [demeþ] þat dowel and dobet arn two Infinites,
Which Infinites wiþ a feiþ fynden out dobest,
Which shal saue mannes soule; þus seiþ Piers þe Plowman.
(*Piers Plowman: The B Version*, B13.124–30)

45. Anne Middleton, "Two Infinites: Grammatical Metaphor in *Piers Plowman*," *ELH: English Literary History* 39 (1972): 170–71, 175.

46. "Dowel" [quod he], "and dobet and dobest þe þridde
Arn þre faire vertues, and ben noȝt fer to fynde
Whoso is [meke of his mouþ, milde of his speche],
Trewe of his tunge, and of his two handes,
And þoruȝ his labour or his land his liflode wynneþ,
Trusty of his tailende, takeþ but his owene,
And is noȝt dronkelewe ne [d]eynous, dowel hym folweþ."
(*Piers Plowman: The B Version*, B8.78–84)

47. *Select Works of Robert Crowley*, 46, line 1388. Printed in Tawney and Power, *Tudor Economic Documents*, 3:62.

48. Most scholars only mention this text briefly: Hudson, "Epilogue," 258–60; Kelen, *Langland's Early Modern Identities*, 61–63; King, *English Reformation Literature*, 324; and Simpson, *Reform and Revolution*, 369–70. Jones discusses it at greater length but mainly within the context of the Marprelate tracts (*Radical Pastoral*, 110–11, 141–46).

49. "I playne Piers which cannot flatter," A3r. Hereafter all references to this work will appear parenthetically in the text.

50. King, *English Reformation Literature*, 323–24.

51. Simpson, *Reform and Revolution*, 365–70.

52. These views appear throughout the *English Wycliffite Sermons* as well as in the far more orthodox John Gower; see his *Vox Clamantis*.

53. Scanlon notes the tendency of scholars to dismiss the radicalism of the *Piers Plowman* tradition as a "misreading" of Langland ("Langland, Apocalypse," 54–55). He aligns Crowley's reading of Piers with the rebel letters (63). See, similarly, Jones, who sets the radicalism of the tradition in direct relation to Langland's poem, although he makes no claims about *Piers Plowman* itself (*Radical Pastoral*, 1–6).

54. Justice, *Writing and Rebellion*, 126. I would hesitate to assign this view to Wyclif. It is unlikely that his views were in wide distribution by 1381, and this perspective is inherent in Christian teaching. Hilton speculates that John Ball was the source; see his *Class Conflict*, 216–26.

55. Rodney Hilton writes, "The rebel demands run entirely counter to the prevailing theory of society which pervaded the sermons of the clergy from bishops to parish clergy; which lay behind much of the penitential system of the church; which was expressed by the lay nobility in Parliamentary petitions and statutes; and which was found in both courtly poetry and that reaching a wider audience (e.g. William Langland's *Piers Plowman*)"—and that is the three estate structure (*Class Conflict*, 222).

56. A late medieval sermon includes a very similar passage in reference to the parable of the talents: "For þow þou kepe wel þe Ten Commaundementis and spende þi v wittes neuer so well—þat is for to sey, be þou neuer so good a lyvere þi-selfe—but ȝiff þou þoroughe þi goodnes brynge oþur men owte of here wickednes in-to goodnes by good prechynge and good techynge, els þou hydes þi besaunde [talent]. And þan woll God sey to þe at þe Day of Dome, 'Wicked seruaunt, I deme þe of þin owne mowthe þat kowdeste and myghtiste teche, and hydeste þi kunnyng and wold not shew it.' How woll þise gret clerkes answere and þise gret persons þat dwellen in lordes courtes þat preche not ons in þre ȝere or foure? I trowe full harde" (Ross, *Middle English Sermons*, 40).

57. *Piers Plowman: The B Version*, B19.183–90.

58. Simpson, *Reform and Cultural Revolution*, 365. On the passage from *Piers Plowman*, see 362–63.

59. Charles Henry Cooper, ed., *Annals of Cambridge* (Cambridge: Warwick and Company, 1843), 2:40–42. Hereafter all references to this dialogue will be to this edition and will appear parenthetically in the text. See also, David Norbrook, ed., *The Penguin Book of Renaissance Verse, 1509–1659* (New York: Penguin, 1992), 387–89; John Lamb, ed., *A Collection of Letters, Statutes, and Other Documents from the MS Library of Corpus Christi College, 1500–1572*

(London: John Parker, 1838), 160–63; and Charles Henry Hartshorne, ed., *Ancient Metrical Tales* (London: William Pickering, 1829), 288–92.

60. Tawney, *Agrarian Problem*, 33–34.

61. In his study *Cambridge Life and the English Eclogue* (Cranbury, NJ: Associated University Presses, 2000), Gary M. Bouchard briefly mentions the dialogue and suggests that it was written by a "university wit" (42). He also claims that the speakers are shepherds (42), but there is no evidence either inside or outside the text to support such a claim.

62. Tawney, *Agrarian Problem*, 333.

63. Piers is less a pure reminder of the past, the nostalgic or ancient figure that other scholars have seen, than he is a figure for the collision between new and old. For the nostalgia of the figure, see Andrew Hadfield, "Foresters, Ploughmen, and Shepherds," 538. For his antiquity, see Kelen, *Langland's Early Modern Identities*, 48, and Jones, *Radical Pastoral*, 111.

Chapter 5. Spenser's Shepheardes Calender *and a Poetry of Rural Labor*

1. On the "medieval" aspects of Alexander Barclay and Barnabe Googe, see Cooper, *Pastoral*, 118–19, 125 and Chaudhuri, *Renaissance Pastoral*, 116–25, 132.

2. Alpers, "Pastoral and the Domain of Lyric," 83. Similarly, in the edition used here, the editor Thomas H. Cain writes, "The *Calender* did indeed inaugurate the New Poetry of England's Renaissance" (*The Shepheardes Calender*, 10).

3. *The Shepheardes Calender*, Epistle, lines 177, 178. Hereafter references to this work will appear parenthetically in the text and, unless otherwise noted, will refer to the eclogue title/epistle and line numbers of the Yale edition.

4. On the relationship between the *Calender* and the *Kalender*, see Richard Halpern, *The Poetics of Primitive Accumulation: English Renaissance Culture and the Genealogy of Capital* (Ithaca, NY: Cornell University Press, 1991), 189–96. Interestingly, the editor of the Yale edition of Spenser's poem describes the *Kalender* as "a homely almanac of astrological and miscellaneous lore, reprinted throughout the sixteenth century" (19n177). This description significantly downplays the religious tenor of the text. As the preface to the *Kalender* states, "thys boke is very profytable bothe for clerkes and for laye people to cause them to haue greate vnderstandyng and in espessyall in that we be bounde to lerne and knowe vpon peyne of euerlastynge deth" (*The Shepherds Kalender* [London, 1506; STC 22408], A2r).

5. Cooper, *Pastoral*, 3; King, *Spenser's Poetry*, 6; Montrose, "'Eliza, Queene of Shepheardes,'" 168.

6. See Bruce Thornton, "Rural Dialectic: Pastoral, Georgic, and the *Shepheardes Calender,*" *Spenser Studies* 9 (1988): 1–20; Fowler, "The Beginnings of English Georgic," 113; and Low, *Georgic Revolution*, 35–70. All of these scholars argue for the influence of georgic but do not offer specific evidence that Spenser is invoking Virgil. See also Jane Tylus, "Spenser, Virgil, and the Politics of Poetic Labor," *ELH: English Literary History* 55 (1988): 53–77, which refers to a georgic influence on Spenser, although Tylus is less interested in rural labor than in the poet/patron relationship.

7. McRae also observes that Spenser's understanding of work goes with a "vernacular tradition" (*God Speed the Plough*, 202).

8. Virgil's *Georgics*, in contrast to the *Eclogues*, did not exert much influence during the sixteenth century: writers did not imitate them until the eighteenth century. Low argues, unconvincingly, that the sixteenth century's lack of interest in Virgil's poem is evidence of "a fundamental contempt for labor, especially manual and agricultural labor" (*Georgic Revolution*, 5). For a response to Low, see Fowler, who argues for the mixture of pastoral and georgic in the sixteenth century ("The Beginnings of English Georgic," 105–25).

9. That these aspects of pastoral appealed to sixteenth-century pastoralists is made clear in Montrose's influential essay, "Of Gentlemen and Shepherds." Similarly, McRae notes, "In a period before the definition of a formal, classically grounded appreciation of pastoral, the rural labourer asserts his potential brusquely to shatter notions of 'a beautiful relation between rich and poor' in the English countryside" (*God Speed the Plough*, 267).

10. Macherey, *A Theory of Literary Production*, 106.

11. Alpers, *What Is Pastoral?*, 27.

12. Anthea Hume, *Edmund Spenser: Protestant Poet* (Cambridge: Cambridge University Press, 1984), 21–26; King, *Spenser's Poetry*, 36, 39.

13. See Murrin, "Mantuan and the English Eclogue," 66. Murrin sets aside the moral eclogues and is, therefore, not directly relevant here.

14. McRae also notes "the elision of rural business" in the *Calender* (*God Speed the Plough*, 270).

15. See, for example, Judith Anderson, *The Growth of a Personal Voice: "Piers Plowman" and "The Faerie Queene"* (New Haven, CT: Yale University Press, 1976), 1–2; Hamilton, "Spenser and Langland"; King, *Spenser's Poetry*, 20–25; Lane, *Shepheards Devises*, 86–88; Norbrook, *Poetry and Politics*, 53–54; Lynn Staley Johnson, *The "Shepheardes Calender": An Introduction* (University Park: Pennsylvania State University Press, 1990), 77.

16. Langland, *Piers Plowman: The B Version*, Prol.9–11.

17. Harry Berger Jr. also finds problems with the relation between the literal and figurative throughout the *Calender* (*Revisionary Play: Studies in the Spenserian Dynamics* [Berkeley: University of California Press, 1988], 306).

18. Leicester, *The Disenchanted Self*, 38.

19. Both Lane and Staley Johnson also note the eclogue's focus on commerce, but neither sees this focus as related to work and its symbolic meanings. See Lane, *Shepheards Devises*, 103 and Johnson, *The "Shepheardes Calender,"* 81.

20. On the mirror, see Roland Greene, "*The Shepheardes Calender*, Dialogue and Periphrasis," *Spenser Studies* 8 (1987): 13–15.

21. "Homily on Good Works," in *Certain Sermons or Homilies*, 50.

22. Lane reads this fable in terms of the failure of "motherly care": "care has been sacrificed for 'hire,' economic transactions substituted for personal relationships between the powerful and their charges" (*Shepheards Devises*, 103). For Lane, Spenser "calls to account its foremost institutions—Crown and church—in the name of their responsibility for the moral integrity and social welfare of that order" (114).

23. Wendy Scase sees the poem *Dauy Dycars Dreame*, with its allusions to Langland's poem, as a "focus for a broader debate about *reading practices* associated with medieval texts, and their potential for subversion" ("*Dauy Dycars Dreame* and Robert Crowley's Prints of *Piers Plowman*," *Yearbook of Langland Studies* 21 [2007]: 177, emphasis in the original). In taking up this poem, then, Spenser is reflecting on the mid-sixteenth-century debate that Scase characterizes.

24. For general comments on this poem and its history, see Scott Lucas, "Diggon Davie and Davy Dicar: Edmund Spenser, Thomas Churchyard, and the Poetics of Public Protest," *Spenser Studies* 16 (2001): 151–65, and Scase, "*Dauy Dycars Dreame*."

25. Langland, *Piers Plowman: The B Version*, 6.321–31.

26. *The contention betwyxte Churchyeard and Camell, vpon Dauid Dycers dreame* (London, 1560; STC 5225), A1r. Hereafter references to this work will appear parenthetically in the text.

27. Lucas establishes Spenser's relationship to Churchyard, arguing that his Diggon Davy is meant to be Churchyard ("Diggon Davie," 157–58). Norbrook also places Spenser in the prophetic tradition (*Poetry and Politics*, 53–81).

28. For the first, see Lucas, "Diggon Davie," and for the second, see Lane, *Shepheards Devises*, 132.

29. For the contradiction between Diggon as "voice of discontent" and the "fears that render that voice unstable," see Annabel Patterson, "Couples, Canons, and the Uncouth: Spenser-and-Milton in Educational Theory," *Critical Inquiry* 16 (1990): 787.

30. Alpers, *What Is Pastoral?*, 138.

31. Montrose, "'The perfecte paterne of a Poete,'" 41–42; Norbrook, *Poetry and Politics*, 78.

32. Montrose, "Of Gentlemen and Shepherds," 433.

33. Norbrook, *Poetry and Politics*, 78.

34. Norbrook notes that this Piers "seems to be a different figure altogether" (ibid., 68), but there seems no reason not to read them as closely linked. Staley Johnson notes that each Piers is a "spokesman for the proper use of language" (*"Shepheardes Calender,"* 77).

35. Cullen, *Spenser, Marvell*, 69; Staley Johnson, *"Shepheardes Calender,"* 85.

36. In his brief introduction to this eclogue, the editor notes that Spenser follows Mantuan's eclogue until line 79 (167).

37. *The eglogs of the poet B. Mantuan Carmelitan*, G2r.

38. Ibid., G2r–G2v. One of Alexander Barclay's shepherds offers a similar complaint in his fourth eclogue. First the shepherd, Minalcas, lists "whole labour / In tending his flockes," labor that gives him no time to write: "In doing all these no respite doth remayne, / But well to indite requireth all the brayne" (Barclay, *Eclogues*, 4.163–80).

39. Barclay, *Eclogues*, 5.808–24.

40. A famous example occurs in Chaucer's *Knight's Tale*, when the Knight states, "I have, God woot, a large feeld to ere, / And wayke been the oxen in my plough" (*Riverside Chaucer*, 1.886–87). But Ethan Knapp reminds us, "metaphors describing writing as agricultural labor are rooted also, of course, in the bucolic tradition. But it is an index to the seriousness of the category of labor in poets such as Hoccleve and Langland that their discussions are marked much less by this highly idealized classical tradition than they are by the conflicts marking the conditions of actual labor in their time" ("Poetic Work and Scribal Labor in Hoccleve and Langland," in *The Middle Ages at Work*, ed. Kellie Robertson and Michael Uebel [New York: Palgrave Macmillan, 2004], 226n7).

41. Langland, *Piers Plowman: The B Version*, 12.16–17.

42. Ibid., B12.25–28.

43. Consider Montrose's statement, "they [the shepherds in October] end by jointly abandoning heroic poetry, the poetry of virtuous action-in-the-world" ("'The perfecte paterne of a Poete,'" 49). Surely the name Piers should suggest that the "poetry of virtuous action-in-the-world" is not only heroic (and, therefore, classical), but the poetry of the *Piers Plowman* tradition.

44. Ibid., 45.

45. I am not, of course, suggesting that *Piers Plowman* had either a real or intended audience of the lower classes. Nevertheless, Langland's debts to homiletic material certainly align him with a more "popular" form of literature than Virgil's *Eclogues*.

46. Greene, "*The Shepheardes Calender*, Dialogue and Periphrasis," 5.

47. For example, Halpern, *Primitive Accumulation*, 176–77; and Alpers, *What Is Pastoral?*, 178.

Chapter 6. Reading Pastoral in Book 6 of Spenser's Faerie Queene

1. Spenser, *The Faerie Queene*, 6.9.19.1–2, emphasis added. Hereafter all references to this work will appear parenthetically in the text.

2. The term *art pastoral* comes from Chaudhuri, *Renaissance Pastoral*, 5, 134, and is used to describe the Italian model. Most scholars use the term *Arcadian* to designate the idyllic (and usually neoclassical) form of pastoral and the *Mantuanesque* to refer to the moral and satiric form, following Cullen, *Spenser, Marvell*, 3.

3. Williams, *The Country and the City*, 18.

4. In his dissertation, "Mantuan and the English Eclogue," Murrin notes that Mantuan's moral eclogue fell out of favor in the 1590s, giving way to the "neoclassical eclogue," which was more courtly in its focus (136, 160–61). Similarly, Cullen sees the moral strand, the Mantuanesque, as "minor" in the history of pastoral (*Spenser, Marvell*, 3).

5. In the 1590 edition Spenser concludes book 3 with quite similar lines, comparing his writing to plowing:

> But now my teme begins to faint and fayle,
> All woxen weary of their iournall toyle:
> Therefore will I their sweatie yokes assoyle
> At this same furrowes end, till a new day:
> And ye faire Swayns, after your long turmoyle,
> Now cease your worke, and at your pleasure play;
> Now cease your worke; to morrow is an holy day.
>   (3.12.47a.3–9)

6. See for example, Low, *Georgic Revolution*, who finds the "georgic spirit" throughout book 6 (43); Andrew Ettin, "The Georgics in *The Faerie Queene*," *Spenser Studies* 3 (1982): 57–71; and Andrew Wallace, "'Nourseld up in life and manners wilde': Spenser's Georgic Educations," *Spenser Studies* 19 (2004): 65–92.

7. The comparison resembles a medieval text known to Spenser, Geoffrey Chaucer's *Knight's Tale*, far more closely than Virgil. Near the opening of Chaucer's tale, the narrator interrupts himself to say "I have, God woot, a large feeld to ere, / And wayke been the oxen in my plough" (*Riverside Chaucer*, 1.886–87).

8. Humphrey Tonkin, *Spenser's Courteous Pastoral: Book 6 of the Faerie Queene* (Oxford: Oxford University Press, 1972), 117.

9. Williams, *The Country and the City*, 18.

10. Julia Reinhard Lupton reads this episode persuasively in terms of colonialism in Ireland—not the New World—and a dialectic between home and exile that Spenser draws from Virgil's First Eclogue. See her "Home Mak-

ing in Ireland: Virgil's Eclogue 1 and Book 6 of the *Faerie Queene*," *Spenser Studies* 8 (1987): 119–45.

11. *The eglogs of the poet B. Mantuan Carmelitan*, D2r–D2v.

12. *Oxford English Dictionary*, definition 1a.

13. Calidore's selfishness and his mistakes are well-known to readers. See, for example, Paul Alpers, *The Poetry of "The Faerie Queene"* (Princeton, NJ: Princeton University Press, 1967), 292; and Tonkin, *Spenser's Courteous Pastoral*, 119.

14. Alpers, *What Is Pastoral?*, 6–7, 194.

15. Tonkin, *Spenser's Courteous Pastoral*, 116.

16. *Faerie Queene*, 1224n29–30.

17. As the editor notes, Spenser is here following the old shepherd's speech in Torquato Tasso, *Gerusalemme Liberata*, canto 7, stanzas 8–13 (1224n19–25). I've consulted the English translation, *The Jerusalem Delivered of Torquato Tasso*, trans. J. H. Wiffen (New York: Hurst, 1858).

18. On the modification of Golden Age topoi, see also Alpers, *What Is Pastoral?*, 189.

19. Alpers, *Poetry of "The Faerie Queene,"* 295.

20. Ibid., 296.

21. On the way in which "Spenserian pastoral fails the rustic" because the poet is "unable or unwilling to represent him in the full sense," see Alpers, *What Is Pastoral?*, 194. Alpers, however, is uninterested in the link to the "reality" of rural labor at this time.

22. Lupton suggests that this link restores the contrast between the dispossession of Virgil's First Eclogue and the celebration of his Fourth, but she does not tie this violence to labor (slavery) ("Home Making," 138–41).

23. Tonkin, for example, writes that the dance is "a representation of artistic form" (*Spenser's Courteous Pastoral*, 112).

24. Alpers, *What Is Pastoral?* 186.

25. As Tonkin writes, the brigands are "an infernal parody" of the shepherds (*Spenser's Courteous Pastoral*, 144–45).

26. It is unclear whether Spenser could have known, but pirates were an important source of slaves in the Roman period. See Keith Bradley, *Slavery and Society at Rome* (Cambridge: Cambridge University Press, 1994), 37.

27. The Romans' "derogatory attitudes toward work" are a scholarly commonplace: see Sandra Joshel, *Work, Identity, and Legal Status at Rome: A Study of the Occupational Inscriptions* (Norman: University of Oklahoma Press, 1992), from whom the quotation is taken (63), and John D'Arms, *Commerce and Social Standing in Ancient Rome* (Cambridge, MA: Harvard University Press, 1981).

28. *The bucolikes of Publius Virgilius Maro*, C1v.

29. On the sixteenth-century interest in classical agricultural treatises, see Thirsk, "Making a Fresh Start," 15–34.

30. Joshel, *Work, Identity, and Legal Status*, 49.

31. On this association, see Bradley, *Slavery and Society at Rome*, who notes that labor came predominantly from slaves, who formed about one-third of the population (13). See also Joshel, *Work, Identity, and Legal Status*, 49.

32. See, for example, Poggioli, *The Oaten Flute*, 23.

33. A. C. Hamilton, ed., *The Spenser Encyclopedia* (Toronto: University of Toronto Press, 1990), 112.

34. See Longus, *Daphnis and Chloe: The Elizabethan Version from Amyot's Translation by Angel Day*, ed. Joseph Jacobs (London: Nutt, 1890).

35. The editor notes that "Spenser bases this episode on the story of Isabel in *Orlando Furioso* 12.91 ff" (1229n2 ff).

36. Isabella relates her story at the beginning of book 13 in Ariosto's *Orlando Furioso*. I have referred to *Orlando Furioso: A New Verse Translation*, trans. David Slavitt (Cambridge, MA: Harvard University Press, 2009).

37. Montrose, "Of Gentlemen and Shepherds," 427.

38. The quotation comes from *The Journals of All the Parliaments During the Reign of Queen Elizabeth*, ed. Sir Simonds D'Ewes (London, 1682), 674, and appears in McRae, *God Speed the Plough*, 8.

39. See, for example, *Piracy, Slavery, and Redemption: Barbary Captivity Narratives from Early Modern England*, ed. Daniel J. Vitkus (New York: Columbia University Press, 2001), which includes John Fox, "The Worthy Enterprise of John Fox, in delivering 266 Christians out of the Captivity of the Turks," in Richard Hakluyt's *Principal Navigations*, 55–70. In the introduction, Nabil Matar writes that before the 1620s, there were more Britons in North Africa than in America (2).

40. Ibid., 3.

41. Ibid., 66 and 67.

42. Ibid., 7.

43. Lupton, "Home Making," 135.

44. Indeed, Alpers claims that this pun shows that Calidore has renounced the pastoral (Alpers, *What Is Pastoral?*, 194).

45. Tonkin also observes the interesting confluence of events: Coridon accepts money at the end of the pastoral episode (*Spenser's Courteous Pastoral*, 146).

46. Greg, *Pastoral Poetry*, 3.

Afterword

1. On the special relationship between the Renaissance and beginnings and the difficulty of overcoming the division between the Middle Ages and Renaissance, see Margareta de Grazia, "The Modern Divide: From Either

Side," *Journal for Medieval and Early Modern Studies* 37 (Fall 2007): 453–67. For attempts to revise the boundary between medieval and early modern, see the additional essays collected in Jennifer Summit and David Wallace, eds., "Medieval/Renaissance: After Periodization," special issue, *Journal of Medieval and Early Modern Studies* 37 (Fall 2007).

2. *Shepheardes Calender*, 19.
3. Alpers, *What Is Pastoral?*, 27.
4. Barrell, *The Dark Side of the Landscape*, 5.
5. Jean E. Howard's introduction to the play in *The Norton Shakespeare* is typical: "The play thus participates in the rich tradition of Renaissance pastoral literature in which the rustic world of forest and field offers an alternative to and a sanctuary from the urban or courtly milieu to which it is contrasted" (*The Norton Shakespeare*, ed. Stephen Greenblatt et al. [New York: W. W. Norton and Company, 1997], 1591). For a somewhat polemical survey of how critics have approached pastoral in the play, see Linda Woodbridge, "Country Matters: *As You Like It* and the Pastoral-Bashing Impulse," in *Revisions of Shakespeare: Essays in Honor of Robert Ornstein*, ed. Evelyn Gajowski (Newark, NJ: University of Delaware Press, 2004), 189–214.
6. See Richard Wilson, "'Like the Old Robin Hood': *As You Like It* and the Enclosure Riots," *Shakespeare Quarterly* 43 (1992): 1–19.
7. Alpers, *What Is Pastoral?*, 71–78; 123–34.
8. *As You Like It*, in *The Norton Shakespeare*, act 2, scene 4, lines 70–77.
9. The influential essay that discusses the play in terms of enclosure and agrarian capitalism reads the conflict in terms of topicality, the forest rioters, and not in terms of the older, plowman tradition. See Wilson, "'Like the Old Robin Hood.'"
10. *As You Like It*, act 3, scene 2, lines 64–67.

WORKS CITED

Primary Sources

Andrew, Malcolm, and Ronald Waldron, eds. *The Poems of the Pearl Manuscript: Pearl, Cleanness, Patience, Sir Gawain and the Green Knight.* Exeter: University of Exeter Press, 1997.
Arber, Edward, ed. *The First English Printed New Testament.* Translated by William Tyndale. London: Selwood Printing Works, 1871.
Ariosto, Ludovico. *Orlando Furioso: A New Verse Translation.* Translated by David Slavitt. Cambridge, MA: Harvard University Press, 2009.
Barclay, Alexander. *The Eclogues of Alexander Barclay from the Original Edition by John Cawood.* Edited by Beatrice White. Early English Text Society, original series, vol. 175. 1928. Reprint, London: Oxford University Press, 1960.
Brinton, Thomas. *The Sermons of Thomas Brinton, Bishop of Rochester (1373–1389).* 2 vols. Edited by Sister Mary Aquinas Devlin. Camden Society 3rd Series, vols. 85–86. London: Offices of the Royal Historical Society, 1954.
Certain Sermons or Homilies Appointed to Be Read in Churches in the Time of the Late Queen Elizabeth. Oxford: Oxford University Press, 1840.
Certayne Causes gathered together. . . London, 1552; STC 9980.
Chaucer, Geoffrey. *The Riverside Chaucer.* Edited by Larry D. Benson. Boston: Houghton Mifflin, 1987.
Cigman, Gloria, ed. *Lollard Sermons.* Early English Text Society, original series, vol. 294. Oxford: Oxford University Press, 1989.
The contention betwyxte Churchyeard and Camell, vpon Dauid Dycers dreame. London, 1560; STC 5225.

Cooper, Charles Henry, ed. *Annals of Cambridge*. 2 vols. Cambridge: Warwick and Company, 1843.
Crowley, Robert. *Select Works of Robert Crowley*. Edited by J. M. Cowper. Early English Text Society, extra series, vol. 15. London: Trübner, 1872.
———. *The Way to Wealth*. London, 1550; STC 6096.
Dean, James, ed. *Piers the Plowman's Crede*. In *Six Ecclesiastical Satires*. Kalamazoo, MI: Medieval Institute Publications, 1991.
———. *The Plowman's Tale*. In *Six Ecclesiastical Satires*. Kalamazoo, MI: Medieval Institute Publications, 1991.
———. *Song of the Husbandman*. In *Medieval English Political Writings*. Kalamazoo, MI: Medieval Institute Publications, 1996.
de Meun, Jean, and Guillaume de Lorris. *The Romance of the Rose*. Translated by Charles Dahlberg. Hanover, NH: University Press of New England, 1983.
Froehlich, Karlfried, ed. *Biblia Latina cum Glossa Ordinaria*. 4 vols. Turnhout: Brepols, 1992.
Gilpin, Bernard. *A Godly Sermon preached in the court at Greenwitch before King Edvvard the sixth, the first Sunday after the Epiphany, anno Domini 1552*. London, 1630; STC 11898.
Googe, Barnabe. *Eglogs, epytaphes, and sonettes*. London, 1563; STC 12048.
———. *Eclogues, Epitaphs, and Sonnets*. Edited by Judith M. Kennedy. Toronto: University of Toronto Press, 1989.
Gower, John. *Confessio Amantis*. In *John Gower's English Works*. 2 vols. Edited by G. C. Macaulay. Early English Text Society, extra series, vols. 81 and 82. London: Kegan Paul, 1900–1901.
———. *Vox Clamantis*. In *The Complete Works of John Gower: Latin Works*. Edited by G. C. Macaulay. London: Oxford University Press, 1902.
———. *Vox Clamantis*. In *The Major Latin Works of John Gower*. Translated by Eric Stockton. Seattle: University of Washington Press, 1962.
Grosart, A. B., ed. *The Poems, English and Latin, of the Rev. Thomas Bastard*. Manchester: C. E. Simms, 1880.
Hartshorne, Charles Henry, ed. *Ancient Metrical Tales*. London: William Pickering, 1829.
Hudson, Anne, and Pamela Gradon, eds. *English Wycliffite Sermons*. 5 vols. Oxford: Oxford University Press, 1983–96.
"I playne Piers which cannot flatter." London, ?1547; STC 19903a.
Johnson, Samuel. *Rambler* 37, July 24, 1750. In *The Works of Samuel Johnson*, 4:238–44. Edited by Arthur Murphy. London: J. Haddon, 1820.
The Journals of All the Parliaments During the Reign of Queen Elizabeth. Edited by Sir Simonds D'Ewes. London, 1682.
Lamb, John, ed. *A Collection of Letters, Statutes, and Other Documents from the MS Library of Corpus Christi College, 1500–1572*. London: John Parker, 1838.

Langland, William. *Piers Plowman: The A Version*. Edited by George Kane. Berkeley: University of California Press, 1988.

———. *Piers Plowman: The B Version*. Edited by George Kane and E. Talbot Donaldson. London: Athlone Press, 1975.

———. *Piers Plowman: The C-text*. Edited by Derek Pearsall. 1978. Reprint, Exeter: University of Exeter Press, 1994.

———. *The vision of Pierce Plowman nowe the second time imprinted by Roberte Crowlye*. London, 1550; STC 19907.

———. *The Vision of Piers Plowman*. Edited by A. V. C. Schmidt. Rutland, VT: Charles E. Tuttle Company, 1987.

Latimer, Hugh. *Selected Sermons of Hugh Latimer*. Washington, DC: Folger Shakespeare Library; Charlottesville: University of Virginia Press, 1968.

———. *Sermons by Hugh Latimer, Sometime Bishop of Worcester*. London: Dent, 1906.

Longus. *Daphnis and Chloe: The Elizabethan Version from Amyot's Translation by Angel Day*. Edited by Joseph Jacobs. London: Nutt, 1890.

Lumiansky, R. M., and David Mills, eds. *The Chester Mystery Cycle*. 2 vols. Early English Text Society, supplementary series, vols. 3 and 9. London: Oxford University Press, 1974, 1986.

Luther, Martin. "Treatise on Good Works." In vol. 4 of *Works*. Edited by Jaroslav Pelikan. Saint Louis, MO: Concordia, 1955–86.

Mantuanus. *The Eclogues of Baptista Mantuanus*. Edited by Wilfred P. Mustard. Baltimore, MD: Johns Hopkins University Press, 1911.

———. *The Eclogues of Mantuan*. Translated by George Turberville. Edited by Douglas Bush. New York: Scholars' Facsimiles and Reprints, 1977.

———. *The eglogs of the poet B. Mantuan Carmelitan*. Translated by George Turberville. London, 1567; STC 22990.

Mirk, John. *John Mirk's Festial*. Edited by Susan Powell. 2 vols. Early English Text Society, original series, vol. 334. New York: Oxford University Press, 2009.

More, Sir Thomas. *Utopia*. Translated by Ralphe Robynson. Edited by J. Rawson Lumby. Cambridge: Cambridge University Press, 1908.

Norbrook, David, ed. *The Penguin Book of Renaissance Verse, 1509–1659*. New York: Penguin, 1992.

Oschinsky, Dorothea, ed. *Walter of Henley and Other Treatises of Estate Management*. Oxford: Clarendon Press, 1971.

Pyers plowmans exhortation, vnto the lordes, knightes and burgoysses of the Parlyamenthouse. London, 1550; STC 19905.

Ross, Woodburn O., ed. *Middle English Sermons*. Early English Text Society, original series, vol. 209. London: Humphrey Milford, Oxford University Press, 1960.

Shakespeare, William. *As You Like It*. In *The Norton Shakespeare*. Edited by Stephen Greenblatt, et al. New York: W. W. Norton and Company, 1997.
The Shepherds Kalender. London, 1506; STC 22408.
Smith, Lucy Toulmin, ed. *York Plays*. Oxford: Clarendon Press, 1885.
Spenser, Edmund. *The Faerie Queene*. Edited by Thomas P. Roche. New York: Penguin, 1978.
———. *The Shepheardes Calender*. In *The Yale Edition of the Shorter Poems of Edmund Spenser*. Edited by William A. Oram, Einar Bjorvand, Ronald Bond, Thomas H. Cain, Alexander Dunlop, and Richard Schell. New Haven, CT: Yale University Press, 1989.
Stevens, Martin, and A. C. Cawley, eds. *The Towneley Plays*. 2 vols. Early English Text Society, supplementary series, vols. 13 and 14. Oxford: Oxford University Press, 1994.
Tasso, Torquato. *The Jerusalem Delivered of Torquato Tasso*. Translated by J. H. Wiffen. New York: Hurst, 1858.
Tawney, R. H., and Eileen Power, eds. *Tudor Economic Documents*. 3 vols. London: Longmans, 1924.
Tyndale, William. *Expositions and Notes on Sundry Portions of Holy Scriptures Together with the Practice of Prelates*. Edited by Rev. Henry Walter. Cambridge: Cambridge University Press, 1896.
———. *The Parable of the Wicked Mammon in Doctrinal Treatises and Introductions to Different Portions of the Holy Scriptures*. Edited by Henry Walter. Cambridge: Cambridge University Press, 1848.
Virgil. *Bucolica Virgilii*. London, 1512; STC 24813.
———. *Bucolica Virgilii*. London, 1514; STC 24814.
———. *The bucolikes of Publius Virgilius Maro*. Translated by Abraham Fleming. London, 1575; STC 24816.
———. *The Eclogues*. Translated by Guy Lee. New York: Penguin, 1980.
Vitkus, Daniel J., ed. *Piracy, Slavery, and Redemption: Barbary Captivity Narratives from Early Modern England*. New York: Columbia University Press, 2001.
Walsingham, Thomas. *The St. Albans Chronicle: The Chronica Maiora of Thomas Walsingham*. 2 vols. Edited by John Taylor, Wendy R. Childs, and Leslie Watkiss. New York: Oxford University Press, 2003.
Whiting, Bartlett Jere, ed. *Proverbs, Sentences, and Proverbial Phrases from English Writings Mainly Before 1500*. Cambridge, MA: Harvard University Press, 1968.
Wilkinson, Robert. "A sermon preached at North-Hampton . . ." London 1607; STC 25662.
Wimbledon, Thomas. *Redde Rationem Vilicationis Tue: A Middle English Sermon of the Fourteenth Century*. Edited by Ione K. Knight. Pittsburgh, PA: Duquesne University Press, 1967.
Wyclif, John. *Sermones*. 4 vols. Edited by Johann Loserth. London: Wyclif Society, 1887–90.

Secondary Sources

Adams, Robert. "Langland's Theology." In *A Companion to "Piers Plowman,"* edited by John A. Alford, 87–114. Berkeley: University of California Press, 1988.
Aers, David. *Community, Gender, and Individual Identity*. New York: Routledge, 1988.
———. *Faith, Ethics, and Church: Writing in England, 1360–1409*. Rochester, NY: Boydell and Brewer, 1999.
———. *Piers Plowman and Christian Allegory*. London: Edward Arnold, 1975.
———. *Salvation and Sin: Augustine, Langland, and Fourteenth-Century Theology*. Notre Dame, IN: University of Notre Dame Press, 2009.
Allen, Robert. *Enclosure and the Yeoman*. Oxford: Clarendon Press, 1992.
Alpers, Paul. "Pastoral and the Domain of Lyric in Spenser's *Shepheardes Calender*." *Representations* 12 (1983): 83–100.
———. *The Poetry of "The Faerie Queene."* Princeton, NJ: Princeton University Press, 1967.
———. *What Is Pastoral?* Chicago: University of Chicago Press, 1996.
Anderson, Judith. *The Growth of a Personal Voice: "Piers Plowman" and "The Faerie Queene."* New Haven, CT: Yale University Press, 1976.
Aston, T. H., and C. H. E. Philpin, eds. *The Brenner Debate: Agrarian Class Structure and Economic Development in Pre-Industrial Europe*. New York: Cambridge University Press, 1985.
Barney, Stephen. "The Plowshare of the Tongue: The Progress of a Symbol from the Bible to *Piers Plowman*." *Mediaeval Studies* 35 (1973): 261–93.
Barrell, John. *The Dark Side of the Landscape: The Rural Poor in English Painting, 1730–1840*. New York: Cambridge University Press, 1980.
Baswell, Christopher. *Virgil in Medieval England*. Cambridge: Cambridge University Press, 1995.
Beckwith, Sarah. *Christ's Body: Identity, Culture, and Society in Late Medieval Writing*. London: Routledge, 1993.
Berger, Harry, Jr. *Revisionary Play: Studies in the Spenserian Dynamics*. Berkeley: University of California Press, 1988.
Berger, Peter L., and Thomas Luckmann. *The Social Construction of Reality: A Treatise in the Sociology of Knowledge*. Garden City, NY: Anchor Books, 1967.
Bothwell, James, P. J. P. Goldberg, and W. M. Ormrod, eds. *The Problem of Labour in Fourteenth-Century England*. Rochester, NY: Boydell and Brewer, 2000.
Bouchard, Gary M. *Cambridge Life and the English Eclogue*. Cranbury, NJ: Associated University Presses, 2000.
Bradley, Keith. *Slavery and Society at Rome*. Cambridge: Cambridge University Press, 1994.

Brenner, Robert. "Agrarian Class Structure and Economic Development in Pre-Industrial Europe." *Past and Present* 70 (1976): 30–75.
Burrow, J. A. "The Action of Langland's Second Vision." *Essays in Criticism* 15 (1965): 247–68.
Camille, Michael. *Mirror in Parchment: The Luttrell Psalter and the Making of Medieval England*. Chicago: University of Chicago Press, 1998.
Chaudhuri, Sukanta. *Renaissance Pastoral and Its English Developments*. Oxford: Clarendon Press, 1989.
Clebsch, William. *England's Earliest Protestants, 1520–1535*. New Haven, CT: Yale University Press, 1964.
Clopper, Lawrence. "Need Men and Women Labor? Langland's Wanderer and the Labor Ordinances." In *Chaucer's England: Literature in Historical Context*, edited by Barbara Hanawalt, 110–29. Minneapolis: University of Minnesota Press, 1992.
Cooper, Helen. *Pastoral: Mediaeval into Renaissance*. Ipswich: Brewer, 1977.
Cullen, Patrick. *Spenser, Marvell, and Renaissance Pastoral*. Cambridge, MA: Harvard University Press, 1970.
D'Arms, John. *Commerce and Social Standing in Ancient Rome*. Cambridge, MA: Harvard University Press, 1981.
de Grazia, Margareta. "The Modern Divide: From Either Side." *Journal for Medieval and Early Modern Studies* 37 (2007): 453–67.
Emmerson, Richard K., and P. J. P. Goldberg. "'The Lord Geoffrey had me made': Lordship and Labour in the Luttrell Psalter." In *The Problem of Labour in Fourteenth-Century England*, edited by James Bothwell, P. J. P. Goldberg, and W. M. Ormrod, 43–63. Rochester, NY: Boydell and Brewer, 2000.
Empson, William. *Some Versions of Pastoral*. New York: New Directions, 1974.
Ettin, Andrew. "The Georgics in *The Faerie Queene*." *Spenser Studies* 3 (1982): 57–71.
———. *Literature and Pastoral*. New Haven, CT: Yale University Press, 1984.
Everitt, Alan. "Farm Labourers." In vol. 4 of *The Agrarian History of England and Wales*, edited by Joan Thirsk, 396–465. Cambridge: Cambridge University Press, 1967.
Fowler, Alastair. "The Beginnings of English Georgic." In *Renaissance Genres: Essays on Theory, History, and Interpretation*, edited by Barbara Kiefer Lewalski, 105–25. Cambridge, MA: Harvard University Press, 1986.
———. "Georgic and Pastoral: Laws of Genre in the Seventeenth Century." In *Culture and Cultivation in Early Modern England: Writing and the Land*, edited by Michael Leslie and Timothy Raylor, 81–88. Leicester: Leicester University Press, 1992.
Freedman, Paul. *Images of the Medieval Peasant*. Stanford: Stanford University Press, 1999.

Galloway, Andrew. "Chaucer's 'Former Age' and the Fourteenth-Century Anthropology of Craft: The Social Logic of a Premodernist Lyric." *ELH: English Literary History* 63 (1996): 535–53.
Graham, Kenneth J. E. "Distributive Measures: Theology and Economics in the Writings of Robert Crowley." *Criticism* 47 (2006): 137–58.
Green, R. F. "John Ball's Letters: Literary History and Historical Literature." In *Chaucer's England: Literature in Historical Context*, edited by Barbara Hanawalt, 176–200. Minneapolis: University of Minnesota Press, 1992.
Greene, Roland. "*The Shepheardes Calender*, Dialogue and Periphrasis." *Spenser Studies* 8 (1987): 1–33.
Greg, W. W. *Pastoral Poetry and Pastoral Drama*. London: Bullen, 1906.
Haber, Judith. *Pastoral and the Poetics of Self-Contradiction*. Cambridge: Cambridge University Press, 1994.
Hadfield, Andrew. "Foresters, Ploughmen, and Shepherds: Versions of Tudor Pastoral." In *The Oxford Handbook of Tudor Literature, 1485–1603*, edited by Mike Pincombe and Cathy Shrank, 537–54. New York: Oxford University Press, 2009.
Hailey, R. Carter. "'Geuying Light to the Reader': Robert Crowley's Editions of *Piers Plowman* (1550)." *Papers of the Bibliographical Society of America* 95 (2001): 483–502.
———. "Robert Crowley and the Editing of *Piers Plowman* (1550)." *Yearbook of Langland Studies* 21 (2007): 143–70.
Halpern, Richard. *The Poetics of Primitive Accumulation: English Renaissance Culture and the Genealogy of Capital*. Ithaca, NY: Cornell University Press, 1991.
Hamilton, A. C. "Spenser and Langland." *Studies in Philology* 55 (1958): 533–48.
———, ed. *The Spenser Encyclopedia*. Toronto: University of Toronto Press, 1990.
Hill, Ordelle G. *The Manor, the Plowman, and the Shepherd: Agrarian Themes and Imagery in Late Medieval and Early Renaissance English Literature*. Cranbury, NJ: Associated University Presses, 1993.
Hilton, Rodney. *Class Conflict and the Crisis of Feudalism: Essays in Medieval Social History*. London: Hambledon Press, 1985.
Holstun, James. "The Giant's Faction: Spenser, Heywood, and the Mid-Tudor Crisis." *Journal of Medieval and Early Modern Studies* 37 (2007): 335–71.
Hudson, Anne. "Epilogue: The Legacy of *Piers Plowman*." In *A Companion to "Piers Plowman*," edited by John A. Alford, 251–66. Berkeley: University of California Press, 1988.
Hume, Anthea. *Edmund Spenser: Protestant Poet*. Cambridge: Cambridge University Press, 1984.
Jameson, Fredric. *The Political Unconscious: Narrative as a Socially Symbolic Act*. Ithaca, NY: Cornell University Press, 1981.

Jones, Mike Rodman. *Radical Pastoral, 1381–1594: Appropriation and the Writing of Religious Controversy*. Burlington, VT: Ashgate, 2011.
Joshel, Sandra. *Work, Identity, and Legal Status at Rome: A Study of the Occupational Inscriptions*. Norman: University of Oklahoma Press, 1992.
Justice, Steven. *Writing and Rebellion: England in 1381*. Berkeley: University of California Press, 1996.
Kelen, Sarah. *Langland's Early Modern Identities*. New York: Palgrave MacMillan, 2007.
King, John. *English Reformation Literature: The Tudor Origins of the Protestant Tradition*. Princeton, NJ: Princeton University Press, 1982.
———. *Spenser's Poetry and the Reformation Tradition*. Princeton, NJ: Princeton University Press, 1990.
Kirk, Elizabeth. "Langland's Plowman and the Recreation of Fourteenth-Century Religious Metaphor." *Yearbook of Langland Studies* 2 (1988): 1–21.
Knapp, Ethan. "Poetic Work and Scribal Labor in Hoccleve and Langland." In *The Middle Ages at Work*, edited by Kellie Robertson and Michael Uebel, 209–28. New York: Palgrave Macmillan, 2004.
Knight, Stephen. "The Voice of Labour in Fourteenth-Century Literature." In *The Problem of Labour in Fourteenth-Century England*, edited by James Bothwell, P. J. P. Goldberg, and W. M. Ormrod, 101–22. Rochester, NY: Boydell and Brewer, 2000.
Land, Stephen K. *Kett's Rebellion: The Norfolk Rising of 1549*. Ipswich: Boydell, 1977.
Lane, Robert. *Shepheards Devises: Edmund Spenser's "Shepheardes Calender" and the Institutions of Elizabethan Society*. Athens: University of Georgia Press, 1993.
Leicester, H. Marshall, Jr. *The Disenchanted Self: Representing the Subject in the Canterbury Tales*. Berkeley: University of California Press, 1990.
Low, Anthony. *The Georgic Revolution*. Princeton, NJ: Princeton University Press, 1985.
Lucas, Scott. "Diggon Davie and Davy Dicar: Edmund Spenser, Thomas Churchyard, and the Poetics of Public Protest." *Spenser Studies* 16 (2001): 151–65.
Lumiansky, Robert Mayer, and David Mills, eds. *The Chester Mystery Cycle: Essays and Documents*. Chapel Hill: University of North Carolina Press, 1983.
Lupton, Julia Reinhard. "Home Making in Ireland: Virgil's Eclogue 1 and Book 6 of the *Faerie Queene*." *Spenser Studies* 8 (1987): 119–45.
Macherey, Pierre. *A Theory of Literary Production*. Translated by Geoffrey Wall. 1978. Reprint, London: Routledge and Kegan Paul, 2006.
Mann, Jill. *Chaucer and Medieval Estates Satire*. Cambridge: Cambridge University Press, 1973.

Marshall, Peter, and Alec Ryrie, eds. *The Beginnings of English Protestantism*. Cambridge: Cambridge University Press, 2002.
Marx, Karl. "So-Called Primitive Accumulation." In *Capital*, vol. 1, translated by Ben Fowkes. New York: Random House, 1976.
Masciandaro, Nicola. *The Voice of the Hammer: The Meaning of Work in Middle English Literature*. Notre Dame, IN: University of Notre Dame Press, 2007.
McGrath, Alister E. *Iustitia Dei: A History of the Christian Doctrine of Justification*. 3rd ed. Cambridge: Cambridge University Press, 2005.
McRae, Andrew. *God Speed the Plough: The Representation of Agrarian England, 1500–1660*. Cambridge: Cambridge University Press, 1996.
Middleton, Anne. "Acts of Vagrancy: The C Version 'Autobiography' and the Statute of 1388." In *Written Work: Langland, Labor, and Authorship*, edited by Steven Justice and Kathryn Kerby-Fulton, 208–317. Philadelphia: University of Pennsylvania Press, 1997.
———. "Two Infinites: Grammatical Metaphor in *Piers Plowman*." *ELH: English Literary History* 39 (1972): 169–88.
Montrose, Louis. "'Eliza, Queene of Shepheardes' and the Pastoral of Power." *English Literary Renaissance* 10 (1980): 153–82.
———. "Of Gentlemen and Shepherds: The Politics of Elizabethan Pastoral Form." *ELH: English Literary History* 50 (1983): 415–59.
———. "'The perfecte paterne of a Poete': The Poetics of Courtship in *The Shepheardes Calender*." *Texas Studies in Literature and Language* 21 (1979): 34–67.
Murrin, Michael. "Mantuan and the English Eclogue." Ph.D. diss., Yale University, 1965.
Nisse, Ruth. *Defining Acts: Drama and the Politics of Interpretation in Late Medieval England*. Notre Dame, IN: University of Notre Dame Press, 2005.
Norbrook, David. *Poetry and Politics in the English Renaissance*. Rev. ed. Oxford: Oxford University Press, 2002.
Owst, G. R. *Literature and Pulpit in Medieval England*. Cambridge: Cambridge University Press, 1933.
Patterson, Annabel. "Couples, Canons, and the Uncouth: Spenser-and-Milton in Educational Theory." *Critical Inquiry* 16 (1990): 773–93.
———. *Pastoral and Ideology: Virgil to Valéry*. Berkeley: University of California Press, 1987.
Patterson, Lee. *Negotiating the Past*. Madison: University of Wisconsin Press, 1987.
Piepho, Lee. *Holofernes' Mantuan: Italian Humanism in Early Modern England*. New York: Peter Lang, 2001.
Poggioli, Renato. *The Oaten Flute: Essays on Pastoral Poetry and the Pastoral Ideal*. Cambridge, MA: Harvard University Press, 1975.

Robertson, D. W., Jr. *A Preface to Chaucer: Studies in Medieval Perspectives.* Princeton, NJ: Princeton University Press, 1962.

Robertson, D. W., Jr., and Bernard F. Huppé. *Piers Plowman and Scriptural Tradition.* Princeton, NJ: Princeton University Press, 1951.

Robertson, Kellie. *The Laborer's Two Bodies: Labor and the "Work" of the Text in Medieval Britain, 1350–1500.* New York: Palgrave Macmillan, 2006.

Sahlins, Marshall. *Islands of History.* Chicago: University of Chicago Press, 1985.

Salter, Elizabeth. "The Annunciation of the Shepherds in Later Medieval Art and Drama." In *English and International: Studies in the Literature, Art and Patronage of Medieval England*, edited by Derek Pearsall and Nicolette Zeeman, 272–92. Cambridge: Cambridge University Press, 1988.

Scanlon, Larry. "Langland, Apocalypse, and the Early Modern Editor." In *Reading the Medieval in Early Modern England*, edited by Gordon McMullan and David Matthews, 51–73. Cambridge: Cambridge University Press, 2007.

Scase, Wendy. "*Dauy Dycars Dreame* and Robert Crowley's Prints of *Piers Plowman*." *Yearbook of Langland Studies* 21 (2007): 171–98.

Scattergood, V. J. "The Short Poems." In *Oxford Guides to Chaucer: The Shorter Poems*, A. J. Minnis with V. J. Scattergood and J. J. Smith. New York: Oxford University Press, 1995.

Schmidt, A. V. C. "Chaucer's Golden Age." *Essays in Criticism* 26 (1976): 99–115.

Schultz, John Richie. "The Method of Barclay's Eclogues." *Journal of English and Germanic Philology* 32 (1933): 549–71.

Shagan, Ethan. *Popular Politics and the English Reformation.* Cambridge: Cambridge University Press, 2003.

Simpson, James. *1350–1547: Reform and Cultural Revolution.* Vol. 2 of *The Oxford English Literary History.* Oxford: Oxford University Press, 2002.

———. *Piers Plowman: An Introduction to the B-text.* London: Longman, 1990.

———. "Spirituality and Economics in Passus 1–7 of the B Text." *Yearbook of Langland Studies* 1 (1987): 83–103.

Snyder, Susan. *Pastoral Process: Spenser, Marvell, Milton.* Stanford: Stanford University Press, 1998.

Somerset, Fiona. *Clerical Discourse and Lay Audience in Late Medieval England.* Cambridge: Cambridge University Press, 1998.

Staley Johnson, Lynn. *The "Shepheardes Calender": An Introduction.* University Park: Pennsylvania State University Press, 1990.

Steiner, Emily. *Documentary Culture and the Making of Medieval English Literature.* Cambridge: Cambridge University Press, 2003.

Stevens, Martin. *Four Middle English Mystery Cycles: Textual, Contextual, and Critical Interpretations.* Princeton, NJ: Princeton University Press, 1987.

Summit, Jennifer, and David Wallace, eds. "Medieval/Renaissance: After Periodization." Special issue, *Journal of Medieval and Early Modern Studies* 37 (Fall 2007).

Tawney, R. H. *The Agrarian Problem in the Sixteenth Century.* 1912. Reprint, New York: Harper and Row, 1967.

———. *Religion and the Rise of Capitalism.* 1926. Reprint, New Brunswick, NJ: Transaction, 1998.

Taylor, Charles. *A Secular Age.* Cambridge, MA: Harvard University Press, 2007.

Thirsk, Joan. "Enclosing and Engrossing." In *The Agrarian History of England and Wales*, edited by Joan Thirsk, 4:200–255. Cambridge: Cambridge University Press, 1967.

———. "Making a Fresh Start: Sixteenth-Century Agriculture and the Classical Inspiration." In *Culture and Cultivation in Early Modern England: Writing and the Land*, edited by Michael Leslie and Timothy Raylor, 15–34. Leicester: University of Leicester Press, 1992.

Thornton, Bruce. "Rural Dialectic: Pastoral, Georgic, and the *Shepheardes Calender.*" *Spenser Studies* 9 (1988): 1–20.

Tonkin, Humphrey. *Spenser's Courteous Pastoral: Book 6 of the Faerie Queene.* Oxford: Oxford University Press, 1972.

Trueman, Carl R. *Luther's Legacy: Salvation and English Reformers, 1525–1556.* New York: Oxford University Press, 1994.

Tylus, Jane. "Spenser, Virgil, and the Politics of Poetic Labor." *ELH: English Literary History* 55 (1988): 53–77.

Wailes, Stephen. *Medieval Allegories of Jesus' Parables: An Introduction.* Berkeley: University of California Press, 1987.

Wallace, Andrew. "'Nourseled up in life and manners wilde': Spenser's Georgic Educations." *Spenser Studies* 19 (2004): 65–92.

Watson, Nicholas. "Censorship and Cultural Change in Late-Medieval England: Vernacular Theology, the Oxford Translation Debate, and Arundel's Constitutions of 1409." *Speculum* 70 (1995): 822–64.

Wawn, Andrew N. "The Genesis of *The Plowman's Tale.*" *Yearbook of English Studies* 2 (1972): 21–40.

Weber, Max. *The Protestant Ethic and the Spirit of Capitalism.* Translated by Talcott Parsons. New York: Scribner's, 1958.

White, Helen. *Social Criticism in Popular Religious Literature.* New York: Macmillan, 1944.

Whittle, Jane. *The Development of Agrarian Capitalism: Land and Labour in Norfolk, 1440–1580.* Oxford: Oxford University Press, 2000.

Williams, Raymond. *The Country and the City*. New York: Oxford University Press, 1973.
Wilson, Richard. "'Like the Old Robin Hood': *As You Like It* and the Enclosure Riots." *Shakespeare Quarterly* 43 (1992): 1–19.
Wood, Andy. *The 1549 Rebellions and the Making of Early Modern England*. Cambridge: Cambridge University Press, 2007.
Woodbridge, Linda. "Country Matters: *As You Like It* and the Pastoral-Bashing Impulse." In *Re-visions of Shakespeare: Essays in Honor of Robert Ornstein*, edited by Evelyn Gajowski, 189–214. Newark: University of Delaware Press, 2004.

INDEX

Abraham and Isaac, 119
Adam and Eve, 26–27, 63–66
Adams, Robert, 222n9
Aeneas Sylvius
　Miseriae Curialium, 53, 59
Aers, David, 31, 210n48, 222nn8–9
agrarian capitalism
　emergence in the sixteenth
　　century, 11, 12, 87–89
　—polemic against, 93–98
　pastoral mode and, 86, 100–10,
　　197–99
　See also enclosure
allegorical pastoral. *See* ecclesiastical
　pastoral
Allen, Robert, 88
Alpers, Paul
　definition of pastoral, 7, 15–16, 50
　—*agrestis* vs. *silvestris*, 184
　—ecclesiastical pastoral, 203n15
　—freedom from poverty, 101, 108
　—novelty, 1
　—*otium*, 206n3, 206n7
　—poet as shepherd, 161
　—representative anecdote, 145,
　　196, 204n25, 214n9

on Mantuan's *Eclogues*, 9
on Shakespeare's *As You Like It*,
　197
on Spenser's *Faerie Queene*, 183,
　233n21
on Spenser's *Shepheardes Calender*,
　143, 213n5
Arcadian pastoral, 3, 4, 13–14, 16,
　53, 171–73, 187, 190–91,
　202n9
Ariosto, Ludovico
　Orlando Furioso, 188

Ball, John, 37–38, 65–66, 227n54
ballads (sixteenth-century), 98–99
Barbary Coast pirates, 189–90
Barclay, Alexander
　Eclogues
　—compatibility with agrarian
　　capitalism, 86, 101–5, 109–10,
　　159
　—contrast between country and
　　town in, 159, 181–82
　—ecclesiastical pastoral in, 67–68
　—as first pastoral poetry in
　　English, 3, 12, 49–51, 54–68

249

Barclay, Alexander (*cont.*)
— medieval influences on, 6, 51–53, 213n6, 214n11, 214n13
— poet as shepherd in, 161, 163–65, 231n38
— rural labor and *otium* in, 55–61
— rural labor and social radicalism in, 62–68, 108
Barney, Stephen, 24, 28
Barrell, John, 196, 205n38
Baswell, Christopher, 202n5
Bible, expositions
  Exodus 3:8, 153
  Matthew 6:25, 32
  Matthew 7:16–20, 117
  Matthew 18:12, 134
  Matthew 25:31–46, 135–36
  James 2:26, 115–16, 125
  Romans 2:6, 119
  Romans 8:29–31, 131–32
Bible, rural labor and reform
  Matthew 18:28 (*Redde quod debes*), 134–35
  Matthew 20:1–16 (Parable of the Laborers in the Vineyard), 26–27, 30, 36, 115
  Luke 16:1–10 (Parable of the Unjust Steward), 27–28
  Luke 5:8 (Parable of the Sower), 121, 137
  John 10:11–18 (Parable of the Good Shepherd), 21, 39–40, 118
  See also ecclesiastical pastoral
biblical pastoral. *See* ecclesiastical pastoral
Boccaccio, 4, 203n13
Boethius. *See* Chaucer, *Boece*
Bouchard, Gary M., 228n61
Brenner, Robert, 109
  Brenner debate, 218n21
Brinton, Bishop Thomas
  Sermons, 39–40
Bush, Douglas, 65

Cain and Abel, 67, 219n38
Camille, Michael, 209n35
Certayne Causes gathered together, 93–99, 106
Chaucer, Geoffrey, 144
  Boece, 21–23
  Clerk's Tale, 61
  "Former Age," 20–24, 165
  General Prologue
  —Parson, 3, 76, 102, 151
  —Plowman, 51, 76, 90–91, 97, 102, 199
  Knight's Tale, 231n40, 232n7
  Pardoner's *Prologue* and *Tale*, 153
Chaudhuri, Sukanta
  on Barclay's *Eclogues*, 213nn5–6, 214n11, 214n13
  on Googe's *Eclogues*, 216n35
Churchyard, Thomas
  Davy Dycar's Dreme, 156–60
class conflict, 15, 63–66, 72–76, 98, 101, 108–10, 145. *See also* Brenner, Robert; Hilton, Rodney
Clebsch, William, 114, 222n1
Cooper, Helen
  account of pastoral, 2–3, 11, 16, 202n9, 206n6
  on Barclay's *Eclogues*, 213n6, 214n11
  on Googe's *Eclogues*, 216n35
  on Shepherds' Plays, 202n6
Cranmer, Thomas, 116
Crowley, Robert, 6, 113
  as editor of *Piers Plowman*, 124–30
  Epigrams, 126, 130
  Way to Wealth, 95
Cullen, Patrick, 4–5, 16

Daphnis and Chloe (Longus), 187–88
de Grazia, Margareta, 234n1

Diggon Davy (Spenser), 144, 145, 161
  source in Churchyard's *Davy Dycar's Dreme*, 156–60
  source in Langland's *Piers Plowman*, 156–57
Drayton, Michael, 49
Dudley, Edmund
  "Warning to the People against Rebellion," 66

ecclesiastical pastoral
  in Barclay's *Eclogues*, 67–68
  defined, 3–5
  in Googe's *Eclogues*, 69, 75–76
  influence of Boccaccio and Petrarch, 4, 203n13
  in Langland's *Piers Plowman*, 6, 41
  in Mantuan's *Eclogues*, 4, 67–68, 215n33
  medieval versions of, 15–16, 39–41, 42–45
  —intersections with later pastoral, 50–51, 203n15
  in the *Piers Plowman* tradition, 149–50
  —"I playne Piers which cannot flatter," 137–38
  in Spenser's *Shepheardes Calender*, 144, 146–56, 157, 161
Emmerson, Richard K., 209n35
Empson, William, 55, 74, 108
enclosure, 11, 43, 79
  historians' accounts of, 83–86, 216n47
  pastoral as response to, 84–87, 100–110
  in Shakespeare's *As You Like It*, 197–98, 235n9
  sixteenth-century polemic on, 12, 52, 87–89, 92–100, 123, 138–40, 159
  See also agrarian capitalism

English Wycliffite Sermons, 40, 227n52
Everitt, Alan, 104, 221n60
exegetical criticism, 24–25, 28

Fowler, Alastair, 8, 9, 205n35, 229n8
Fox, John, 189
Freedman, Paul, 29, 64–65, 210n44, 215n26, 221n70

Galloway, Andrew, 24
georgic, 9–10, 144, 172–73, 205n35. *See also* Virgil, *Georgics*
Goldberg, P. J. P., 209n35
Googe, Barnabe
  Eclogues
  —compatibility with agrarian capitalism, 86, 103–4
  —contentment in, 110, 198
  —ecclesiastical pastoral in, 75–78
  —as first pastoral poetry in English, 3, 12, 49–51
  —medieval influences on, 6, 51–53, 214n11, 216n35
  —poet as shepherd in, 162
  —rural labor in, 68–73
  —rural labor and social radicalism in, 73–76
  —woodcut in, 69–70
  "An Epitaph of the Lord Sheffield's Death," 78–81
Gower, John
  Confessio Amantis, 40, 65, 91–92
  Vox Clamantis, 64, 80–81, 90, 219n38
Graham, Kenneth J. E., 225n37
Green, R. F., 212n70
Greene, Roland, 169
Greg, W. W., 2, 4, 7–8, 193

Hadfield, Andrew, 204n22, 228n63
Hailey, R. Carter, 225n36

Hakluyt, Richard
  Principal Navigations, 189
Harrison, William
  Description of England, 98, 106
Hill, Ordelle G., 204n22
Hilton, Rodney, 38, 74, 227nn54–55
Holstun, James, 88–89, 97
Homily on Good Works, 116, 154, 155
Hudson, Anne, 113
husbandry manuals, 25, 90–91, 208n29
  Roman treatises on agriculture, 187, 217n1
  See also *Seneschaucie*

"I playne Piers which cannot flatter," 6, 13, 51, 102, 113, 121, 124, 130–38

"Jack of the North," 138–41
Jameson, Fredric, 25, 27, 50, 100–101, 218n14
Johnson, Samuel, 8
Jones, Mike Rodman, 204n21, 222n4, 223n10, 225n33
Justice, Steven, 37–38, 132, 212n70, 217n51

Kelen, Sarah, 225n33, 228n63
Kett's Rebellion, 71, 79–81, 88
King, John, 124, 130
Kirk, Elizabeth, 34, 211n61
Knapp, Ethan, 231n40
Knight, Stephen, 25, 208n26

laborers
  in the Bible (*see* Bible, expositions; Bible, rural labor and reform)
  denigration of, 64, 105, 187
  holy simplicity of, 34–35, 89, 121, 211n61
  in the three-estate structure, 91–92
  in Tyndale's writings, 118–20
  See also rural labor; shepherds
Lane, Richard, 230n19, 230n22
Langland, William. See *Piers Plowman*
Latimer, Hugh
  Sermons, 92–93, 112, 120–23, 137
Leicester, H. Marshall, Jr., 25, 153
Lincolnshire Rising of 1536, 93
Lollard Sermons, 120
Lollards. *See* Wycliffites
Low, Anthony, 9–10, 229n8
Lucas, Scott, 230n27
Lupton, Julia Reinhard, 232n10, 233n22
Luther, Martin, 116, 223n18, 224n24
Luttrell Psalter, 209n35

Macherey, Pierre, 52, 100–101, 145
Mantuan (Baptista Spagnoli Mantuanus)
  Eclogues
  —compatibility with agrarian capitalism, 104, 107
  —contrast between country and town in, 53, 62–65, 77
  —ecclesiastical pastoral in, 4–5, 67–68, 203n13, 215n33
  —influence of, 2–3, 49–51, 58, 147, 232n4
  —*otium* in, 56–57, 105
  —realism of, 9, 54, 56, 176–77
  —rural labor in, 9–10, 181
  —shepherd as poet in, 53, 163–64
  See also Turberville, George
Mantuanesque pastoral, 4, 53, 72, 171, 214n18, 232n2
Marx, Karl, 83–84, 87–88, 218n21
Masciandaro, Nicola, 207n14, 208n24

Matar, Nabil, 189
McRae, Andrew
  on England's agrarian identity, 189
  on pastoral, 217n10, 219n27, 229n9
  on sixteenth-century complaint, 112, 123, 124, 204n22, 204n28, 218n19
medieval pastoral, 2–3, 11–12, 15–17, 38–47, 202n6. *See also* ecclesiastical pastoral, medieval versions of; Shepherds' Plays
Middle English Sermons, 29, 33, 115–16, 117, 119, 224n23, 227n56
Middleton, Anne, 128–29
Mirk, John
  Festial, 26–27
Montemayor, Jorge
  Diana, 69
Montrose, Louis
  definition of pastoral, 7, 15, 50, 69, 72, 143
  —*otium*, 17, 105–6, 188–89
  on pastoral and agrarian controversy, 85–86
  on pastoral and the court, 1, 70, 162
  on Shepherds' Plays, 202n8
  on Spenser's *Shepheardes Calender*, 231n43
More, Sir Thomas
  Utopia, 87–88, 96, 108
Murder of Abel (Towneley cycle), 219n38
Murrin, Michael, 204n26, 214n18, 232n4

nativity plays. *See* Shepherds' Plays
Nisse, Ruth, 41–42, 212n79
Norbrook, David, 163, 225n33, 230n27, 231n34
"Nowe a Dayes," 98–99

Owst, G. R., 24

Palavicino, Sir Horatio, 106
pastoral conventions
  contrast between country and town, 53, 57–58, 62–68, 72–76, 77, 109–10, 181–82, 197
  courtliness of, 69–70, 71, 84–85, 162, 168, 173, 192
  decorum, 55
  Golden Age, 20–24, 107–8, 180, 197, 207n14, 233n18 (*see also* Virgil, *Eclogues*)
  literalization of the shepherd, 50–51, 54–55, 86, 147–48, 170
  otium, 4, 12, 17, 56–61, 104–6, 148, 165, 171, 174–78, 185–91, 204n26
  poet as shepherd, 161–69
  See also Alpers, Paul, definition of pastoral; Montrose, Louis, definition of pastoral
Patterson, Annabel, 7–8, 217n52, 230n29
Pearl, 115–16, 117, 120
Peasants' Revolt of 1381, 26–27, 52, 74, 79–81, 140
  John Ball's sermon in, 37–38, 65–66, 212n70
  Langland's *Piers Plowman* and, 29, 132–33
Petrarch, 4, 203n13
Piers (as figure)
  for the critique of agrarian capitalism, 110
  —in "Jack of the North," 138–39
  —in *Pyers plowmans exhortation*, 94, 97, 98
  in Langland's *Piers Plowman*, 94, 113–14, 120–21

Piers (as figure) (*cont.*)
   for negotiating Protestant ideas, 114, 124
   —in Crowley's edition, 127–28
   —in "I playne Piers which cannot flatter," 130–31, 135, 137–38
   nostalgia of, 228n63
   in the Peasants' Revolt of 1381, 52, 132
   in Spenser's *Shepheardes Calender*, 6, 13, 144, 145, 149–50
Piers Plowman
   A-text, 34, 211n63
   C-text, 210n55, 211n64
   class conflict in, 109
   early eclogues and, 5–6
   ecclesiastical pastoral in, 6, 41
   rural laborer as reformer in, 12, 28–29, 33–35, 65, 94
   —founding of the church (B-text, Passus 19), 35–36, 134–35
   —Plowing of the Half Acre (B-text, Passus 6), 29–33
   shepherds as laborers in, 89
   Shepherds' Plays and, 42
   sixteenth-century popularity of, 6, 13, 113
   as source for Churchyard, *Davy Dycar's Dreme*, 156–57
   and Spenser's *Shepheardes Calender*, 151, 166–68
   works in, 41, 113, 117, 125, 152, 222n9
   See also Crowley, Robert; Piers
Piers the Plowman's Crede, 6, 33–34, 51, 54
Piers Plowman tradition, 5–6, 51–52, 113–14, 120, 123–41. *See also* "I playne Piers which cannot flatter"; *Piers the Plowman's Crede*; *The Plowman's Tale*; *Pyers plowmans exhortation*

The Plowman's Tale, 5–6, 41, 51, 113, 150, 151, 162–63, 173
Poggioli, Renato, 5, 105
Protestantism (sixteenth century)
   faith vs. works in, 111–12, 114–23
   in the *Piers Plowman* tradition, 123–25
   —Crowley's edition of *Piers Plowman*, 125–30
   —"I playne Piers which cannot flatter," 130–38
   in Spenser's *Shepheardes Calender*, 146, 152, 154–56, 163
   See also Latimer, Hugh; Luther, Martin; Tyndale, William
Pyers plowmans exhortation, 12, 51–52, 93–98, 113, 139

Reformation, 6, 11, 12–13, 111–14, 125, 138, 199. *See also* Protestantism
reformism (medieval)
   defined, 12, 24, 27, 40
   in Spenser's *Shepheardes Calender*, 157–61, 162–63
   See also rural labor
Renaissance, 195
Robertson, Kellie, 209n36
Roman de la Rose, 21–22
rural labor
   as metaphor for poetry, 162–63, 166–67, 172–73
   writing of, 16–17, 89–92, 143–45, 171–72
   —reformism of, 10, 27–41, 137–38, 146 (see also *Piers Plowman*)
   See also under individual authors; georgic

Sahlins, Marshall, 11, 114–15
Salter, Elizabeth, 41, 206n6

Scanlon, Larry, 29, 225n36, 226n43, 227n53
Scase, Wendy, 230n23
Scattergood, V. J., 21, 207n16
Schmidt, A. V. C., 21
Schulz, John Richie, 214n17
Seneschaucie, 90–91
Shakespeare, William
   As You Like It, 172, 197–99
shepherds
   as definitive of pastoral mode, 2, 15–16, 50–51
   as distinct from other rural laborers, 83, 86, 92–98
   recreation of, 19–20, 206n6
   as rural laborers, 7–10, 12, 17–20, 38–47, 89–91
   See also ecclesiastical pastoral; pastoral conventions
The Shepherds Kalender, 70, 143–44, 228n4
Shepherds' Plays, 2, 17, 202n6, 202n8
   The Angels and the Shepherds (York), 90
   and ecclesiastical pastoral, 39, 77
   First Shepherds' Play (Towneley), 18–20, 41–47, 90, 109, 212n79
   Second Shepherds' Play (Towneley), 6
   Shepherds' Play (Chester), 18–20, 41–47
Simpson, James, 30, 124, 135, 210n51, 211n67
slavery, 173–74, 186–90
Somerset, Fiona, 211n65
Song of the Husbandman, 17, 43, 92, 108
Spenser, Edmund
   The Faerie Queene, Book 6, 13–14
   —compatibility with agrarian capitalism, 107–8, 110, 199
   —*otium* in, 171, 174–81
   —*otium* of the brigands, 184–86
   —*otium*, slavery in relation to, 186–93
   —rural labor in, 172–74, 179–82, 191–93
   —shepherd as disguise in, 182–84
   The Shepheardes Calender,
   —ecclesiastical pastoral in, 4, 146–49, 160–61
   —as first pastoral poetry in English, 1, 3, 50, 195
   —georgic in, 144
   —influence of medieval tradition, 6, 13, 143–45, 151
   —influence of Virgilian pastoral, 145–46
   —poet as shepherd in, 161–69
   —rural labor in, 149–52, 156–61
   —works in, 152–56
Staley Johnson, Lynn, 230n19, 231n34
Statutes of Laborers, 31
Steiner, Emily, 210n54
Stevens, Martin, 18
symbolic imagination
   defined, 10–11
   of labor in medieval texts, 24–28
   in Shakespeare's *As You Like It*, 198–99
   sixteenth-century disruption of, 86, 92, 110
   —Reformation, 111, 113, 114–17, 133, 139, 140
   in Spenser's *Shepheardes Calender*, 144–45, 152

Tasso, Torquato
   Gerusalemme Liberata, 180
Tawney, R. H.
   The Agrarian Problem in the Sixteenth Century, 11, 83, 88, 93, 95, 138, 139
   Religion and the Rise of Capitalism, 112, 114

Taylor, Charles, 225n35
Thirsk, Joan, 84–85, 95, 99–100
three-estate structure
  attack on, 132–33, 140
  medieval views of, 12, 26–28, 89, 94
  plowman/rural laborer in, 6, 102
  Reformation views on, 113, 114, 123
Tonkin, Humphrey, 233n23, 234n45
Trueman, Carl, 222n1, 224n24
Turberville, George, 55. *See also* Mantuan
Tusser, Thomas
  Five Hundred Pointes, 95
Tyndale, William, 13, 130, 131
  Exposition on Matthew, 117–20
  The Parable of the Wicked Mammon, 114, 116–20

Virgil
  Eclogues, 101–3
  —in England, 2, 49, 202n5
  —Fourth Eclogue, 21–23, 44–45
  —rural labor in, 7–8, 54,
  —slavery in, 187, 221n64
  Georgics, 9–10, 144, 172–73, 229n8
"Vox Populi Vox Dei," 99

Walsingham, Thomas, 37–38, 74
Weber, Max, 112, 116, 152

Whittle, Jane, 88, 94
Williams, Raymond, 14, 54, 84–85, 100, 172, 218n20
Wilson, Richard, 235n9
Wimbledon, Thomas, 27–28
Wood, Andy, 88, 223n11
works, 12–13, 111–12
  in "Jack of the North," 138–40
  medieval views of, 20, 26, 115–16, 125
  —in Langland's *Piers Plowman*, 41, 113, 117, 125, 152, 166–67
  in the *Piers Plowman* tradition, 113–14, 124
  —Crowley's edition of *Piers Plowman*, 125–30
  —"I playne Piers which cannot flatter," 132–36
  redefined in the Reformation, 116–17
  in Shakespeare's *As You Like It*, 197–99
  in sixteenth-century polemic, 121–23
  and Spenser's *Shepheardes Calender*, 144, 153–56, 163, 166–67
  as things, 117, 125, 154–55
  See also Protestantism, faith vs. works in
Wyclif, John, 224n23
Wycliffites, 24, 33–34, 41, 131

KATHERINE C. LITTLE

is associate professor of English at the University of Colorado Boulder.
She is the author of *Confession and Resistance: Defining the Self
in Late Medieval England* (University of Notre Dame Press, 2006).